SOUL SOUNDS

Soul Sounds

THE AFTERLIFE IN AFRICAN AMERICAN LITERATURE AND MUSIC

Daylanne K. English

FORDHAM UNIVERSITY PRESS NEW YORK 2027

Fordham University Press also publishes its books in a variety of electronic formats. Some content that appears in print may not be available in electronic books.
Visit us online at www.fordhampress.com.

For EU safety / GPSR concerns: Mare Nostrum Group B.V., Doelen 72, 4831 GR Breda, The Netherlands, gpsr@mare-nostrum.co.uk

Library of Congress Cataloging-in-Publication Data available online at https://catalog.loc.gov.

Printed in the United States of America
29 28 27 5 4 3 2 1
First edition

I dedicate this book to Dr. Deborah E. McDowell,
Alice Griffin Professor Emerita of English
at the University of Virginia.

Contents

Let's start living our lives
Living for the future paradise.
—STEVIE WONDER, "PASTIME PARADISE," ON *Songs in the Key of Life*

Introduction

Let's Not Wait for the Afterlife

This book's title comes from the poem "Georgia Dusk" in Jean Toomer's *Cane*, a work that emerged from his time spent in the rural South. In the dusk of the poem, "men and barking hounds" pursue a Black man who works at a sawmill. They have "surprised [him] in making folk-songs from soul sounds."[1] Like "Georgia Dusk," *Cane* as a whole seeks to preserve and honor the voices, the arts, and the often harsh lived experiences of poor Southern Black Americans—to lend them an afterlife. Literary scholar Daniel Barlow has succinctly described Toomer's creative process in *Cane*, noting that he "converted his aural experiences into scribal text and combined that musical text with several previously written works," thereby producing a "literary ethnomusicology."[2] Such a blending of genres, sensory experiences, and aesthetic forms models the content, the methodology, and even the argument of this book. *Soul Sounds* combines literary studies, historical studies, religious studies, time studies, and sound studies while ranging across genres, media, and eras—even as it remains firmly planted in the urgency of the now. *Soul Sounds* thereby offers an interdisciplinary revision of our understanding of African American literary and musical representations of the afterlife across time, foregrounding their power and their potentiality in the present.

With this transtemporal method, this book implicitly argues that there is no "was" regarding African American literature.[3] *Soul Sounds* argues for literary and cultural studies, particularly African American literary studies, that are less bound to and by particular periods, while calling, too, for a literary-critical approach that honors the work of scholars of the tradition who have gone before.[4] In other words, contra both Kenneth Warren and T. S. Eliot, *Soul Sounds* advocates for tradition and *collective* talent among both artists and scholars. The intertwined project of creating, documenting, and studying Black literature and culture has taken on fresh, even vital, importance in the face of assaults on Black history and art, especially as they are studied in public schools and colleges and universities and preserved in museums. *Soul Sounds* contends that recurrent representations of the afterlife in African American literature and music can aid in that project and can shape contemporary activisms, along with contemporary scholarship.

As for how the afterlife shapes this particular project: Because it has been repeatedly imagined by African American writers and musicians, *Soul Sounds* can range widely by genre and by time period. This book considers literary texts ranging from life narratives of formerly enslaved persons to Spiritualist tracts to novels to poetry, and musical texts ranging from sorrow songs to funk to hip hop to Afrofuturist songs and music videos, spanning the mid-nineteenth century to the present. To unearth this sustained aesthetic tradition of the afterlife, *Soul Sounds* blends interdisciplinary method with form-based argument, locating in aesthetic form a means to reimagine and rebuild our present-day world. In this argument for the reparative power of the afterlife and its representation, *Soul Sounds* engages and challenges Black studies scholarship that has advanced strictly metaphorical understandings and applications of the terms "afterlife" and "afterlives." This book argues, above all, that Black studies and African Americanist literary and cultural studies scholars need to take the afterlife *seriously* as a location and as an idea—and a politically, aesthetically, and personally empowering one at that. But what exactly lends the afterlife this power?

The afterlife is, as a concept, transtemporal. It also recurs, as an image, across time in African American literary and musical works. As I argue in Chapter 1 and in the coda, the afterlife has always been there, and it is and always will be there. And although the afterlife may seem to lie ahead, only for those of us still living (or yet to be born) in this secular world does the afterlife necessarily reside in the future. So, an afterlife is a future, yes, but it also is "coeval," to use Johannes Fabian's anthropological term.[5] *Soul Sounds* contends that this temporal complexity, this layered-ness, of the afterlife underlies its power in that it offers us continuous access to other, possibly better, times—enabling us to reimagine and re-create our present. *Soul Sounds* thereby counters Saidiya Hartman's highly influential concept of the "afterlives of slavery" and her sense of the damage wrought by contemporary Black people's being "coeval with the dead."[6] I contend that this coeval state does not necessarily signify what Hartman terms "a horizon of loss" or "irreparability."[7] If Hartman is correct that Black people are "coeval with the dead," then it follows logically that time is neither linear nor earthbound in African American literature and culture. The afterlife is eternal, *and* it is fully available in the present. As Soyica Colbert tells us, "To hold onto the past and not be held by it, Black people have long created practices of communing with the dead, of learning to live in a land filled with shadows but not ghosted by the past."[8]

Yet Black studies scholarship on death and the afterlife continues to draw on and extend Hartman's work, consistently framing the afterlife as purely metaphorical. For example, Sampada Aranke's insightful book of 2023, *Death's Futurity: The Visual Life of Black Power*, argues for the power of the "afterlife" of "Black radical death as it is pictured in and through mediation."[9] Here again, we see a nonliteral afterlife, one Aranke identifies with visual representations of murdered Black radicals—as in a photograph of Bobby Hutton, living, but with images of bullet holes overlaying his image and altering the photo and, in the process, lending both it and Hutton an "afterlife." Although at least part of my argument is quite compatible with Aranke's thesis that there is a "generative capacity of death in Black radical life [that works] toward the egalitarian promise of Black liberation,"[10] *Soul Sounds* centers not so much on death as on the "generative capacity" of an afterlife understood literally. This book thus locates liberatory potential not in death or in representations of the dead but in actually *living on after death*. The key representation here is of a very real afterlife. This elevation of the afterlife's generative quality pushes against Afropessimism, a school of African Americanist cultural and literary theory produced by scholars such as Hartman and Frank B. Wilderson III, who emphasize the suffering, terror, and "subjection," to use Hartman's term, that accompany Black life in the United States. In Wilderson's words, "Blackness is coterminous with Slaveness," such that "the Black is a sentient being though not a Human being," as a result of sustained, systemic violence against Black people in the United States.[11]

I wish to suggest that downplaying the power of *form*, especially seemingly conventional aesthetic form, within Afropessimism helps explain why the movement overlooks the positive potentiality of a nonmetaphorical afterlife, in favor of the "scenes of subjection" associated with a metaphorical afterlife of enslavement, as the title of Hartman's 1997 book suggests.[12] In his brilliant 2025 book, *The Disturbing Profane*, Joseph R. Winters refers to this tendency in Wilderson's work as "form-shattering."[13] For Fred Moten, it is the "blur," the "deformational," that produces a necessary "oppositional collision" in Black art and performance.[14] Following this pattern, Hartman, in *Scenes of Subjection*, presents an acute (and, granted, to some degree formal) analysis of *Incidents in the Life of a Slave Girl*, focusing on Jacobs's conventional, even obvious, choice to address a white audience. Hartman interprets that choice as Jacobs's "seduction" of a white reader by "conforming to their desires."[15]

However, Hartman overlooks a subtle (that is, perhaps not shattering) shift in address in *Incidents* that signals Jacobs's investment in another audience altogether. In describing her resistance to racism and segregation on board a "Jim Crow train," Jacobs writes:

> My answer was that the colored servants ought to be dissatisfied with themselves, for not having too much self-respect to submit to such treatment; that there was no difference in the price of board for colored and white servants, and there was no justification for difference of treatment. I staid a month after this, and finding I was resolved to stand up for my rights, they concluded to treat me well. Let every colored man and woman do this, and eventually we shall cease to be trampled under foot [*sic*] by our oppressors.[16]

As Anna Kornbluh has argued, what distinguishes literary texts is "their formalization of other, different, better ideas and relations than what is already here."[17] In a better world, Jacobs's "we," meaning that formal shift to address Black people, signifies the possibility, in fact the necessity, of rising up *together*. The sociality of form produced by her "we" corresponds to a real-life sociality, what I term "collective agency." In other words, that "we" points directly to the work that art can perform in rebuilding our world. I would argue that the afterlife, too, works as a "social form" and as a partner to literature and the arts, in that all tap into a nonlinear form of time that, in itself, aids collective creating and imaginative rebuilding. As I show in Chapter 2, Jacobs expands upon her alternative audience—Black people—and her alternative purpose—collective resistance by that audience—via representation of an afterlife inhabited by and presided over by her own family members.

To return here to my title, *Soul Sounds*, Toomer's "Georgia Dusk" in *Cane* offers an ideal case study to develop an argument for the sociality of form and the sociality of a temporally complex afterlife. The poem's form and content alike are deeply rooted in the varied material experiences of Black people expressed via remixed literary and musical/aural registers. A kind of ballad-elegy with seven pentameter ABBA quatrains, the poem combines folk music forms with traditional lyric poetic ones. The poem's content likewise offers a series of striking combinations, including white terroristic-racial violence set alongside rich oral-cultural traditions and practices of African American people, all taking place and sounding in a rural—yet also modern and industrial—American South. As I mentioned at the outset, in the poem, at Southern dusk, "men and barking hounds" pursue a Black man as he works, surprising him "in making folk-songs from soul sounds."[18] On the one hand, this line—the word "soul," especially—suggests an inherent Black musicality that could tend toward essentialism. On the other hand, it also points toward a shared oral tradition unbound by time that expresses precisely the connections between ballad and elegy, between folk music (living tradition) and poetic commemoration (eternity), and therefore the connections between a quotidian this-life and an afterlife for the Black characters in *Cane*. *Any*time—at work or at leisure or at liminal times, such as dusk or "the end of the workday," to use Barbara Foley's phrase[19]—they might meet death in Georgia, with sounds/music filtered through the poetic serving as an ideal form for expressing that dreadful living-dead reality. Indeed, the poem, along with the first section of *Cane* as a whole, turns on sounds of multiple kinds, including the horrifying sounds that accompany violence done to Black men through lynching and to trees through logging, calling to mind Charles Chesnutt's short story "Po' Sandy."[20] So it would seem that the Afropessimists are correct: "Georgia Dusk" apparently records subjection.

However, in addition to recording these sounds of trauma, the poem represents those sounds both heard and created by the sawmill workers themselves: that is, *soul sounds*. As Black men with royalty in their African history ("vestiges of pomp, / Race memories of king and caravan"), though now manual laborers in Georgia, they are "singing through the footpaths of the swamp." Through their singing, they are contributing substantially to the sociality of form and to material sociality. Or, as Kendrick Lamar sings, "I got loyalty / got royalty / inside my DNA."[21] In the American South, these still-royal men are collectively subject to the sonics and temporalities of industry, "whistle" and "buzz-saws," but also to the less-oppressive sounds and rhythms of nature: "the pine trees are guitars, / Strumming."

Together, these mechanical and natural sounds produce modern *and* ancestral versions of what Barlow aptly terms the "soundscape" in the first part of *Cane* (208), underscoring a cultural tradition of long durée. Coined by R. Murray Schafer, "soundscapes," a foundational term in sound studies, signifies, in Schafer's words, a "definition of space by acoustic means of a society [which] can be read as an indicator of social conditions which produce it."[22] Just so, in the poem, the workers contribute their own music in response to their social conditions, their temporally layered soundscape, by offering up an evening hymn to the heavens, a "vesper to the stars." They look up at and sing to an afterlife above that offers them a welcome alternative to an earthbound world that holds always the possibility of their imminent violent death and therefore their own entry into that very afterlife, "above the sacred whisper of the pines." But this art not only responds to particular social conditions; it also establishes the workers as part of a collective and ongoing tradition of talent *and* a tradition of an afterlife that offers different and better social conditions.

Granted, "Georgia Dusk" does seem to suggest that the Black singers with their "soul sounds" are not working toward this-world justice but are instead simply waiting for their ascendance into heaven. Such passive patience appears to support Barbara Foley's argument in her classic essay on *Cane*, "'In the Land of Cotton': Economics and Violence in Jean Toomer's *Cane*," regarding the book's far-from-progressive and insufficiently historical-materialist politics.[23] The singers' waiting also seems to support Barlow's assertion that the book as a whole, as a preservation project, remains largely elegiac and nostalgic rather than being materially effective or engaging with the present (Barlow, 202, 205, 208). Just so, in the last stanza, the workers' "resinous and soft" songs deliver "Dreams of Christ" rather than, say, dreams of freedom or of reparations for Black people. In this view, these songs offer, to use Toomer's words, a "swan-song"[24] for ways of life and musics that, as vestiges of the past, have largely passed on and that *Cane*, just as Barlow claims, seeks to preserve solely in print.[25]

However, in another poem from *Cane*, "Cotton Song," heaven and the afterlife signify something altogether different, with both patience and nostalgia notably absent. Foley rightly notes that "Cotton Song" "replicates the rhythms and imagery of a work song chanted by laborers heaving bales of cotton," but then argues that it therefore fails to reflect the material and economic realities faced by Black workers in the US South in the 1920s, when cotton was no longer king.[26] So *Cane* appears once again to be politically and historically-materially out-of-touch. But Foley's analysis of "Cotton Song," rather like Hartman's reading of *Incidents*, overlooks another political message delivered by the poem's *form* in conjunction with its *content*, namely its insistent and repetitive representation of the afterlife. Beginning with the very first stanza, this work song/poem supplants any version of the afterlife that derails this-life resistance:

Come, brother, come. Lets lift it;
Come now, hew it! roll away!
Shackles fall upon the Judgment Day
But lets not wait for it.[27]

"Cotton Song" is in fact more explicitly resistant and militant than many traditional Black work songs, with the hard sounds and quick meter in this stanza echoing the fast-paced rhythms of modernity's systems of industrial labor, as well as the intensity of the poem's call to action. The first stanza's last line, "But lets [*sic*] not wait for it," departs from the meters of a work song in favor of a spondaic declaration. Such urgency suggests that the "work" the song calls for is not picking cotton but rather demanding justice, in keeping with Barlow's argument that in *Cane* "African American musics [work] as an incisive mode of criticism, one especially relevant to literary discussions of trauma, fluctuating racial identities, and the cultural politics of modernization" (194).

And yet "Cotton Song" refutes other parts of Barlow's argument, particularly his assertion that *Cane* consistently represents primarily the "nostalgia" of its characters (194, 196). The poem says, twice, "God's body's got a soul, / Bodies like to roll the soul, / Cant blame God if we dont roll." These lines link Godliness with the bodies and souls (and "soul") of Black people, in a powerful combination of this-life and the afterlife. "Cotton Song" calls upon Black people collectively to "roll," not cotton into bales, but bodies into action. Such a call amplifies neither nostalgia nor patience and neither looking back nor waiting. Instead, the poem plainly urges Black people not to wait for God to render them justice in heaven. "Brothers" must understand Godly justice rendered in the afterlife as a goal to work toward in *this* life. Just so, the last line of both the second and third stanzas, "We aint agwine t wait until th Judgment Day!" works as a chorus reinforcing the poem's representation, at the level of form, of a more-just afterlife to be enacted now. As H. William Rice has observed of this line, "Not only do these words reflect black dialect, but they also create spontaneity and make the line move quickly."[28]

As in this analysis of Toomer's poems, throughout *Soul Sounds* I ally close reading of literary and musical form with representations of the afterlife in order to document and foreground an optimistic, empowering understanding of an African American literary and musical tradition, even as I acknowledge the ongoing explanatory and critical power of Afropessimism. As I show in Chapter 3, contemporary Black poetic representations of the afterlife actually mediate tensions between Afropessimism and what we might term Afro-Optimism. Represented in the work of scholars such as Badia Ahad-Legardy, Michelle Commander, and Kevin Quashie, this optimism turns on what Quashie has termed "black aliveness," or the power and potentialities of Black life and Black art in the United States.[29] Activist Black Optimism and joy have been explored in popular culture, too; for example, a 2020 *British Vogue* article identifies "revelling in joy [as] an act of resistance" for Black people.[30] Ultimately landing on confidence in the power of artists and scholars to help make our world a better place, *Soul Sounds* in all its chapters offers formal analysis that supports an argument for the shared pain, yes, but more so the collective agency represented in and by the afterlife—that is, an *agential* afterlife.

Chapter 1, "*Dealings with the Dead*," focuses on a now little-known nineteenth-century African American writer, Spiritualist, and figure of the occult, Paschal Beverly Randolph (1825–1875). Randolph, like many American Spiritualists, promoted the idea of a utopian afterlife that could provide a corrective model for this world. As he writes in his 1868 book *After Death*, "Thank God for death! And thank him for life beyond the gloomy sea! . . . If the agony protracted called life, that most of us . . . endure on earth, was *all*, then indeed existence were an awful tragedy, and terrible beyond all bearing."[31] "*Dealings with the Dead*" argues that Randolph, despite his often strange and sometimes troubling beliefs, constructed an afterlife to remedy that "agony protracted." In his imagined alleviation of present-day miseries through a Spiritualist afterlife, Randolph also offers an early model for contemporary Afrofuturist revisioning of a United States that remains in shaky recovery from an agonizing pandemic that has to date claimed over a million American lives and that continues to suffer from a second presidency that is seeking to complete the mission of the first to destroy the nation's democratic and legal structures, particularly those that protect Black people and their right to vote.

In his novels and in what we might now term his creative nonfiction, Randolph represented an afterlife, along with other alternative realities, that implicitly critiqued the United States of his lifetime, which spanned the devastation of the Civil War and a series of deadly epidemics of cholera and tuberculosis that caused disproportionate suffering among the nation's urban poor. Like millions of contemporary Americans, and like so many during his lifetime, Randolph experienced devastating losses from epidemics and preventable illnesses. His mother died in New York in an 1830s cholera epidemic when he was just five years old; he also experienced the death of two of his children (he had four children from two of his three marriages).[32] It is perhaps not surprising, then, that Randolph, like the many Americans who participated in the Spiritualist movement of the mid- to late nineteenth century, would take the notion of an afterlife seriously as a site where loved ones reside and as a real alternative to the painful realities, the *protracted agonies*, of their this-world lives.

For us now, taking the afterlife seriously in this way—both as a real place founded on strongly held belief and as an imagined place that enables liberatory thought and action—has taken on new importance and usefulness. In the context of historical epidemics coupled with the differential and ongoing impacts of the COVID-19 pandemic on Black communities, along with the likewise ongoing, indeed continuous, murders of Black people by the police, the afterlife can (and I predict will) matter anew to families, individuals, communities, and collectives. Of course, in these devastating contemporary contexts, so thoroughly explored by Hartman, Wilderson, and other Afropessimists, death and the afterlife can also take on deeply traumatic meanings for the loved ones whom the departed have left behind, full of "longing and loss" to use Hartman's apt words, particularly when they could not be with their beloved now-dead at their passing.[33] And yet the afterlife also holds potentially healing meanings even, and perhaps especially, in these contexts of pandemic and police violence and their terribly disproportionate effects on Black people, Indigenous people, and other people of color. As Mary T. Bassett, health commissioner of the New York State Department of Health, succinctly puts it, "COVID-19 pulled back the curtain on the extent of racialized inequality in the United States."[34]

Among the finest of literary responses to the COVID epidemic and its profound revelation of structural inequity is Victor LaValle's short story "Recognition,"[35] set in New York City in the summer of 2020.[36] In the story, a woman of color, the dynamic and stylish Cuban American Mirta, befriends the narrator, an unnamed and self-described "shy" and unfashionable Black woman (LaValle, 2). The two live in the same Washington Heights apartment building where the landlord checks daily for deaths from COVID, spray-painting a "V" for "vacant" on the doors of those apartments where the tenants have died (6–7). He explains to the narrator that this is now the policy for buildings in COVID "hot spots" in New York in the Bronx, Queens, Harlem—where less-affluent, majority nonwhite neighborhoods, like their own, are concentrated (8). As Mirta says to the narrator, "The ones who could leave, left. The rest of us? We were abandoned" (11). Eventually Mirta herself dies of COVID; nonetheless, she speaks to the narrator from the afterlife, affirming her (Mirta's) belief in past lives and lending the story its title: "I knew we met before. Recognition. Like seeing a member of my family." The now-dead Mirta has left a pair of her shoes for the narrator, saying "*Give them back when you see me again*" (15).

LaValle's story records the trauma and the differential impacts of COVID, while locating a source of solidarity and heightened political awareness among people, particularly women of color, in the pandemic's unfolding and in its aftermath. The sustained existence and influence of Mirta, even after death, provides equally sustained solace for the narrator, as the last line of the story suggests: "I have to slip on an extra pair of socks to make them fit, but I wear them everywhere I go" (15). If the residents of this building have been "abandoned," the interpersonal and ethical commitments of the two women of color, continued on into the afterlife, hold the possibility of challenging the social and political policies and practices that produced such abandonment in the first place.

Chapter 2, "Marvels of Inventiveness," considers how Black women, as early as Harriet Jacobs in *Incidents in the Life of Slave Girl* (1861), have long advanced feminist models of an agential afterlife that creates and sustains such connections between and among them—and they continue to do so. As I argue in this chapter, Black feminist representations of heavenly justice continue in the present, as in the work of Janelle Monáe. In Monáe's version of a Black Feminist afterlife, or at least an alternative post-death reality, Black queer women, transgender women, and nonbinary people can experience thriving individual being as well as vibrant collectivity. For example, at the end of their (Monáe's preferred pronoun) 2010 video *Many Moons*, Monáe's alter ego, android performer Cindi Mayweather, short-circuits as a result of an increasingly frenzied recitation of historical and contemporary sufferings—including "Welfare, bubonic plague" and "HIV, lost hope"—only to be welcomed "home" to "Shangri-La" by others of their kind, namely other androids replicated on the model of Mayweather.[37] Together all the androids sing, "And when the world just treats you wrong / Just come with us and we'll take you home / Shang, shang, shang, Shangri-la."[38] If Mayweather has in fact "died," then they will never be alone in the afterlife.

As I argue in Chapter 3, "Scaled Perfectly to Eternity," such collectivity in death and in the afterlife emerges perhaps most vividly in contemporary African American poetry, as in Danez Smith's 2017 collection *Don't Call Us Dead* and in their (Smith's preferred pronoun) 2020 poetry collection, *HOMIE*. For example, *HOMIE*, from title on, imagines the dead as being like the self. In a three-part poem included in the collection titled "for Andrew," Smith eulogizes and elegizes a friend, a Black man who has died by suicide. The poetic speaker longs to "edit and loop" back in time to when their vibrant and vital friend "wore the rainbow / beaded crown à la Stevie in the '70s," walking "like some Southside Buddha" with a "boombox dangling from your neck old Radio Raheem / looking ass dude blasting" music.[39] The combination of past and present-participial verb forms in these lines serves as the formal expression of how the speaker's friend, like all the dead who are remembered and memorialized by their loved ones, embodies and evokes multiple time periods. In this poem, those periods include the timelessness of Buddha, Stevie Wonder during the 1970s, and Spike Lee's 1989 film, *Do the Right Thing*. The speaker goes on to reflect on the potentialities of such time-blending, particularly when it extends into the afterlife: "we have no word for, only myth / & faith & doubt about the place that lives—we hope lives—after the body / spits out the soul like a seed" (45). As Chapter 3 argues, we see again and again in contemporary Black poetry precisely this motif of death as part of an organic process, one that begins with dirt-bound pain and loss ("when you went i choked on dirt," 47), yet is followed by rebirth through an afterlife marked by sound, as the departed loved one in "for Andrew" has "nothing left to leave me / but sound" (49). The dirt, the seed, the sound: these are the elements of what I term in Chapter 3 "a contemporary Black poetics of the afterlife," an afterlife where, for Smith, "the wind is tangled / with the dust of dead homies."[40]

Chapter 4, "Wade in the Water," on hip hop and sorrow songs, particularly "Wade in the Water," draws on and weaves together many of the terms and arguments of the preceding chapters. It also returns to the first chapter on Spiritualism and to this introduction's discussion of Toomer's "Cotton Song." The chapter thus offers a structural-methodological mirroring of hip hop's own primary musical modality of *sampling*, which, as Alex Weheliye has observed of DJ's mixing and sampling, combines "the archival and the sonic," resulting in a "sonic projection of temporality."[41] This temporal-sonic-archival triad matches the afterlife itself as it is theorized by so many hip hop artists. Indeed, given the nearly overwhelming prevalence of hip hop lyrics about anticipated death, death itself, and the afterlife—particularly in the 1990s—this chapter, rather than advancing an argument based on an exhaustive survey, takes a case study approach via the works of Kendrick Lamar, Notorious B.I.G., and Tupac Shakur. These three artists repeatedly turn and return to death—but also to *resurrection*. The term *resurrection* and the idea of resurrection recur throughout their song titles, lyrics, album titles. *Resurrection* is also the subtitle of a posthumous biographical documentary about Shakur made up entirely of his own words, sampled and repurposed, seemingly in order to bring him back, sonically at least, from the dead.[42]

As I argue in Chapter 1, while the afterlife certainly works across multiple sensory registers, the sonic served as its primary sensory modality, at least as Spiritualists understood the afterlife in the nineteenth century. In its own theorizing of the afterlife, hip hop retains sonic technologies but layers visual technologies onto them, as in Kendrick Lamar's use of AI to bring Kobe Bryant and Nipsey Hussle back, facially-visually, in the 2022 video *The Heart Part 5* and as in the well-known video for Tupac Shakur's song *I Wonder If Heaven Got a Ghetto* (released in 1997 after his death in 1996), wherein heaven is peopled with actors who look like Black celebrities who have passed on.[43] This song prophesied Shakur's own death by shooting, while the video includes visual evidence of multiple faith traditions, including Catholicism, Islam, and Judaism. Chapter 4 explores this sampling of multiple technologies and religions at length, adding Spiritualism to the roster of hip hop's religious-spiritual samplings. For *Soul Sounds*, as is often the case in hip hop, heaven and the afterlife are neither strictly secular nor strictly Christian but rather consist of a conglomeration of sounds and sights/sites that could help build a new world in the now.

In its application of sound studies across time periods, *Soul Sounds* is arguing implicitly for a transhistorical sound studies, just as it is arguing for transhistorical literary studies. As Paul Gilroy writes, "Black Atlantic self-making and sociality can be explored through organised sound: music and song."[44] By contrast, the field of sound studies has generally advanced period- and location-specific analyses of sound, sound technologies, and soundscapes. For instance, Schafer's definition of "soundscape" points to its "definition of space" and its connection to particular "social conditions."[45] To give just one example of this place- and time-based form of sound studies, Mark M. Smith's brilliant 2001 book, *Listening to Nineteenth-Century America*, offers a sustained analysis of what US "slavery sounded like" in the South, drawing on representations of the sounds of whips, of bells, and the cries of the enslaved.[46] In *Soul Sounds*, sound across time and genre offers, rather than a record of subjection, a sonic-formal means to hear and draw on the power of eternal life.

Throughout *Soul Sounds*, my sustained analysis of form, whether sonic, musical, or literary, emerges out of that central premise: that African American literature and music and their representations of the afterlife through particular aesthetic forms across a long tradition can help build the world anew. As we shall see, especially in Chapter 4, the afterlife thus becomes at once a technology and an art that permits the imagination and construction of that "better place" in the here and now. That here and now may be "filled with shadows," as Colbert says, yet those shadows may also leave shoes for us, shoes that, even if we "have to slip on an extra pair of socks to make them fit," we can "wear . . . everywhere" we go. Then we may be able to construct a new world that truly fits.

1

Dealings with the Dead

Paschal Beverly Randolph and Afrofuturism

This chapter's title is taken from the 1861 book *Dealings with the Dead: The Human Soul, Its Migrations and Its Transmigrations* by the nineteenth-century African American author, occultist, and sex magician Paschal Beverly Randolph (1825–1875).[1] Randolph was a remarkable—and remarkably strange—figure. According to his biographer, John Patrick Deveney, one of Randolph's friends once wrote to another friend: "Randolph is the weirdest person I ever met in my life."[2] Randolph was well known during his lifetime not only for his weirdness but also for his work as trance medium, clairvoyant physician, and consultant for sexual ailments. He wrote and spoke publicly for abolition, too, and seems to have, like Frederick Douglass, helped recruit Black soldiers for the Civil War. Over the course of this wide-ranging career, Randolph achieved a significant degree of national and international fame. He traveled widely in the United States, Europe, and the Middle East and emerged as a prominent Spiritualist in Boston, San Francisco, London, and Paris. Unfortunately, he also experienced a number of failed business and publishing ventures; adding to his trials, he was disabled in 1873 as a result of an accident at a train track that left his left side partially paralyzed.[3] These experiences, in combination with a lifelong struggle with depression, contributed to Randolph's deep despair in the final years of his life. On July 29, 1875, at age fifty he took his own life by shooting himself with a revolver (see figure 1).[4]

Such a compelling life and death certainly merits the attention of historians of Spiritualism and the occult, and Randolph's prolific writing career would seem to compel it from literary scholars. He published or, more often, self-published a great deal of fiction and nonfiction, including many

Figure 1
Photographic portrait of Paschal Beverly Randolph.
Rodney Poole, Public domain, via Wikimedia Commons.

Spiritualist and Rosicrucian books, essays, and pamphlets. This frequent self-publication, along with the publishing difficulties that contributed to the downward spiral at the end of Randolph's life, are, to a degree, representative of the extraordinary challenges Black authors faced in the nineteenth-century US publishing world. As Alex Black points out in an article on William Still's writings, the publication of "much of early African American print culture . . . was a matter of self-direction as well as of self-defense," while "the demand that Black writers self-finance their books often meant that they depended on white publishers or forms of publication that had become outmoded," such that Randolph's being both "Author and Publisher" for several of his books should come as no surprise.[5] What distinguishes Randolph from Still, however, is a lack of the sustained Black network that Still had in place to support his publishing efforts, as Alex Black shows.

Randolph nonetheless managed to put into print an astonishing volume of writings, self-published or not.[6] In 1863, he published two novels: *The Wonderful Story of Ravalette* and *Tom Clark and His Wife, Their Double Dreams and the Curious Things That Befell Them Therein; or, The Rosicrucian's Story*.[7] Near the end of his life, in 1872, he published an autobiography, *The "Learned Pundit" and "Man With Two Souls": His Curious Life, Works, and Career. The Great Free-Love Trial. Randolph's Grand Defence. His Address to the Jury, and Mankind. The Verdict* (a title that suggests the book's strange blend of fiction and nonfiction). Despite this substantial body of writing, only a small handful of literary scholars have studied his literary output.[8] Even a 2020 special issue of *American Literary History* on "the genealogies of Black modernity in the nineteenth century,"[9] as capacious as it is, contains no mention of Randolph, even though it does consider nineteenth-century Black print culture quite broadly and includes consideration of many other nineteenth-century Black authors in the Americas, including the very canonical (e.g., Douglass) and the much less so (e.g., Florence Hall). Other than his biographer, Patrick Deveney, those scholars who have attended closely to Randolph's work include a few anthropologists, religious studies scholars, and historians of Spiritualism, all of whom have focused, not on his fiction or his autobiography, but rather on his participation in the Spiritualist movement and the occult or on his contributions to the literature of sexual magic.[10]

This neglect of Randolph as a writer, coupled with the recovery of his literary writings, usefully complicates a number of prominent debates within contemporary literary and cultural studies. For instance, given how intensely scholars have, for decades, debated which texts constitute the earliest African American–authored novels, it is astonishing that Randolph's have, to date, garnered almost no attention.[11] So why this scholarly neglect? The strangeness and inconsistency of Randolph's beliefs and his convoluted prose style go some way toward explaining it.[12] But perhaps most damning for his legacy, at least as an African American writer, are his inconsistent racial self-identification and his not infrequent expressions of anti-Black and anti-Asian prejudice. One need not be Eve Kosofsky Sedgwick's paranoid reader to discern the problems with Randolph's writings on race.[13] To give just one example, he once wrote, "A true negro [*sic*]" can "never surpass in capacity the adolescent average Anglo-Saxon."[14] Lana Finley, one of the few literary scholars to have focused on Randolph's writings, reasonably concludes that Randolph's "legacy was not preserved by the Black community on account of his radical spiritual beliefs and questionable racial politics."[15] Randolph uncomfortably throws into relief still in-play questions of whether an author's chosen racial identity, or their sustained contact with a Black community, or the presence of Black characters and overtly racial content in their writings, or particular political or cultural views, ought to serve as criteria for inclusion in an African American literary tradition or canon.

And yet Randolph's writing, however troubling it may be, at times does offer some distinctly reparative possibilities as well as substantial evidence that his writings belong within a canon of African American literature. Thus I am suggesting here that we work toward a recovery of Randolph's vexing legacy, and I do so for three reasons in addition to how his work intervenes in contemporary literary-scholarly debates. First, his biography intersects with an astonishingly wide range of circumstances in the nineteenth-century United States, from cholera epidemics to abolitionism to Civil War to Spiritualism, such that his life effectively metonymizes the period.[16] To study Randolph is to enable a better understanding of the nation and its enduring failure to deliver on its promises of democracy and egalitarianism, particularly because Randolph's writings alternatively challenge and reinforce the social hierarchies of his day. To put this more plainly, like his publishing record, his life and work more broadly are representative of the paranoia and the reparation, the problems and the potentialities of his time—and, as we shall see, of ours. Second, Randolph's fantastic beliefs and writings stand as an important, yet heretofore overlooked, antecedent for Afrofuturism.[17] Afrofuturism, a flourishing contemporary cultural and political movement, represents, theorizes, and centers Black subjectivity and Black vitality via complex temporalities and fantastic modalities, both of which likewise characterized US Spiritualism, particularly Randolph's version of it. Finally, and perhaps most important, a long-standing Black temporal-fantastic tradition, to which I contend in this chapter that Randolph and his writings belong, can be tapped in our present to support and sustain global protests against structural, indeed national-foundational, racism and the violent and traumatic deaths of Black people—whether at the hands of the police or by COVID-19.

Spiritualism and Afrofuturism, Black afterlives and Black futures, can help us imagine and build a better world, after the toppling and the burning that come before.[18] As Anna Kornbluh has argued, "Theory must prepare to build things up, and literature models that building."[19] Afrofuturism and what Richard Iton termed "the black fantastic," which includes "the conjunctions made possible by the artist-activist," operate at once as theory and art, offering us a double model for (re)building.[20] To adapt Hortense Spillers's words about African American sermons, "the role" of the fantastic as written about by Randolph—and later advanced, albeit in substantially revised form, by contemporary Afrofuturists like Janelle Monáe —is to "replay not only *this* narrative but its *outcome* on the other side of disaster."[21]

In order to recover Randolph and his legacy and (re)place him within histories of African American literature, Spiritualism, and Afrofuturism, I use a combination of time studies and sound studies. Although time studies may seem obviously suited for the study of a figure preoccupied with the afterlife, how might *sound* and sound theory also suit such a recovery project? As I have argued elsewhere, "It makes perfect sense that sound studies would follow on from the recent temporal turn in American and African American literary studies, itself a post-spatial turn development."[22] In fact, it is a commonplace in sound studies that sound indexes both time and space, as in Alain Corbin's classic study of church bells in nineteenth-century rural France, *Village Bells*, in which he noted, "A bell was supposed to be audible everywhere within the bounds of a specific territory," serving to alert everyone within that territory so that they could, for example, arrive for church service on time.[23] In a more recent study of sound in early America, historian Richard Rath argues that ringing bells offered "a way of belonging to something larger than the face-to-face community, whether that something was located in space, as was the nation, or in time, as was [*sic*] the calendar and the seasons."[24] Conventional sound studies, then, understands that sound spans and measures time both socially and spatially. Historian of the senses Mark M. Smith succinctly expresses this idea with his compelling phrase "the sound of time."[25]

However, as I discussed in the introduction, in this chapter, by placing Spiritualism next to Afrofuturism, I am forging sonic connections across time. Such a transhistorical, nonterritorial approach works especially well in this case because both movements advance a nonlinear sense of time and center sound and music. Certainly, a privileging of sound among Spiritualists has been well established. As sound studies scholar Jonathan Sterne has argued, "Not only did writers in the Spiritualist tradition claim to account for the difference between hearing and seeing: they claimed that the hallmarks of the modern era—reason, rationalism, the subject/object split, science, and capitalism—all emerged from the privilege of sight over audition."[26]

As a consequence, Randolph, along with many Spiritualists, represented the afterlife as being full of sound, with bells often either signifying the transition to the spirit world or announcing the presence of spirits during séances. According to Randolph, "The world we live in is full of the pattering of ghostly feet, and the music of spiritual singers."[27] A later Spiritualist writer in a 1918 issue of *The Occult Review* claimed, "Is it not . . . a fact that bells are among the few material things that we *can*, without any grotesque effort, imagine as present among things spiritual?"[28] Similarly, an anonymous article in the January 1, 1868, issue of *The Spiritual Magazine*, titled "Ring Out the Old, Ring in the New," begins by interpreting the sound of bells at the New Year as a sonic bridge between the past and the future and between the dead and the living.[29] Confirming Sterne's argument about the corrective primacy of sound in Spiritualism, the article goes on to contend that such aural, sense-based evidence of the afterlife permits "modern Spiritualism . . . [to meet] the Materialist on his own ground. He clamors for facts which his senses can take note of. Spiritualism meets this demand in the most simple and direct way" (3). This combination of "facts" and "statistics," along with Spiritualism's "new outpouring of the Divine Spirit" will lead, the writer hopes, to "the entire renovation of the individual and collective life of humanity," thus preparing humans for "the immortal life of the Spirit" (2, 3), with immortality obviating the time- and location-bound nature of sound as habitually theorized.

Of course, it is no coincidence that bells and the sense of hearing frame such ambitious Spiritualist arguments and agendas: The Spiritualist movement in the United States had actually been launched by sound. The movement, at least in its most widespread and popular incarnation, was sparked in 1848 when two Hydesville, New York, sisters declared that they had contacted the spirit world.[30] According to one nineteenth-century skeptic, Kate Fox and Maggie Fox discovered that by cracking their toe knuckles "against a 'substance which is a good conductor of sound,'" as one sister described it, they could create a loud rapping that seemed to come from nowhere in particular.[31] The sisters claimed that these sounds were communications from the dead. This news stoked the Spiritualist movement in the United States; it quickly spread to England, with believers and practitioners as eminent and varied as William James, Francis Galton, Sojourner Truth, and Arthur Conan Doyle. As many scholars of mid- and late nineteenth-century American literature and culture have noted, a Spiritualist vogue persisted in the United States throughout the second half of the nineteenth century.[32] Even well before then, during the late eighteenth and early nineteenth centuries, "new age" beliefs and alternative religions and Spiritualist or occult practices had emerged in Europe and the United States, including Mesmerism, Mormonism, Millerism, Shakerism, and others.[33]

Among all these movements, what enabled Spiritualism's exceptional success in the United States during Randolph's lifetime? The devastating loss of life brought about by the Civil War, cholera and tuberculosis epidemics, and a high infant mortality rate stand as perhaps the clearest causes for American Spiritualism's rise and longevity.[34] In David Nartonis's words, "Bereaved [American] citizens were seeking new assurance of continuity and justice after death."[35] Or, as McGarry succinctly puts it, "Nineteenth-century Spiritualism was a movement of consolation."[36] Like the millions of Americans mourning the loss of loved ones to COVID-19, Randolph and Harriet Wilson, both active in the Spiritualist movement, had *personal* reasons to seek consolation and to yearn for a continuity of life after death—and to try to communicate with the spirit world. Two of Randolph's three children from his first marriage died during the 1850s and 1860s.[37] Wilson's son died in 1860 at the age of seven. Around 1866, Wilson moved to Boston, becoming involved in the thriving Spiritualism movement there and working as a trance medium.[38] For Randolph, however, the losses had begun much earlier.

Randolph was born in 1825 in New York's Five Points district, in dire poverty, to a single Black mother who died of cholera when he was five. Five Points, a Lower Manhattan neighborhood densely populated by Black people and Irish people, was the epicenter of the 1830s New York cholera outbreak that claimed 14 percent of the city's population.[39] As Sari Altschuler and Priscilla Wald have noted, "Like COVID-19, cholera was a wholly new disease in the United States (although considerably deadlier), and it was, like the novel coronavirus, a poorly understood one that disproportionately affected immigrants and African Americans."[40] We can readily see the connection of this epidemiological history to our present, what Altschuler and Wald term our "strangely similar times,"[41] even a kind of awful repetition, with Queens and the Bronx nearly a hundred years later taking Five Points' epidemiological place in New York City. Will we likewise enter a new age of Spiritualism in the wake of such sustained and widespread suffering and death?

But nineteenth-century Spiritualism did not address solely the traumatic material-bodily realities, the prevailing loss and grief, of a post–Civil War United States. It also helped finesse the period's cultural debates. For instance, Spiritualism engaged with all sorts of modern material technologies, including telegraphy and photography, but did so as a means to interact with an immaterial afterworld. A number of scholars of the movement have pointed out the appeal of just this combination of materialism and immaterialism, of science/technology and religion. Religious studies scholar David Walker, for one, has argued that "mediums' own modernity lay neither in singularity of affiliation or diction, nor in ability to collapse or harmonize cultural dichotomies, but rather in their navigations and encampments between them."[42] McGarry concurs: "Many Spiritualists denied basic categorical binaries."[43] Similarly, Christine Ferguson has observed that "Spiritualism was a maverick faith that combined the traditional Christian tenet of the soul's post-life survival with a zealous, albeit flawed, modern empiricism."[44] Spiritualism thus works both as a counter to the period's materialist positivism and as a futurist and spiritual complement to various scientific discourses of the period, including evolution and eugenics, similarly future-oriented bodies of thought.

In precisely this dual fashion, Paschal Beverly Randolph contributed to the period's material scientific and racial discourses, even as he wrote of an immaterial post-death realm. That realm turns out to have been a kind of eugenic spirit-world—that is, a racist and ableist utopia. In *Dealings with the Dead*, Randolph explains that there are "no maimed forms" in the afterlife; all souls "possess excellent health, exhilarant youth, concentration and power."[45] In *After Death*, he offers a more detailed description of the body, ironically enough, of a "disembodied man" in the afterlife:

> Who has bad teeth here, or one eye only, or club feet, or doubtful eyes, find them all right and straight when they get there [and there are] no deformities . . . no matter how crooked, maimed, hacked up, or misshapen one may have been here, he finds himself perfectly whole and sound when he arrives there.[46]

He even asserts that, after death, "negroes [*sic*] lose their crisp, wooly hair, and they are no longer black" (108). Here, Randolph seems to position Blackness itself as a disability.[47] But such a eugenic and racist version of the afterlife was not at all unusual among Spiritualists; again ironically, Randolph was thus representative of the movement as a whole.[48]

But Randolph does stand out among Spiritualists, including other Black Spiritualists, in that he purges not just the afterlife but, at times, *even his own genealogy* of Blackness. That is, Randolph sometimes claimed but at other times denied his Blackness. His mother, he writes in his autobiography, *Curious Life*, using third person, "had not a single drop of Negro in her veins, nor consequently has her son, the subject of this memoir."[49] Perhaps surprisingly, then, Randolph, now in first person, ascribes his "successes" to "my conglomerate blood" (3). Shifting back to third person, he writes:

> The so-called "angularity," and genius with it, of her son, had its origin in the fact that in his veins run no less than seven distinct varieties, or strains of blood, true negro, or continental African *not* constituting one of them; hence, he is not a mulatto, or quadroon, or octoroon, as has been stated, but is probably the most perfect specimen of the composite, or concrete man now living, for it is unquestionably this mingling of various nationalities in him that constitutes the source of his peculiar mental power and almost marvelous versatility. (18)

In this passage, Randolph challenges the period's mainline eugenic thinking by associating racial mixture with superiority, indeed with genius. Yet he excludes Blackness from that mixture, claiming that his father was the wealthy (white) early Virginia colonizer William Randolph (18). There is no evidence to support either claim regarding his parentage. As Deveney points out, Randolph was biracial (Black-white) and had no verifiable connection to William Randolph.[50] Here we see the obstacle to placing Randolph in any African American literary tradition that centers on anti-racist writing by clearly and positively Black-identified authors.[51]

And yet some of Randolph's writings do fit readily into such a canon; likewise, he himself does, at times, comport with conventional notions of African American authorship. For example, in his abolitionist and race work Randolph consistently identified himself as being "of color." In 1864, the *New Orleans Tribune* published a letter from Randolph in which he opposed any colonization scheme for emancipated people:

> We men of color were born here; so were our fathers, and our mothers down a long line of ancestry: Our blood, bones, nerves—every particle of our bodies was and is composed of American soil, air, water, and our souls are American all the way through, all of which, so it seems to me, constitutes us Americans.[52]

One of his novels, too, argued explicitly for full and unfettered Black citizenship. The byzantine plot of his 1863 *Tom Clark and His Wife* offers a remarkable defense of African American civil rights alongside an equally remarkable (at least for his period) feminist argument for companionate marriage, though admittedly in the context of an anti-divorce screed. I turn now to a close analysis of *Tom Clark*, and in doing so I am in agreement with Anna Kornbluh's eloquent rebuttal of "anti-critique" and "post-critique" arguments and with her advocacy of novels and their form as an avenue for the critique necessary to improve a world in dire need of improvement. In her words, novels' "special kind of world making and world interpreting" can aid "imaginative rebuilding."[53] Randolph's novels certainly engage in "imaginative rebuilding," as we shall see, with *Tom Clark* offering some remarkable and clearly allegorical "world making and world interpreting." Randolph's novel critiques fraught unions between two people that quickly come to stand for a United States riven in what were then and are now familiar ways.

The novel begins as a frame narrative in which a Randolph-like first-person narrator, who is traveling from San Francisco to Panama on a steamboat—tellingly named the *Uncle Sam*—introduces readers to an also Randolph-like character, a storyteller who is identified twice in the story as "Paschal." Echoing the over-the-top self-descriptions of Randolph's autobiography, the narrator describes the storyteller-character as "some sort of a mystic, a dreamer, or some such out-of-the-ordinary style of person, because everything he said or did bore an unmistakable ghostly impress."[54] In Part I of the novel, this mystical storyteller details his dream of an afterlife encounter with his beautiful long-dead lover, Lara, during which he must demonstrate his mastery of proper moral action in order to be worthy of her love and to establish their eternal bond. In Part II, the storyteller, now identified as "the Rosicrucian," tells a seemingly unrelated tale of an unhappy marriage between Tom Clark and his wife, Betsey, both of whom—like the Rosicrucian in his dream—must learn to be worthy of their partner. Preoccupied with their spouse's faults, each contemplates murdering the other. As they fall into separate dream states, Tom and Betsey both encounter in their dreams the same terrible shadowy creature that embodies the evil of their mutual disdain.

At this point, the story makes what seems at first to be a wholly unrelated digression. The Rosicrucian storyteller interrupts the narrative flow to offer an impassioned plea for the civil rights of African American men because of their Civil War service (Part II). He calls out the names of battles in which Black soldiers fought valiantly for the Union: "Remember Milliken's Bend, Port Hudson, Fort Wagner, and the Black Heroes of the war—Noble men—Black, too, but the bravest of the brave—yet treated not as heroes ought to be. Forget not Fredericksburg!" He then chastises white Northerners for their racism and for their failure to remember and to honor these Black heroes:

> Bear in mind that this gorgon of your own creation will not quit you, day or night—not even on your dying day, when it will hiss into your ears, "Father, behold, embrace me!"—and its slime will fall upon and choke you, as you have choked our country. And the sheeted ghosts of six hundred thousand heroes, slaughtered by a whim, will mournfully upbraid, and—perhaps—forgive you. (Part II, para. 38)

What makes this passage *not* a digression is the fact that both marriages—that is, the Rosicrucian's and the Clarks'—allegorize a split within the Union, with Tom and Betsey and North and South alike haunted by a terrible beast with its sounds of hissing and rebuking, a sonic "gorgon" of hostile division that will be sustained in the future. Slavery produced one kind of division—a regional one[55]—but white supremacy produces another kind of division—an interracial and national one—that damages and haunts the union and will continue to do so long after the Civil War, on into our present. At this writing, we are mourning well over one million dead, far surpassing the total number of Americans killed in the Civil War (though of course the percentage of the US population dying in the Civil War, around 2.5 percent, is far larger than the population percentage of those dying with COVID-19—to date, about 0.35

percent).[56] Randolph's jeremiad-like revelation of the terrible consequences of a collective failure to truly "reconstruct" a divided nation thus works, for Randolph's own time, as analysis—but for ours, as prophecy.

By way of some consolation, the novel offers its readers an alternative reconstruction: a vision of healing and of reparation. The prophetic narrator in Part II of *Tom Clark and His Wife* imagines a different future, a positive and magical one:

> See, yonder is a plain, miles in extent. In its centre there stands an obelisk. Go, Ministers of State, and plant on its top a banner, upon which shall be emblazoned this magic sentence: "Freedom—Personal, Political, and Social, to the Black man—and protection of his Rights forever," and there will be more magnetic power in it than in ten thousand Ministers, with their little whims; ten thousand "Fancy Generals," with their "pretty little games,"—and such would be History's record when she handed you down the ages. (Part II, para. 39)

Like David Walker in his 1829 *Appeal*, Randolph here invokes the power of the seer, a kind of temporal magic, to reveal the differential consequences of either perpetuating or eliminating white supremacy. Walker in his jeremiad had predicted the Civil War:

> A just and holy Being will at one day appear fully in behalf of the oppressed, and arrest the progress of the avaricious oppressors; for although the destruction of the oppressors God may not effect by the oppressed, yet the Lord our God will bring other destructions upon them—for not unfrequently will he cause them to rise up one against another, to be split and divided, and to oppress each other, and sometimes to open hostilities with sword in hand.[57]

Then, in 1863, in the midst of Walker's prophecy come true, Randolph predicts, via his own jeremiad (the frame narrator repeatedly terms the story a "sermon"), the immortal monstrousness of the nation's and of white liberals' continuous refusal to eradicate white supremacy once and for all. Yet eliminating white supremacy represents the nation's only possible salvation, and, as Albanese argues, "All American magic comes down to salvation, and salvation means healing."[58] Via full and timeless African American citizenship, we may be able to build alternative monuments that carry the magnetism, the magic, required to heal the nation. As the ongoing struggle over Confederate monuments shows, only in a mystical dreamworld can magnetic obelisks readily, and without resistance, heal divisions in marriages/nations such that we achieve what Randolph's storyteller terms a "re-United States" (Part VII, para.

58). Just so, the Clarks ultimately reconcile, awakening from their dreams and deciding to love and appreciate one another, thereby preserving the marriage/union.

We learn at novel's end that the story of the Clarks is actually the Rosicrucian's own story, and therefore also Randolph's, given that the storyteller-Rosicrucian is named Paschal. These layers establish the novel as a double-frame narrative; moreover, the novel begins with a dedication, signed "P. B. Randolph," creating a triple frame. This merging of multiple frames in an 1863 novel points to the long-standing deployment of the fantastic in African American aesthetic forms in order to construct a real, material world wherein the Black artist/writer exerts a magical power to improve that world. As Michelle Commander has argued, "speculation" has long worked to produce "a subversive way of life for Black Americans," one that conjures the possibility of "a global realization of a Black fantastic" that in turn offers a "refutation of the futurelessness promised by life in the United States."[59] In just this way, Randolph's fantastic story builds a novelistic world in which author, narrator, storyteller, and character become one by means of narrative alchemy, a literary-formal magic, creating a fiction that in turn conjures a more perfect future union—one not just inclusive of but represented by and centered on Black people. The result: Randolph capitalized on the reforming and the rebuilding potential of both Spiritualism and the novel.

Similarly, he capitalized on the potentialities of what we might term fantastic *non*fiction to represent the afterlife and its power to reimagine this-life. For instance, in *Dealings with the Dead,* Randolph uses a first-person narrator, once again a stand-in for himself, to describe the afterlife experiences of his real-life close friend, Cynthia, who had died of "consumption" (tuberculosis) in 1854 and then passed "beyond the veil" to enter the spirit world (12). Like *Tom Clark,* then, *Dealings with the Dead* represents and reimagines difficult material conditions of Randolph's time. As Sheila Rothman points out, "Tuberculosis was the leading cause of death in the United States throughout the nineteenth century," being "responsible for one out of every five deaths" at the time of Cynthia's death.[60] Even after Cynthia has passed on, Randolph stays in contact with her as she reports from the afterlife. In sum, the book consists of "the facts of a living, dying, dead and transfigured human being" related by Cynthia and delivered to us by Randolph, as medium, in order to critique the world of the still-living (14).

Perhaps not surprisingly, given Spiritualists' privileging of hearing over seeing, upon realizing that she has died, Cynthia's first experience is one of sound, specifically the sound of a voice: "Not mine," Cynthia says, but "a lower, sweeter, more musical voice, soft and dulcet as the tinkle of a love bell"

(16). As Corbin notes, "One of the functions of the bell was to orient travelers or navigators within the space covered by its sound," that is, its "soundmark."[61] Thus, the bell-like sound that Cynthia hears lets her know that she has entered "the land of the Immortal," once again extracting sound from any particular earthly location and from linear time (16). Religious studies scholar Charles Hirschkind confirms that "for Christians in the nineteenth-century United States, divine acoustics often took the form of thunderclaps, heavenly bells and trumpets, or the sublime voices of angels."[62] But Cynthia is at first surprised that she can hear at all after her death:

> I had, to a certain extent, familiarized myself with Physics, and knew that sounds were supposed to be the result of certain aerial vibrations. Now, supposing this theory to be correct, it struck me, that I, a disembodied soul, ought not to be competent to discern sounds, for there was neither tympanum to *receive*, auditory nerves to *conduct*, nor external ear to *collect* these waves of sound. (16–17, emphasis in original)

As this passage shows, Cynthia has trouble reconciling immaterial spirit with this initial afterlife experience of seemingly material sound. But eventually she comes to understand that "Spirit animates the material things, but itself is not material" (22). This quasi-materiality of the afterlife, like the ringing of a bell (and like sound in general) is experiential, located in perception rather than strictly in the physical body, and thus operates as at once located and unlocated (temporally and spatially) and as both embodied and disembodied. As Julian Henriques aptly puts it, "*The sonic is as disembodying as it is embodying*."[63] It is here that we can begin to find common ground between Randolph and contemporary Afrofuturists, who generally offer much more explicit critique of this world along with visions of an alternative, more just one.

This material, if not precisely or strictly embodied, experience of sound, combined with an immateriality of spirit in *Dealings with the Dead*, bears a remarkable resemblance to Afrofuturist theorist Kodwo Eshun's concept of sonic futurism as laid out in his 1998 book, *More Brilliant Than the Sun*. For Eshun, the sonic is inseparable from nonlinear temporality: "To go back to a sonic past is to go forward into a new future," he argues.[64] Likewise, for Randolph's Cynthia, musical sound is the first sign that she has crossed over to "the other side of time" (255). Moreover, according to Eshun, music *is* the theory that underpins Afrofuturism (00[-004]). Eshun's unorthodox pagination in the introduction, a countdown rather than a count up that goes from 00[-007] to 00[000], disrupts conventional linear print and reading practices right at the start. This strategy, although not sustained throughout the book, reflects Eshun's effort to replicate for his readers sonic futurism's, and especially music's, temporally dislocating yet ultimately empowering effects on listeners. Eshun argues that music precedes and surpasses any other sort of theory precisely because it moves beyond theory's temporal limits, and he aims in *More Brilliant Than the Sun* to encourage "music in its despotic drive to crumple chronology like an empty bag of crisps" (00[-004, -006]). This chronology-crumpling project, like Eshun's initial pagination-crumpling, is liberatory in that it undermines the linear timelines of Western/Enlightenment-based humanism that had rendered Black people as less-than-human objects; as Eshun puts it, "The human is a pointless and treacherous category" (00[-005]).

It is logical, then, to claim, as Eshun does, that the "music of Alice Coltrane and Sun Ra, of Underground Resistance and George Russell, of Tricky and Martina . . . arrives from the future" (00[-006-5]). And, again as in *Dealings with the Dead*, Eshun's Afrofuturism associates the primacy of the sonic with the experiential, with perception and affect that in turn enhance us. As Eshun puts it, "Machines don't distance you from your emotions, in fact quite the opposite. Sound machines make you feel more intensely, along a broader band of emotional spectra than ever before. . . . Sonically speaking, the posthuman era is not one of disembodiment, but the exact opposite: it's a hyperembodiment (00[-002])." Eshun's rejection of "disembodiment" may at first seem incompatible with Randolph's "disembodied soul"; however, *Dealings with the Dead* likewise "crumples chronology" by associating a particular kind of "hyperembodiment" with the afterlife. Cynthia reports that a human spirit "has thirst, hunger, and amatory love, all of which have their appropriate gratification in the Spirit-world," which is, like Eshun's, a world enhanced and liberated from a particular time-place and its physical laws (21).

Randolph, as medium and frame narrator, stays in contact with Cynthia as she details that "amatory love." Because the usual physical laws do not apply in the afterlife, sex in the afterworld does not result in pregnancy but rather works as the expression of soul-mate love among equals: "Every one [*sic*] has a conjugal mate in the universe" (31). And sex in the afterlife, it turns out, is far better than ante-mortem sex. Here in the afterlife, reports Cynthia, sex "reaches a point of fullness, completion and intensity . . . [such that] No body [in the living world] is capable of either giving or receiving . . . even a foretaste of the joys which the soul, freed therefrom, can and does spontaneously" (52). In this radical challenge to his period's predominant models of marriage and sex, Randolph, once again, represents Spiritualism more broadly. As Braude has argued, the companionate marriage that many Spiritualists promoted, and that appeared in their versions of the afterlife, served to critique marriage in their earthbound present.[65] Thus, we can read Randolph's afterlife, with its mutually enjoyable nonreproductive heterosexual sex between equals (or soulmates), as a critique of his material present with its restrictive, heteropatriarchal notions of sexuality and marriage.[66]

But Randolph's ideas about sex went much farther than a relatively straightforward critique of his period's strictures regarding marriage and sexuality. He was an enthusiastic practitioner of sex magic, which religious studies scholar Hugh B. Urban succinctly defines as "the explicit use of sexual intercourse and genital orgasm as a source of creative magical power that can be harnessed and manipulated by the practitioner."[67] For example, Randolph advocated the use of magic mirrors—made magic in part by the application of "magnetic effluvium from the eyes," menstrual blood, or semen.[68] These "magnetic" or "magic" mirrors," as described in his 1874 book, *Eulis!*, granted a range of special powers, depending upon their particular formulae, including becoming clairvoyant, finding true love, and, for men, being able to hone their sperm in order to achieve "the most magnificent results."[69] Randolph coyly leaves out of the book the formula for this process, directing readers to one of his for-sale pamphlets should they want the details. Like Harriet Wilson, he was "forced to some experiment," it would appear, to make a living.[70] This spermatic process, available to "such noble souls as can appreciate it," guarantees more perfect "generation" (offspring) and possibly even immortality (176). Randolph regularly links love and sex, done right at least, with power, more specifically with "Master-Potency, Power, Energy" (31)—and with soul and thus with immortality and the afterlife, in accordance with what Christine Ferguson has termed Randolph's "occult form of sexual science."[71] "They who waste love, waste soul," he writes in *Eulis!*, and will therefore be kept "patiently waiting" back on earth until they can reach the "glittering, golden, sunny shores beyond" (185).

Like his unsteady racial identification and his racial prejudices, Randolph's fantastic sexual-spirit world distinguishes him from other African American writers of the period. Pauline Hopkins and Harriet Wilson, for example, engaged in more conventional forms of Spiritualism, and Hopkins, at least, represented far more traditional forms of marriage, as well, in what Ann duCille has famously termed "the coupling convention."[72] DuCille does argue convincingly that Wilson, unlike Hopkins, offered "inversions and subversions" of conventional marriage and marriage plots.[73] And yet neither Hopkins nor Wilson invented radical alternatives to those forms, as did Randolph. So, although sex magic certainly sets Randolph apart from conventional constructions of a nineteenth-century African American literary tradition, it does, as we shall see, help him fit into a genealogy of Afrofuturism.

Just as sound and (hyper)embodiment brought Randolph into conversation with Eshun, sex magic brings him into conversation with the quintessential twenty-first-century Afrofuturist: Janelle Monáe.[74] At the same time, Monáe, too, is in conversation with Eshun. In a kind of contemporary version of sex magic, Monáe sings in the song "Screwed" from *Dirty Computer*, "Everything is sex / Except sex, which is power."[75] Similarly, in a privately circulated pamphlet, Randolph wrote, "True Sex-Power is God-power."[76] And Eshun's Randolph-like temporal-sonic argument, particularly his point that "machines don't distance you from your emotions, in fact quite the opposite" (00[-002]), finds expression in Monáe's cross-album persona as the clearly *feeling* rebel-android Cindi Mayweather. Mayweather has time-traveled to our present from the year 2719 and has created a new form of music called "cyber-soul,"[77] with soul carrying the double meaning of soul music and the soul of a cyborg who, like Randolph's Cynthia, experiences "the other side of time." Monáe's 2018 album and "emotion picture" (the film's subtitle) *Dirty Computer*, like both Randolph's sex magic and Eshun's sonic futurism, link an improved this-world with sexual agency and with the power of the fantastic, while advancing the revelatory and liberatory potential of an emotional human-as-computer—and this remains so even after Monáe left behind their Mayweather alter ego with *Dirty Computer*.

In "Screwed," song and video together deliver a musically and visually layered critique of the present, with its class, racial, economic, gender, and sexual politics and oppressions. It also represents the joyful power of Black queer love. The music in "Screwed" mirrors that layered complexity, modulating from upbeat major, a kind of summer-anthem sound, to slower minor sections and to relatively brief rapping/spoken word by Monáe in which they deliver the song's most explicit critique of the present: "Hundred men telling me cover up my areolas / While they blocking equal pay, sippin' on they Coca Colas (oh) . . . / The devil met with Russia and they just made a deal / We was marching through the street / They were blocking every bill (oh) / I'm tired of hoteps tryna tell me how to feel / For real."[78] These lyrics deliver a thorough and efficient send-up of US neoliberalism and misogyny as well as of intra-racial (Black) masculinism ("hoteps") and of misogynoir.[79] For most of "Screwed," however, Monáe sings and dances joyfully with their "electric ladies"[80]—all Black women, including Tessa Thompson (who may or may not have been Monáe's real-life lover). These scenes are interspersed with scenes of Monáe's character's tender and passionate interaction with two lovers, one man and one woman (not Thompson), all while the three are pursued by state agents of surveillance, control, and punishment (the drone surveillance in the video is eerily prescient of the surveillance of Black Lives Matter protesters after Derek Chauvin's murder of George Floyd).[81] In some of these scenes, Monáe's character wears a shirt that reads, "subject not object."

Of course, there are also significant, even extreme, disconnections between Monáe's Afrofuturism and Randolph's version of Spiritualism. For one thing, Randolph's sex magic is both masculinist and heterosexist (heteropatriarchal), while he viewed those with nonbinary gender expression as "monstrosities" who were "born wrong."[82] Monáe constructs a very different version of sexual magic, one that alchemizes the sexual and political power of Black women and of Black queer women in particular, including trans-women, as subjects engaged in collective action inseparable from sex.[83] As they sing, "You fucked the world up now/we'll fuck it all back down."[84] Monáe's songs and videos and their time-traveling persona Cindi Mayweather harmonize perfectly, then, with much contemporary queer performance and time theory. In José Muñoz's words, this is "queerness as collectivity," as utopia[85]—or, in Monáe's words in "Screwed," "paradise found."[86] Just as Elizabeth Freeman noted so brilliantly, "Temporality has inflected queer theory from the outset."[87] For Freeman, queer temporality emerged most vividly in those "moments" in queer cultural production during which "an established temporal order"—or "chrononormativity"—is "interrupted" (3, xxii). She concluded that "performance, affect, and even sex itself, through the work they [queer people] do with time and history, might be knowledge practices" (173). This is an ideal framework for understanding Monáe's entire body of work as a performative "knowledge practice" that, in the case of *Dirty Computer*, particularly its "PYNK" section, recreates (in both senses of the word) a world in which Black queer women and transgender people collectively build a world so vital that even the desert blooms (24:56–25:03).[88] This is not just sex power and is certainly not "master potency," but rather "Pussy Power" (27:11), with no obelisks in sight. The "weird," it turns out, is *not* the same thing as the queer.[89]

Still, Randolph's entire career and oeuvre, I would argue, testify to his individual struggle to become *subject* rather than *object* in the absence of the Black collectivity that Monáe possesses in abundance. So, are literary scholars right to exclude Randolph and his work in part because, unlike other nineteenth-century authors like William Still, he did not belong to predominantly Black institutions or networks such as the AME church or, in Carla Peterson's words, "an active circle of Black readers and writers"?[90] This is not to say that Randolph utterly lacked Black community. He corresponded with Frederick Douglass, and he attended and spoke at the National Convention of Colored Men held in the city of Syracuse, New York, in 1864, as P. Gabrielle Foreman's major digital humanities project, *Colored Conventions Project*, has documented.[91] Although he more often remained outside such "active circles," Randolph did share with other Black intellectuals and activists of the nineteenth century the impact of dominant, virulently racist discourses (e.g., mainline eugenics) and laws (e.g., *Dred Scott v. Sanford*) that insisted on Black objecthood and noncitizenship. As Deveney puts it, "He was a black man who tried with considerable success to succeed in a white world and to do so on his own terms rather than as the merely symbolical Black Man erected by the forces of organized reform."[92]

In such contexts, Randolph's inconsistency about his racial identity, along with his failure to consistently challenge those racist discourses, becomes more legible. Throughout his lifetime, Blackness was constructed as "dirty," not in the recuperated and Black- and queer-positive sense that Monáe deploys the term, but as part of a process geographer Kathryn Yusoff has described as "a historically constituted and intentionally enacted deformation in the formation of [Black] subjectivity."[93] This enactment, ironically and awfully, includes the workings of nineteenth-century US Spiritualism, in which any blurring of the subject-object binary seemed always to work to the disadvantage of the nonwhite.[94] So Randolph struggled: on the one hand, embracing his Blackness and challenging the racist discourses of his day, and on the other hand, denying his Blackness and reinforcing those discourses. Even his eugenic, ableist version of the afterlife could be interpreted in the context of his own disability and his possible desire to reinhabit, in the afterlife, the body he possessed before the railway accident. Ultimately, however, Spiritualism, with its inseparability from the period's racist and ableist hierarchies, could not supply Randolph with the form of subjecthood he sought; in 1875, he repudiated the movement.[95] So he belonged to the Spiritualist movement, but only up to a point, just as he embraced, only up to a point, a Black identity. Admittedly, then, he seems to belong at most only partially and contingently to a genealogy of a contemporary Afrofuturism that so often centers on Black women and queerness.

And yet I contend that his sex magic, along with the sonic and especially the temporal dimensions of Randolph's afterlife, ultimately secures his place in that genealogy. As McGarry has observed, "Spiritualist practice collapsed time and refused to accept the past as over."[96] In Randolph's words, "Soul, like God, is from forever in the past, to forever in the distance."[97] As I argued in the introduction, the world of the soul, the afterlife, constitutes a future while also being eternal. Only for those of us who are still living does it necessarily reside in the future. Similarly, the figures and texts we currently identify as Afrofuturist do not strictly look to or solely construct a future. Rather, as scholar of Afrofuturism Ytasha Womack has pointed out, "In some cases, it's a total reenvisioning of the past."[98] Eshun offers a similar argument: "The field of Afrofuturism does not seek to deny the tradition of countermemory. Rather, it aims to extend that tradition by reorienting the intercultural vectors of Black

Atlantic temporality towards the proleptic as much as the retrospective."[99] Or, as Walter Benjamin expresses this idea: "It's not that what is past casts its light on what is present, or what is present its light on what is past; rather, image is that wherein what has been comes together in a flash with the now to form a constellation."[100]

Perhaps the quintessential twentieth-century Afrofuturists, George Clinton and Parliament-Funkadelic, sing of precisely that—a constellation of times (and literally of the stars) that reenvisions past, present, and future and that centers on Blackness. In a sonic blend of past and present, Parliament on a classic 1975 album layer horns and electronic music in one of their most iconic songs, "Mothership Connection (Star Child)."[101] In it, they sing of being light years in the future *and* of taking a ride, in the present, on the chariot of a traditional sorrow song. Then, delivering an even more densely layered temporality, they sing that they "have returned to reclaim the pyramids," *while* partying on the mothership, which landed *on the stage* in the late 1970s.[102] The mothership is not, therefore, located solely in the future: Like the afterlife, it exists alongside the United States and the earth in their same temporality (just not in a white space), and the entire audience is invited to take a ride on that mothership, forming a sustained Black collective.

So, like Monáe's androids in their *Many Moons* video, who sing "just come with us and we'll take you home," P-Funk and Clinton are "come for to carry you home."[103] But unlike the collective enterprise implied by "us" in *Many Moons*, in the case of P-Funk, although the audience might be *invited* to take a ride on the mothership, neither anyone in the audience nor anyone in the band other than Clinton himself actually climbs into or disembarks from it. Clinton is then, in this limited way at least, a bit like Randolph: a charismatic male medium who can access other places and times for others who remain left behind.[104] This secondary, earthbound status is reinforced by a particular "Mothership Connection (Star Child)" lyric: "You have overcome, for I am here." This line's verb tenses (the present perfect tense, which connects past and present, plus the present tense) and its pronouns (second person plural plus first-person singular) riff on the pronoun and verb in "We shall overcome" (first-person plural plus formal future), throwing into relief Clinton's individual power over the mothership connection and its liberatory possibilities. But, as Muñoz wrote, "Individual transports are insufficient."[105]

On the other hand, P-Funk's "Mothership Connection" lyrics do point, as well, to the collective power that resides in a rearrangement of timelines, just as Womack and Eshun contend. Contemporary Afrofuturists understand, as did Randolph, that linear chronologies and teleological narratives of progress prevent us from accessing an empowering simultaneity of temporalities and knowledges.[106] Benjamin argued similarly that the "awareness that they are about to make the continuum of history explode is characteristic of the revolutionary classes at the moment of their action."[107] By exploding the calendar and crumpling chronology—for example, by blending 1976 (the year of P-Funk's famous Halloween concert in Houston) and 2719 and 2027 and 1863 (the publication year of Randolph's novels)—we can situate: Afrofuturism, contemporary activisms, an African American literary tradition, and Spiritualism together in time and space, thereby tapping, in Alex Weheliye's words, the "revolutionary potentiality of the oppressed in Benjamin's philosophy."[108]

Just as the blending of times and movements can tap "revolutionary potentiality," so too can the blurring of other boundaries, including disciplinary and institutional ones.[109] It is no coincidence that Randolph was, at best, ambivalent about Blackness and that he largely lacked Black community. Likewise, it is no coincidence that Sun Ra had his Arkestra and that George Clinton and Janelle Monáe both belong to artists' collectives, Parliament-Funkadelic and Wondaland respectively.[110] Contemporary Afrofuturism is characterized by collectivity and collaboration, from its origins in Alondra Nelson's Afrofuturism listserv, begun in 1998, to John Jennings's and Stacey Robinson's "Black Kirby," to the Community Futures Lab, to Camae Ayewa's and Rasheedah Phillips's Black Quantum Futurism Collective, and to Phillips's Metropolarity Queer Sci-fi Collective, to name just a few. As Martin Luther King Jr. argued in 1967, "The future of the deep structural changes we seek will not be found in decaying political machines. It lies in new alliances."[111] In 2019, Kara Keeling—in a powerful recombination of King and Janelle Monáe—pointed out that the "fantastic queer times of our lives support unpredictable alliances, theories, knowledges, and connections."[112] Keeling's apt, and, one hopes, prophetic words point to new constellations, new collectives, and new connections that hold the magical power to rebuild our world. Unlike Randolph but like Monáe, "Now *we'll* fuck the world back down" (emphasis added).

In the following chapter, I explore the work of Black feminist contemporaries of both Randolph and Monáe, each of whom engages or performs a kind of "afterlife" that works to confront and contest white supremacy while deeply valuing Black lives, particularly Black women's lives—something that Randolph, unlike Monáe, did not, and perhaps could not, accomplish.

2

"Marvels of Inventiveness"

Black Feminist Technologies of Time

Since 2000, quite a few literary scholars and queer theorists have focused on time and temporality in US literature and culture. This "temporal turn" is associated with the work of scholars such as Wai Chee Dimock, Dana Luciano, Elizabeth Grosz, Jack Halberstam, Elizabeth Freeman, José Muñoz, Carolyn Dinshaw, and other scholars. Genealogies of the turn generally locate its immediate origins in the early 2000s work of Fredric Jameson, Rita Felski, and Ursula Heise, among others, and in Lee Edelman's innovative 2004 book, *No Future*.[1] In the 2010s and 2020s, Black studies took a similar "temporal turn," perhaps best exemplified by Michelle M. Wright's brilliant 2015 book, *The Physics of Blackness*, which challenges progress narratives with their necessarily linear sense of time, including in accounts of Blackness created by Black people themselves. Wright, in her words, "cautions against overreliance on the exclusive use of linear progress narratives to define blackness," urging "equal consideration" of what she terms epiphenomenal time—that is, Blackness in the here and now, or Blackness as a "when" rather than a what.[2] Such challenges to linear understandings of time—as well as of Blackness and Black cultural production—characterize the temporal turn in virtually all 2000s African American, Black, and Black diasporic literary and cultural scholarship on temporality, including Wright's work, as well as that of Anthony Reed, Kara Keeling, Kodwo Eshun, and Habiba Ibrahim. And yet even this timeline regarding Black studies scholarship may itself be too linear, carrying a sense of progression beyond prior scholarship.

As early as the 1980s and 1990s, Black feminist theorists Karla Holloway and Hortense Spillers had already taken a "temporal turn." Toni Morrison and

John Edgar Wideman had done the same in their historical novels even earlier than that, during the late 1970s and early 1980s. For example, Morrison's well-known neologism "rememory," from the novel *Beloved,* along with the living presence of an embodied past in the figure of the character Beloved, offers a narrative interruption of teleological time, a story that is always both passing on and being passed on, as well as a literary challenge to national narratives of progress regarding race and gender. In a 1999 essay, "The Death of Culture," Holloway theorized this Morrisonian form of time:

> A black death permeates our nationalist sensibilities. Its haunting presence is a cultural accompaniment. The ghostly persistence of our history of dying and its absolute association with the color and character of our national experience assure us that something about African America is a time, "out of joint"—a "CP TIME" that finds our daily lives are a complicated matter of color and death.[3]

I wish to introduce a new term to supplement Holloway's analysis of CP Time/CPT, one that does not emphasize Black forms of time as expressions of "haunting" or "dying" or as modes of resistance to a dominating white national presence. Rather than understand those forms in terms of *difference* at all, a term inflected by deconstruction as in Henry Louis Gates's influential *Critical Inquiry* collection, *"Race," Writing, and Difference,* I offer the term *distinctiveness* so as to mitigate the relational quality of "difference," a term that, when used to describe Black texts or people, implies Blackness understood in relation to whiteness and to a departure from a norm.[4]

Holloway's passage, then, in my reading, shows that racially *distinctive* time does not point to essential forms of either race or time, but rather challenges the temporal structures that undergird US white supremacy while affirming the vitality and the normativity of nondominant practices of time and timekeeping. In the same essay, Holloway expresses exactly that idea: "Cultural black time," she writes, "subverts the Occidental moment of our national location and insists [on] a way of imagining ourselves as both here and not here, and then fixing this particular imaginary to the (re)construction of black culture."[5] In her classic 1987 essay, "Mama's Baby, Papa's Maybe," Spillers summed up her own similar cultural-temporal and aesthetic-critical project in this way: "In order for me to speak a truer word concerning myself, I must strip down through layers of attenuated meanings, made an excess in time, over time, assigned by a particular historical order, and there await whatever marvels of my own inventiveness."[6] Here, Spillers describes the critical and creative distinctiveness of a timeline (re)shaped by Blackness and womanhood, quite apart from Holloway's version of CPT.

In what follows, I argue for Black women's historical and present-day use of a range of technologies—including print, sound, cellphone video, and live-streaming—in order to "speak truer words" about themselves and others as they document violent acts of white supremacy and patriarchy and, only seemingly paradoxically, as they also represent an agential afterlife. Black women's documentation of the violent deaths of other Black people offers those who have passed on an afterlife by memorializing them, in perpetuity, while inspiring resistance and activism in others in the present. This is yet another form of legacy, a documentary afterlife designed to make *this* life anew in an act of what Minneapolis-based theologian and activist Barbara A. Holmes termed "radical creativity."[7]

But early Black writers also imagined, particularly in nineteenth-century life narratives such as Harriet Jacobs's and Frederick Douglass's, a more literal Christian afterlife that likewise held the promise of an improved this-world. As James Cone argued in his landmark book, *A Black Theology of Liberation*, "The proper eschatological perspective must be grounded in the historical present, thereby forcing the oppressed community to say no to unjust treatment, because its present humiliation is inconsistent with its promised future."[8] Just so, this chapter's combined literary and religious studies methodology reveals how aesthetics, representation, and belief have long worked together in African American culture to imagine a heaven that promotes justice in the present world and on into the future. The result: a long genealogy of an agential afterlife in African American literature, particularly in Black feminist literature and theory, from the nineteenth century to the present.

Two centuries before Holloway's and Spillers's temporal-political-personal formulations, early African American writers had already analyzed the inextricability of race and time while evincing a deep awareness of and longing for Cone's "promised future." First, at the level of genre, nineteenth-century Black life narratives offer substantial evidence to support Holloway's linkage of culture, race, location, and time(s). In fact, the genre of life narratives by formerly enslaved persons is perhaps uniquely positioned simultaneously within multiple temporalities, for it is centrally concerned with "the relationship between the past, present, and future in the context of blackness," to again use Cone's words.[9] These narratives are, like all memoirs and autobiographies, necessarily retrospective and therefore "live" in both past and present. But unlike autobiographies in general, US narratives by formerly enslaved persons are also oriented always toward the future, toward a post-enslavement time of emancipation. The genre in fact exists, at least in part and perhaps even primarily, to *produce* a better material, national future. This technological feature distinguishes it even from other kinds of life narratives written with specific effects in mind, such as conversion narratives that aim to produce more and better Christians.

Second, at the level of content, again like Holloway's and Spillers' writings, narratives by formerly enslaved persons link race, multi-temporality, and material experience, and they do so in ways that remain relevant for futurist movements by people of color, especially Afrofuturism, lending these narratives yet another kind of afterlife.[10] Afrofuturism is a burgeoning contemporary movement that comprises cultural production and intellection (literature, visual art, photography, film/video, multimedia art, performance art, music, and theory) that imagine greater justice and a freer expression of Black, African, African American, and African Diasporic subjectivity in the future or in alternative places or realities, often via representations of time blending or time traveling. Although the connections between Afrofuturism and what have been conventionally termed "slave narratives" may not be readily apparent, the movement and the genre actually offer quite compatible treatments of time. Take, for example, the narratives' frequent representation of death and the afterlife as sanctuary for the enslaved. An afterlife, is, after all, as I have already established, a kind of *future*. As represented in these narratives, it is a future that can produce the "contra-modernity," the anti-teleological and nonlinear temporalities that Homi Bhabha has associated with the "signifying time-lag of cultural difference" that, in turn, undergirds "subaltern and postcolonial agency."[11]

Admittedly, this "signifying," agential quality of the afterlife does not come through in all narratives by formerly enslaved persons. Scholars who study nineteenth-century African American literature may actually be more likely to understand a Christian belief in the afterlife as a means to undermine resistance in this life. For example, Harriet Jacobs, writing as Linda Brent in *Incidents in the Life of a Slave Girl*, offers this description of her Uncle Benjamin and his defiance of their religious grandmother: "She [her grandmother] asked if he did not also think of God. I fancied I saw his face grow fierce in the moonlight. He answered, 'No, I did not think of him. When a man is hunted like a wild beast he forgets there is a God, a heaven. He forgets every thing in his struggle to get beyond the reach of the bloodhounds.'"[12]

Yet we can find other, and far more empowering, representations of the afterlife in other Black life narratives. For, just as Vincent Lloyd has argued in his discussion of Cone's work,

> the struggle for worldly freedom precipitates eschatological freedom. The taste of freedom on earth suggests what might be ahead, at the eschaton. On the other hand, eschatological freedom motivates the

> struggle for worldly freedom. By knowing that one is eschatologically free, one is able to act in this world as if one is already free despite living in a world in which freedom is denied.[13]

In just this way, rather than reject "heaven," Frederick Douglass in *Narrative of the Life* (1845) rewrites a Christian afterlife such that it corresponds to a quite earthly mode of resistance. In the famous passage in which he narrates his life's "turning-point" of winning a physical "battle" with the enslaver Covey, Douglass writes: "I felt as I never felt before. It was a glorious resurrection, from the tomb of slavery, to the heaven of freedom. My long-crushed spirit rose, cowardice departed, bold defiance took its place."[14] Paul Gilroy, in his analysis of the version of this fight that appears in Douglass's second life narrative, *My Bondage, My Freedom* (1855), links the violence and death that Douglass describes with liberation, quoting this passage that describes the immediate aftermath of the fight: "I was no longer a servile coward, trembling under the frown of a brother worm of the dust, but my long-cowed spirit was roused to an attitude of manly independence. I had reached a point at which I was not afraid to die."[15] For Douglass, Gilroy argues, death works as "a release from terror and bondage."[16] In this view, death confers agency; it provides "the moment of jubilee" that "possesses a utopian truth content that projects beyond the limits of the present" (68).

Gilroy thus aptly, if implicitly, links these passages with Afrofuturism; however, he also frames this death-as-jubilee as a "pursuit of utopia" by other than "rational means." This is what Russ Castronovo refers to as "ecstatic irrationality."[17] However, Gilroy does *not* include in his analysis this sentence that *precedes* the passage in *MBMF*: "After resisting him, I felt as I had never felt before. It was a resurrection from the dark and pestiferous tomb of slavery, to the heaven of comparative freedom" (286). Here the move is not, as Gilroy suggests, "towards death and away from bondage" (68), but towards both freedom *and* the afterlife, though an afterlife rendered, seemingly paradoxically, both material and earthly, both in the future and in the present—just as in the corresponding passage from *Narrative* with its "heaven of freedom." Gilroy's reading depends upon death as an ending; it does not accept Douglass's "heaven" as something that Douglass may actually believe in and value.

What happens when we do *not* theorize away heaven, as does Gilroy, but rather take seriously a belief in a Christian afterlife as represented in Black life narratives? And what happens if we accept the dual beliefs in those narratives that, in the words of womanist[18] theologian Monica A. Coleman, "Since God is eternal, we have a kind of eternal life after death within God" *and* that a heavenly afterlife is "correlated with" a "vision of the common good" in this mortal life?[19] In the cases of Jacobs's grandmother and Douglass, if they truly believe in heaven, then for them the rational neither necessarily nor exclusively maps onto the secular. Such a model of timeless resistance exceeds the various dialectics upon which Gilroy's argument rests: rational-Hegelian/irrational-Christian, slavery-life/freedom-death, present-earthly/future-heavenly, and so on. As Coleman succinctly puts this, in Christian theological terms, "All of us have available to us aspects of heaven that can influence what we do and how we shape our world" (63). In much the same way, a both fantastic and rational projection beyond "the limits of the present" constitutes contemporary Afrofuturism along with other contemporary futurisms focused on historically marginalized groups. These futurisms point *not* to ecstatic irrationality but to ecstatic *rationality* unbound by linear time. They are not what Fredric Jameson refers to as "timid spiritualisms" that emphasize eternal immateriality over a bodily present; rather, they are *bold* spiritualisms that posit the inseparability of an imagined future and an embodied present.[20]

This is not then to argue that African American people or other people from historically marginalized groups fail to participate in Western rationality or methods of counting time. Douglass, for one, believes in and inhabits a Western rhetorical time that includes a turning point and a chiasmus, as in the most famous passage in *Narrative of the Life* (1845): "You have seen how a man was made a slave; you shall see how a slave was made a man" (77), itself a narrative time-loop. But he also believes in, or at least represents in the fight scene, the messianic time of the afterlife. This comes close to Agamben's definition of messianic time as signifying "not the end of time, but the *time of the end*."[21] That is, in Agamben's terms, Douglass's time of the afterlife is "neither chronological nor . . . apocalyptic," and it "is no longer linear but three-dimensional" (66). On this model, Douglass himself, along with other enslaved persons, occupies Agamben's time-space of the resurrection, at once just arrived and already "accomplish[ed]" (69, 72). Douglass experiences and describes yet another kind of time in *Narrative of the Life*, the material time of the enslaved in an agricultural setting: "I do not remember to have ever met a slave who could tell of his birthday. They seldom come nearer to it than planting-time, harvest- time, cherry-time, spring-time, or fall-time" (21).

This multiplicity of times and timelines matches, to a degree, Bhabha's notion of "time-lag" in that it signifies difference, or—more precisely—my term, Black *distinctiveness*, along with both oppression and agency. Saidiya Hartman, too, has cited Bhabha on the "time-lag" and has used her own version of it and its challenge to progressive time, though in the process she leaves behind any possibility of agency. In her influential 2004 essay, "The Time of Slavery," Hartman considers what she terms the "belated encounters" of African American tourists with slavery sites in Africa, arguing that "the 'time of slavery' negates the common-sense intuition of time as continuity or progression, then and now coexist; we are coeval with the dead."[22] In this argument, there is no benefit, no agency associated with belatedness or with nonprogressive forms of time, or with being "coeval with the dead." For Hartman, belatedness signifies, not agency or diasporic community, but rather repeated loss and grief in the face of violences and oppressions both past and present. Thus, in her argument, as a result of their encounters with contemporary re-instantiations and memories of the Middle Passage in Africa, the tourists recall: "natal alienation," "broken contracts," "the intransigence of racism," "wounded kinship," and a "state of exile and estrangement" (758, 763, 764, 766). Hartman sums up that inheritance in this way: "Racial subjection, incarceration, impoverishment and second-class citizenship: this is the legacy of slavery that still haunts us" (766). However, as I will argue, it is possible to be "haunted" not only by slavery and its evils, but also by one's Black ancestors, and thus to be "coeval" with *beloved* dead. I would argue that Jacobs, for one, is "haunted" by her parents and grandmother in ways that sustain kinship, create alternative kinds of contracts, and establish a state of grace in community.

As a foundation for that argument, I would like to substitute the term *accretive time* for Bhabha's "time-lag" to connote layers of time and to avoid the sense of tardiness—and therefore temporal linearity and white normativity—that the term "lag" implies, despite the fact that Bhabha understands the "time-lag" as "erasing the compliant past tethered to the myth of progress, ordered in binarisms of its cultural logic: past/present, inside/outside" (363). In this coinage "accretive time," I am invoking the astrophysical term "spherical accretion," which refers to the process by which a gravitational body, such as a star or a black hole, gathers material into itself—or, more precisely, causes material to accelerate toward it, forming a sphere (at least it is a sphere for some period of time). This model strikes me as an apt metaphor for human identity and its layers, in part because "accretion," in astrophysical systems, bears a particular relationship to time, rendering it especially useful for considerations of identity in relation to temporality. For example, rapidly accreting systems, such as black holes, show relativistic effects, with time slowing in proximity to the system. Just so, relativistic notions of time shaped by race in quotidian life—that is, *racial* systems—undergird not only Bhabha's "time-lag" and my "accretive time," but also Holloway's analysis of Black time.[23] It turns out that accretive time is especially compatible with Black feminist considerations of time, including not only Holloway's but also Spillers's rejection of "a particular historical order," and Wright's embrace of "epiphenomenal time." Just as accreting stellar systems show relativistic temporal effects, contemporary Black feminist scholars have developed relativistic notions of time as shaped by race, class, gender, and sexuality in quotidian life—that is, in daily systems that may include misogynoir, homophobia, and transphobia, but that also include Black feminist theory itself, along with other theories and expressions of liberation and community. Once again, there is early precedent for this kind of Black feminist time theory.

Incidents in the Life of a Slave Girl (1861) represents a Black feminist accretive time that challenges Bhabha's "myth of progress"—and, in this, Jacobs's life narrative serves as an early theorization and application of Black women's technologies of time and the afterlife that later Black feminists would also apply. As Coleman observes, "Theology is autobiography" (ix). I would add "theory" to Coleman's equation: for Jacobs, theology = autobiography = theory, and, more specifically, a theory of temporality that puts the lie to linear progress narratives. For example, Jacobs, as Linda Brent, describes her fugitive years hidden in the attic of her grandmother's house: "O, those long, gloomy days, with no object for my eye to rest upon, and no thoughts to occupy my mind, except the dreary past and the uncertain future!" (177). Literally housed in an architecture of marginalization, as Katherine McKittrick has argued,[24] Jacobs is unmoored not only from conventional spatiality but also from steady, linear time and, as a result, inhabits past, present, and future all at once.

In a remarkably similar passage at the very end of the narrative, after her escape, Jacobs tells us: "My thoughts wandered through the dark past, and over the uncertain future. The bill of sale is on record, and future generations will learn from it that women were articles of traffic in New York, late in the nineteenth century of the Christian religion" (300). This passage reassigns atavism, so often ascribed to Black people and Africa (as in Hegel)[25] to white people and New York, and it does so from the perspective of the future, the present, *and* the past, as the various verb tenses in the passage suggest ("wandered," "is," "will," "were"). Jacobs points backward to the origins of Christianity; she points to contemporary (for her) hypocrisies of both South and North regarding slavery; she calls on her contemporary readers to judge her present; she calls on her future readers to judge the sins of a regressive national past. Jacobs is thereby inventing a *marvel*, namely a theory of time that offers future readers a transtemporal and material foundation for Coleman's "vision of the common good." To put this another way, Jacobs, via her own "marvel of inventiveness," rejects "a particular historical order" and a particular narrative order in favor of a specifically Black women's timeline. *Incidents* thus operates according to a Black feminist accretive time that provides a model of resistance and solidarity for Jacobs's future readers.

Jacobs has had, of course, many, many future readers, with the result that *Incidents* itself has had several afterlives. As with a number of pre-emancipation life narratives by formerly enslaved persons, from the time of its publication there were doubts about authenticity and authorship.[26] Jacqueline Goldsby has traced a relatively recent scholarly reception history of *Incidents*, beginning with historian John Blassingame's dismissal of it as a "credible" source because of its orderliness and thus seeming fictionality.[27] But Blassingame did not dismiss all slave narratives in this way; on the contrary, as Goldsby points out, he, along with Eugene Genovese and other historians, made the case in the 1970s for narratives by formerly enslaved persons as vital sources for understanding their experiences, experiences that were not documented elsewhere (13). Thus, the genre as a whole has had an "afterlife," given its recovery as legitimate historical documentation, along with the now-ready availability of so many slave narratives and the degree of scholarly attention paid to them in recent decades.[28]

Jacobs's narrative, too, eventually gained this form of scholarly afterlife in the late 1980s as a result of historian Jean Fagin Yellin's archival verification of the narrative as the true account of Jacobs's life, written by Jacobs herself rather than Lydia Maria Child. Goldsby observes that in the hands of a literary scholar like William Andrews, the status of *Incidents* as literature nonetheless remained paramount. Goldsby considers these competing disciplinary claims:

> Harriet Jacobs trespasses disciplinary boundaries, and the critical reception accorded to her book suggests that the narrative strategies available to and employed by black writers during the antebellum period are themselves a function and evidence of history; or, put another way, history marks and is marked by the writing of narrative itself. (15)

Goldsby also reminds us that Jacobs was reluctant to speak on the abolitionist circuit, preferring instead to produce her narrative first in written form. In choosing print technology, Jacobs could "exercise the modicum of discretion and authority she feared would be denied her . . . should she offer her narrative . . . in the form of oral testimony" (18). *Incidents* thus, as Goldsby puts it, "foregrounds . . . writing as the means to represent black testimony" (19). In other words, Jacobs produces a legacy for the future via the preserving technology of print. Unlike the silver candelabra bought by white enslavers with money borrowed from her then-enslaved grandmother (20), Jacobs's written narrative, as a political and aesthetic inheritance, lies outside—and replaces—the temporalities and exclusivities of (white) genealogy and (white) legal inheritance and its contracts.

Just as she supplants white timelines, legal and otherwise, Jacobs also supplants a white God and a white afterlife—indeed, she supplants all of patriarchal white Christianity. In the final chapter of *Incidents*, titled "Free at Last," Jacobs writes: "I was doing harm to no one; on the contrary, I was doing all the good I could in my small way; yet I could never go out to breathe God's free air without trepidation at my heart. This seemed hard; and I could not think it was a right state of things in any civilized country" (293). Jacobs follows this pointed critique of the hypocrisy, the moral reversal, inherent in the dominant national religion with a quotation from a letter to her from her grandmother:

> Dear Daughter: I cannot hope to see you again on earth; but I pray to God to unite us above, where pain will no more [w]rack this feeble body of mine; where sorrow and parting from my children will be no more. God has promised these things if we are faithful unto the end. My age and feeble health deprive me of going to church now; but God is with me here at home. (293)

But Jacobs is less sanguine than her grandmother about a reunion in any afterlife that could possibly include Dr. Flint, her enslaver and abuser and harasser. When her grandmother writes to her that he has passed, saying "Poor old man! I hope he made his peace with God," Jacobs then writes to us:

> I remembered how he had defrauded my grandmother of the hard earnings she had loaned; how he had tried to cheat her out of the freedom her mistress had promised her, and how he had persecuted her children; and I thought to myself that she was a better Christian than I was, if she could entirely forgive him. I cannot say, with truth, that the news of my old master's death softened my feelings towards him. There are wrongs which even the grave does not bury. The man was odious to me while he lived, and his memory is odious now. (294)

This is an afterlife not of individuals but of *evil*, an undead set of wrongs that matches Hartman's "legacy of slavery that still haunts us" (766).

In the place of any legacy or afterlife that includes enslavers and their evil deeds, Jacobs offers instead a radically creative alternative, one remarkably similar to Coleman's Black womanist afterlife. In Coleman's words, "There is a genuine life after death. . . . In our context, this is the ancestral realm where ancestors commune with one another and with God who is 'looking in' on the activity of the world" (116). Upon learning that she is free, Jacobs writes, "My heart was exceedingly full. I remembered how my poor father had tried to buy me, when I was a small child, and how he had been disappointed. I hoped his spirit was rejoicing over me now" (301). It is not God, then, but her *own family* who is "looking in on the activity of the world." Similarly, Jacobs ends her narrative with memories of her grandmother, who has passed on: "Yet the retrospection is not altogether without solace; for with those gloomy recollections come tender memories of my good old grandmother, like light, fleecy clouds floating over a dark and troubled sea" (303). In the heavens, in the afterlife, Jacobs sees not God, but her own grandmother to whom she owed so much; in Jacobs's words, "I was indebted to *her* for all my comforts, spiritual or temporal" (19).[29] In this passage, Jacobs's grandmother emerges as an emphatic god, a marvelous figure presiding over both this human material world and the next immaterial one, a world peopled by Black ancestors rather than any white male god. Jacobs thereby establishes a radical Black feminist (or womanist, in Coleman's terms) liberation theology through the print technologies of life narrative and letters exchanged between Black women.

Thus, Jacobs's *Incidents*, with its intertwining of grandmother and God, its investment in networks of women—from the Black cook Betty, who was instrumental in Linda's escape, to the white Mrs. Bruce, who purchased her freedom—matches the Black feminist vision of Barbara Holmes, who argued that "social action alone is never enough to create new realities. It will make spaces for temporary changes, but those changes will ultimately collapse unless the unseen scaffolding of spiritual and psychic health provides support."[30] The "scaffolding" particularly of her connections to other Black women, including those who have passed on, sustains Jacobs, as in her memories of her grandmother, and as in the moments she hears her dead mother's voice: "I had received my mother's blessing when she died; and in many an hour of tribulation I had seemed to hear her voice, sometimes chiding me, sometimes whispering loving words into my wounded heart" (138). Here, Jacobs layers onto print technology a technology of *Black feminist sonics*. As sound studies scholar Jennifer Stoever has compellingly argued, in the absence of material inheritances (like candelabras), enslaved people held onto the immateriality of their passed-on loved ones—that is, their voices and memories of them. Jacobs receives immaterial "blessings" from her mother in this life and then holds onto what Stoever terms "heard memories" after her mother's death.[31] A sonic afterlife permits Jacobs to hear the voices of her dead parents, serving as a kind of sound-attic. Or, to adapt Stoever's words, Jacobs finds a "refuge in alternative sonic modes of knowing, being and creating community" that corresponds to her literal space of refuge (35).

However, although in Jacobs's time the sonic may have enabled the formation of Black community both among the living and between the living and the dead, it could not also function in the mid-nineteenth century as a technology of *preservation*, as did print. Of course, the options for preservation and representation via media technologies have multiplied in extraordinary ways in our contemporary era. To give just one example, in a stunning project of converting print into sound, sound artists Mendi + Keith Obadike "sonify," to use their term,[32] the data on lynching that Ida B. Wells-Barnett included in her 1895 book, *The Red Record: Tabulated Statistics and Alleged Causes of Lynching in the United States*. The resulting project, *Numbers Station 2 [Red Record]*, is a series of performance and sound installations they have created and re-created since 2016 in multiple venues, such as the Met Breuer and the Fridman Gallery in New York, among others.[33] Sound studies scholar Julie Beth Napolin explains that Mendi + Keith Obadike have translated Wells-Barnett's lynching statistics into numbers in order "to generate audio frequencies (some of the numbers being below 20 hz, the lowest threshold of human hearing)," signifying the extremeness of the act of lynching and its traumatic consequences.[34] Mendi Obadike then reads the numbers over the sounds of those frequencies as played by Keith Obadike. Napolin succinctly describes one such performance: "Mendi + Keith Obadike sit, chant, and generate sound in this forty-minute live sonification of the data," as "the two performers recite numbers and the tone generator transduces numbers into frequencies."[35] In a 2021 video presentation, Mendi Obadike herself situated *Numbers Station 2 [Red Record]*, along with all their work, within a long technological genealogy: "Technology simply means a tool for us, so although we've worked in a lot of new media, we always connected that to other, older tools and other technologies, including language—language is a technology. So we've always tried to think about the idea of technology across time in a broad sense."[36] It is no coincidence that Mendi + Keith Obadike bring a wide range of technologies to bear on such traumatic and violent content. In Spillers's words, these are traumas "made an excess in time," so excessive and so repetitive that they require all the tools and technologies, at their limits, that can possibly be brought to bear in order to represent those traumas. Yet Wells-Barnett's book, too, despite its late nineteenth-century publication, deploys multiple technologies. As Napolin observes, *The Red Record* "is an act of recitation made graphically legible by tabulation and statistics: violence in and as numerological code."[37] As a result, like Jacobs before her, Ida B. Wells-Barnett offers a model, a technological theory, for contemporary Black women who have repeatedly "made graphically legible" state violence against Black people, although in recent years via digital-binary rather than strictly "numerological" code.

In a remarkable December 2016 essay published on the *Sounding Out!* sound studies blog, titled "Scenes of Subjection: Women's Voices Narrating

Black Death," Napolin explores the power as well as the complex ethical implications of contemporary Black women's "narratives and testimonies" about the deaths of their loved ones, including Rakeyia Scott's and Diamond Reynolds's. Napolin places them within "a long history of black women's acts of testimony," including Wells-Barnett's.[38] For example, Napolin describes Rakeyia Scott's cellphone video of the scene at the September 2016 fatal police shooting of her husband, Keith Lamont Scott, in Charlotte, North Carolina:

> In narrating the scene of her husband's death, Rakeyia Scott becomes the absolute tie between that past of the image and the present of watching; I use the present tense, because it happens again, with each telling. Scott speaks, more silently and spectrally, to the audiences that will later watch and listen to the video she is recording, or read the transcript as synthesized by journalists or other viewers. In holding the camera, she imputes to herself a third voice as narrator, as did Wells in narrating the scene in *A Red Record*.[39]

Napolin also considers Diamond Reynold's live-streaming on Facebook of the July 2016 police killing of her partner Philando Castile in Falcon Heights, Minnesota. Napolin notes the despair of repetition: "*again*, a black woman had been thrust into the position of narrating black death at the hands of a white police officer, while it was unfolding."[40] Just as Napolin argues, Black women have historically and disproportionately been called upon to document, to provide testimony, to preserve these traumas.

In yet another traumatic repetition/preservation, Darnella Frazier documented, via cellphone video, Derek Chauvin's murder of George Floyd in Minneapolis on May 25, 2020. There is no clearer instance of a Black woman's deployment of the technologies of the afterlife, with all the overwhelming power and impact those technologies can hold. Like Jacobs and Wells-Barnett before them, Scott, Reynolds, and Frazier chose representational technologies that permitted them, in Goldsby's words, to "exercise the modicum of discretion and authority [they] feared would be denied" them, should they offer their narratives and evidence solely in other media or settings, such as in a newspaper interview or in a courtroom. All these women *preserve* injustice via technologies that inhabit both "real time" and the future. Those preserved narratives/testimonies critique our present while implicitly imagining a better future, one in which Rakeyia Scott's recorded, audible, and repeated insistence that her husband *doesn't have a gun* becomes a truth that can interrupt the state-sponsored killing of unarmed Black people. In all of these recent testimonies, Black women use the technologies of their present to lend afterlives to dead loved ones and other Black people lost to violence in ways that, to use Cone's words, "say no to unjust treatment" and that inspire a "struggle for worldly freedom," to use Lloyd's.

This is precisely the model that Jacobs and Wells-Barnett provided for Scott, Reynolds, and Frazier, as well as for today's futurisms and other activisms. A wide range of late twentieth-century and early twenty-first-century technologies—from performance, to film, to visual and digital art, to music, and to the print culture that was also available to Jacobs—have delivered blistering critiques of current socioeconomic, national, and racial orders, along with powerful imaginings of more just times and spaces. To give just a handful of examples: El Teatro Campesino's "acto Los Vendidos," according to Catherine Ramírez, "first performed in 1967 and thus one of the earliest examples of Chicanafuturism";[41] Sun Ra's 1974 film *Space Is the Place*; Wangechi Mutu's Afrofuturist collages; Larissa Sansour's Arabfuturist photographs, posters, and films, including *A Space Exodus* (2008); Alex Rivera's film *Sleep Dealer* (2009); Indigenous Futurism as represented in Grace Dillon's edited short story collection, *Walking the Clouds*; and Janelle Monáe's *ArchAndroid* concept album. In Curtis Marez's words, such works may show us a grim "projection of a particular, determinist future social order" and/or "an open-ended desire for a world beyond the limits of the present."[42]

In Black feminist accretive time, one can always circle back (or forward), imagining and accessing other times, and people, "beyond the limits of the present." As Jacobs writes at the end of *Incidents*, despite the pain of recalling her days of enslavement, "the retrospection is not altogether without solace" when she remembers her "good grandmother" (303). It is through such returns and recollections that we ourselves could find some solace now. Janelle Monáe performs precisely this kind of retrospection via combined technologies through their characteristic time-traveling rebellion-as-celebration. For example, they connect with powerful Black women from the past, as in their *Q.U.E.E.N* video, with the invocation of Queen Nefertiti and Harriet Tubman in the spoken-word section at video's end.[43] And in their futuristic *and* anachronistic *Electric Lady* video[44] (the title, of course, riffs on and revises Jimi Hendrix's *Electric Ladyland*), Monáe invokes a Black feminist past, present, and future all at once in a joyful performance of Black sorority, as they sing and dance along with their present-day, real-life Black sisters in art—including their own mother. As *Pitchfork* explains, the video is "set at a somewhat-futuristic college party and features cameos from T.I., Estelle, Esperanza Spalding, T-T.I., T-Boz, Monica, Kimbra, Joi, choreographer Fatima Robinson, and Monáe's mother (at the beginning), among others."[45]

I wish to conclude by circling back from Monáe to Spillers, who has argued that to closely read and interpret Black texts, both past and present, is to engage in what she terms a "process [of] encounter and potential transformation."[46] Spillers focuses on the transformative "role" specifically of print forms of African American sermons, as being able to "replay not only *this* narrative but its *outcome* on the other side of disaster."[47] Like these sermons, all the texts I have considered in this chapter, both despite and because of their generally traumatic and repetitive, played and replayed, and *preserved* content, have the power to forge community, to catalyze, to transform: They have afterlives. Monáe's *Dirty Computer* "emotion picture," for instance, with its thrilling concluding scene of shared escape after state surveillance, pursuit, and capture,[48] is clearly representing an "*outcome* on the other side of disaster." By opening ourselves up to transformation and action through close reading of Black feminist texts, times, and technologies, we may reach that "other side," what Spillers calls "that good time coming":[49] an inclusive world of electric ladies, a Wondaland, Holmes's "new realities," and Coleman's "vision of the common good." As Holmes expresses this idea, "Art opens a portal to new realities."[50] All the Black women who appear in this chapter—Jacobs, Wells-Barnett, Morrison, Spillers, Holloway, Goldsby, Wright, Coleman, Holmes, Monáe, Scott, Reynolds, and Frazier—have opened a portal. We must step through it.

In the following chapter, I turn to poetry and to poetic form as means to "open a portal" to other realities, most especially the afterlife, that can in turn, like Monáe's music and emotion pictures, help forge Black solidarity and that hold the promise of new worlds to come.

3
"Scaled Perfectly to Eternity"
A Contemporary Black Poetics

Shovels appear remarkably often in poems by contemporary Black American poets. Ross Gay titled his 2011 collection *Bringing the Shovel Down*,[1] also the title of the book's fifth poem, which Gay returns to and revises in the collection's last poem titled, aptly, "Again." The shovel image returns in the title poem of Gay's 2015 collection *Catalog of Unabashed Gratitude*.[2] Shovels also appear in his 2019 essay collection, *The Book of Delights*.[3] Although the shovel would seem to work as an especially fitting poetic—and literal—tool for Gay, an avid organic gardener and a founding board member of the Bloomington Community Orchard, he is far from alone in wielding it. Jericho Brown includes a poem titled "Shovel" in his 2019 poetry collection, *The Tradition*.[4] Danez Smith's *Don't Call Us Dead* (2017)[5] offers multiple shovel images, including what could even be an allusion to Gay's "Bringing the Shovel Down" in their own poem "every day a funeral and a miracle": "if i try to get up, she brings the shovel down / saying i miss you so much, my sweetest boy" (64). Smith's title and these two extraordinary lines powerfully and compactly express the double meaning (or, more precisely, the multiple meanings) of the shovel that Gay had established structurally via the two versions of "Bringing the Shovel Down." The love and the violence, the connections and lineages, the losses and mourning, implied in Smith's lines resound throughout contemporary African American poetry and would therefore seem to provide clear evidence of Claudia Rankine's chilling, rather Afropessimistic, insight that the "condition of black life is one of mourning."[6] And although it is true that recent Black American poetry frequently represents death and mourning, at the same time it imagines an afterlife, one that, like the shovel, carries multiple meanings and potentialities expressed via an astonishing range of poetic forms.

Indeed, a conspicuous formalism characterizes this contemporary Black poetics of the afterlife. As a result, this chapter offers sustained analysis of poetic form and the personal and political meanings that form can produce. As Caroline Levine has argued, "Formalist analysis turns out to be as valuable to understanding sociopolitical institutions as it is to reading literature. Forms are at work everywhere."[7] This is not to say that literary forms, regardless of whether they are familiar, or revised, or entirely new, can be neatly characterized as either constraining or liberating in relation to those institutions. As I have argued elsewhere, "Radicalism of literary form does not comfortably or consistently correspond to the representation of radicalized social formations."[8]

Nonetheless, forms are clearly hard at work—and in revisionary, progressive, and ethical ways—in both versions of Gay's repeated poem in *Bringing the Shovel Down*. The first version, "Bringing the Shovel Down" (7–9), consists of thirty stanzas, almost all of them couplets. This stanzaic form delivers meaning throughout; even the poem's content functions as a kind of "couplet." "Bringing the Shovel Down" begins as a "Love" poem, with an intimate pairing of lovers together in bed mirrored by the couplet form: "as you and I, Love, the fine hairs/on your upper thigh nearly glistening in the night, and the boy,/the night . . ." (7). However, in these lines, the enjambment of "boy" together with the repetition of "night" produce another kind of content: a horror story, with these formal qualities, these pairings, forging a deep connection between the two "coupleted" stories. In other words, the love poem becomes a horror story, one that nevertheless still hinges on "Love." The word "love" appears five times in the poem, including in one of its only two non-couplet stanzas (in this case, the second stanza), thereby drawing our attention to it:

> I want to tell you a story I shouldn't but will, and in the meantime, neglect,
> Love,
> the discordant melody spilling from my ears but attend, (7)

"Love" stands alone, hinging the two lines on either side. The word works here most obviously as a form of address to the lover within the poem as well as to the reader outside it, such that the poetic speaker's "love" is renewed as each new reader encounters the poem, repeatedly staging an intimate encounter between poet and reader. And yet the word's placement also uncomfortably connects "love" to both "neglect" and "discordant" sound. The speaker goes on after this love-hinge to tell a terrible story about a child who, having been misled by still other stories, kills a dog. The boy "brings the shovel down" onto the pathetic Max, a name the speaker imagines for the "unnamed dog," so as not to minimize "heartbreak." The poem thereby also *brings the shovel down*, metaphorically of course, on the reader, who reels from the stark shift in content and the intense description of the boy's awful act. Hinging and naming together pull the speaker and the reader into that act; poet and poem are entirely willing to break our hearts—*and* to implicate us.

There are still more pairings, more couplets, in "Bringing the Shovel Down" that deepen the speaker's—and the reader's—implication in violence. For example, the poem links the speaker and his lover with the parents of the boy: "and more quietly he [the boy] leaves the house where upstairs his father lies dreamless, / and his mother bends her body into his," mirroring the initial lovers in bed together (8). These lines also recall Tracy K. Smith's poetry collection titled *The Body's Question*,[9] as the body of the mother in "Bringing the Shovel Down" bends, as if into a question mark. Gay is in fact posing an ethical question here, as poet, storyteller, characters, readers, and actions—along with love and horror—blend into one another via the poem's various pairings, represented formally by its couplets. Those of us both inside and outside the poem (the speaker's "Loves") hear about a terrible violence and the death that results, but we are seemingly helpless to prevent them, because we are trapped within in endless pairing by this one-sentence poem.

Perhaps the collection's most crucial pairing, along with a possible answer to these questions of poetic form and of ethics, comes with the last poem, the alternative version of "Bringing the Shovel Down," titled "Again" (59–61). This second version is identical to the first version—that is, until the twenty-first stanza. The changes there give us a different outcome and therefore a different answer to "the body's question." Where the boy would bring the shovel down in the first version, in "Again" the line reads instead: "Max raises his head to look at the unnamed boy," establishing a bond that leads, not to the boy's killing Max, but rather to his freeing the dog from his chain (59). This alteration implies that it is insufficient to simply *hear* a story about violence; we must also truly *see* and value one another—and then *act*—in order to avert tragic and fatal outcomes, including those produced by what Levine terms "sociopolitical institutions."

Gay's holding out this possibility of connecting and acting seems to contradict Saidiya Hartman's argument about the shortcomings of the "empathy" that is produced by representations of Black suffering; for example, when a nineteenth-century American white writer represents the pain of the enslaved, sentiment and identification do not "expand the space of the other" but rather "place . . . the self in its stead."[10] But "Again" does not restrict its representation of suffering or the inflicting of that suffering by identity or subject position, that is, by a particular self. It does not advance what Hartman terms that "thin line between witness and spectator," in large part because of *form*, which, as I argued in the introduction, Hartman and other Afropessimists sometimes overlook or underestimate.[11] Instead, the poem insists that we blur the "unnamed boy" with the speaker, or with any other boy, *and* with ourselves; *in every instance*, we must face the named dog. The "shovel" is being wielded, not with self-centering empathy, but with direct confrontation. Gay's poem thus works not to bury but to acknowledge and to "raise" (rather than bring down), to liberate, to save, and perhaps even to offer redemption. In this poetic ethics, it is not sufficient simply to spectate or even to witness. Here we see clearly that in Gay's poetry, as Kevin Quashie elegantly expresses it, "Aesthetics makes the ethical possible."[12]

In Gay's poems, this dual meaning of the shovel, as that which buries and uncovers, and mourns and confronts, suggests *apocalypse* in its likewise dual meanings: a tragic ending of life plus a redemptive unveiling followed by a resurrection—that is, an afterlife. And yet the second version of the poem ends exactly as the first did, with raspberries: "that he [the boy] could pull from the earth that which could make you smile," suggesting that to unearth, to use both the shovel and poetry ethically, will consistently lead to interpersonal, even interspecies and human-nature, connections. Taken together, all these connections lend both the first poem and Max the dog a post-apocalyptic afterlife. On a literary level, they create a metapoetic afterlife. As Linda Gregerson has pointed out, "Bringing the Shovel Down" ends with connections among the boy in the poem, who picks raspberries after killing Max, the poetic speaker, and his lover.[13] Gay establishes all these relationships in part via an allusion to William Carlos Williams's famous poem "This Is Just to Say" with its "plums / that were in / the icebox." At the end of "Again" we encounter these lines:

> that he could pull from the earth that which might make you smile,
> Love, which you'll find in the fridge, on the bottom shelf, behind the milk,
>
> in the bowl you made with your own lovely hands. (61)

As Levine has observed, "No form operates in isolation," such that "we need to attend to the specificity of particular historical situations to understand the ways in which forms overlap and collide" (7–8). With the raspberries reappearing in "Again," Gay not only "overlaps" with his own prior poem but also "collides" with modernist poetic form as it is concentrated in Williams's brief, fully enjambed, "This Is Just to Say." This metapoetic revisitation/collision is heightened by Gay's end-stopped single verse line: "the bowl that you made with your own lovely hands." This single verse line distinguishes "Again" from "Bringing the Shovel Down," which had sustained the couplet form all the way to the end. The final standalone line in "Again," which ends with a period, *points* to art and to love, to tactile, sensual, personal, and aesthetic connections grounded in earthly delights unearthed. To put this another way, those delights *resurrect*, certainly the dog (along with Gay's own initial poem), but also Williams's modernist poetic form into a richer, and perhaps more humane, afterlife.

Whereas Williams offered a highly interior and individualist (and therefore potentially solipsistic) poetics without end, with the "you" absent though addressed,[14] Gay punctuates Williams in the name of couplets/connections. Just so, enjambment disappears in the last three lines of "Again." The poem also rearranges the final couplets of "Bringing the Shovel Down" such that the boy and the speaker's "Love" are brought together into one stanza; the raspberries thereby inextricably link boy and speaker, speaker and love. "You" is not just addressed by the poem, but is present within it—*and they will get to eat the fruit*! In the process, the interiority of the speaker's story is coupled with the exteriority of both his listeners and the natural world: These raspberries were picked "from a thorny fruit bush" in the "fields"; they were not always in a fridge (or an icebox). As Gay himself has said of his last two books of poetry, "the *you* is a caretaking gesture."[15] This caretaking exemplifies Quashie's "Black aliveness" as being "of relation" (141).

Jericho Brown, in a poem titled "Shovel" from *The Tradition* (2019),[16] deploys metapoetics to refer not to a past poetic tradition, as Gay does in "Again," but to Brown's own poetry, and, perhaps more broadly, to all contemporary Black representations of Black suffering. Brown thereby extends Hartman's argument about white representations of the pain of enslaved Black persons. In other words, in "Shovel," Brown is "unburying" the ethics of writing verse about the violent deaths of Black people, and he is doing so via form. For instance, Brown *unpunctuates* in this highly enjambed poem, which carries what Anahid Nersessian terms enjambment's "dynamic impulse."[17] Like Gay's "Bringing the Shovel Down" forcing us to face Max, Brown's "Shovel" does not allow either poet or reader to pause or to simply empathize in the face of the trauma the poem reveals. "Shovel" lays bare the burdens and obligations, along with the pain and potentiality, of being "not the man who put a bullet in" the "brain" of a "corpse," but rather the one who must "dig and dig and dig" (36). The poet-speaker thus wields a shovel/"Shovel" that, as is typical in a contemporary Black poetics of the afterlife, both uncovers and buries: "I dump the body in a hole / I myself made," making "love songs" as "I sweat into the earth as I repair it. / I completely cover the dead . . ." (36–37). Notably, after the title, the word "shovel" never appears again, rendering the *poem itself* a digging, a burying/unburying, tool. By its end, "Shovel" and its forms have propelled us through a poem that carefully considers how poetry can lead to revelation and reparation and/or to burial and solace. But that solace can edge toward a denial that, in turn, risks denying the dead their afterlife: "And I sing, again, those songs because I know / The value of sweet music when we need to pass / The time without wondering what rots beneath our feet" (37). In these final lines of the poem, the enjambment of "pass / The time," in combination with the dual meaning of "pass," blurs the boundary between living and dead. At the same time, these lines connect the I/poet-speaker with readers ("we"), connecting both poet-speaker and readers with those who have died and lie beneath us. The result is a choir ("sing") of the dead and the living collectivized by an earth that, like the corpse within it, is so rotted that it produces devastating shared trauma. In Calvin Warren's terms, this is Black "~~being~~" that is "buried deeply beneath layers of metaphysical [and physical] violence."[18]

Such a highly connective and multilayered poetics of burying and unburying recurs throughout much contemporary African American poetry, as concentrated in the image of the shovel. For Ross Gay, Jericho Brown, and Danez Smith, the image stands at once for planting; for organic renewal and revitalization; for sustained and sustaining genealogies of plants and people; for often (though not always) violent or otherwise traumatic death; and for illness, loss, burial, mourning, and remembering. It works, then, as a synecdoche for the ways that Gay, Brown, and Smith—along with Tracy K. Smith in her two collections *Life on Mars* (2011) and *Wade in the Water* (2018)—are, collectively, inventing and developing a Black poetics of the afterlife. This poetics effectively mediates between this-life and the afterlife; at the same time, it both partakes of and mediates between an Afropessimism that emphasizes Black subjection, as represented in the work of Saidiya Hartman, Christina Sharpe, Calvin L. Warren, and Frank B. Wilderson III, among others, and what might be termed an Afro-Optimism that emphasizes Black agency and joy, as represented in the work of Badia Ahad-Legardy, Stephen Best, Michelle Commander, and Kevin Quashie, among others. A poetics of the afterlife thus blurs the boundaries of these two only apparently opposed schools of thought, just as it blurs the boundaries between the dead and the living.

That poetics imagines the afterlife as both a literal place for the dead and as a conceit for lineages, inheritances, and natural cycles that necessarily include death and rebirth, just as in a garden. The shovel thus reveals how we are, in Hartman's words, "coeval with the dead."[19] That is, the dead in their eternity live in and alongside those of us who are still alive, yet they also exist in a place-time of their own. Those we have seemingly lost to death are always being buried, are never fully dying either in our memory or in their afterlife. In other words, they dwell in an immaterial afterlife and in a more literal, even material, afterlife. Such a sustained existence enables "Afro-nostalgia," in Ahad-Legardy's's terms, or "*saudade*," the Portuguese term for nostalgia that Commander uses.[20] Both scholars frame such looking back not as an escape or a reminder of subjection or abjection, as does Hartman, but rather as an empowering mode of connecting Black people to their past and their ancestors.

Tracy K. Smith's "Shadow Poem" from *The Body's Question* (83–84) expresses this same idea: "We were souls together once / Wave after wave of ether / Alive outside of time" (83). In this tercet, the enjambment, the internal repetition ("wave") and near-rhyme or assonance ("Alive," "time") match our unending connections with those who are not quite us yet are very close to us. Like Gay's couplets and like Brown's dynamic propulsion, these formal qualities in Smith's poetry deliver the poet's particular version of the afterlife. These lines show that Tracy K. Smith, as Nersessian says of Keats (having learned from Milton), knows well "how to highlight a thought by towing it over enjambment" (Nersessian, 145). "Shadow Poem" highlights the thought that we are very nearly our children and our parents, including those who have passed on: all three together, "outside of time" in a perpetual cycle of birth, death, and afterlife—without end(stops). The poem's next two tercets underscore that continuity: "I'm still there / Though twice I curled / Into a speck-sized marvel / And waited / In the wet earth of you / Briefly human" (83). Thus, although Smith's fully enjambed stanzas in "Shadow Poem" might seem to express ongoing loss, their tercet form[21] actually reflects tripartite connection, just as Ross Gay's couplets suggested dual connection. In *The Body's Question*, we are all, at some time, being buried in and emerging from "wet earth," coeval, "outside of time."

In Tracy K. Smith's particular poetics of the afterlife, this coeval-ness with the dead—their eternity alongside our present—does not generally signify a negative or pessimistic state or a perpetually traumatic burial. For instance, *The Body's Question* ends with a poem titled "Prayer," quite literally a prayer-poem *to* "a Lord that is always listening" and *for* the speaker's "Mother," "and the mornings / You feed me" (85). Unlike Hartman, with her "afterlife of slavery" that passes on "skewed life chances, limited access to health and education, premature death, incarceration, and impoverishment,"[22] Smith, along with all the poets I am considering here, constructs an afterlife that does pass on grief and trauma but that also delivers joy through our connections to and love for others, including our memories of them. Mourning thus becomes *morning*, as in "Prayer." As Ross Gay wrote in *Lace & Pyrite*, a garden-based "poem correspondence" ("Introduction," unpaginated) between himself and fellow poet-gardener Aimee Nezhukumatathil (yet another pairing), "I think we have an obligation, like an ethical obligation, to study what we love, what we want to preserve and keep with us and grow. Joy strikes me as one of the ways we know that we are in the midst of such things."[23]

Ross Gay's "ethical obligation" to preserve the love and joy he found in two beloved and departed people—his father and his friend Don Belton—threads through five of his books: *Be Holding* (2020) (where Belton appears in the acknowledgments), *The Book of Delights* (2019), *Catalog of Unabashed Gratitude* (2015), *Lace & Pyrite* (2014), and *Bringing the Shovel Down* (2011). In all these books, Gay creates a poetics of the afterlife in order to honor these men. One vivid example, "Spoon" from *Gratitude* (33–41), is dedicated to Belton, a fellow creative writing professor at Indiana University who was murdered in December 2009. The poem's dedication "*for Don Belton*" works as an introductory prepositional clause that flows directly to the first line, "Who sits like this on the kitchen floor," that then works at once as an independent, completing clause and as a question (perhaps a body's question) that in turn launches the entire poem, which as a result becomes one long answer about who Don Belton was, particularly in relation to the speaker. Whereas Gay had dedicated the earlier collection *Bringing the Shovel Down* (2011) in part, "to the memory of Don Belton," *Gratitude* brings Belton back to vivid life and to *living*. As Kevin Quashie has asked, "What would it mean to consider black aliveness, especially given how readily—and literally—blackness is indexed to death?" (1).

"Spoon" is full of participial forms and couplets that, for Belton and for Gay's readers, lend his friend *aliveness*. The poem consists of seventy-one couplets across nine pages and ends with a single concluding verse line. As with "Again," the couplet form suggests a pairing, in this case a friendship: "arm in arm, shoulder to shoulder" (36), an intensely sustained spooning between himself and Belton. The first eight pages are made up of one long flowing sentence that carries us headlong through the poem, with what Quashie describes as "a flare of feeling" produced by Gay's "continuous" verse forms (125). "Spoon" begins with an ekphrastic meditation on Belton's holding a spoon; its "small, silent body" carries with it a sibilance that signifies both sorrow and beauty (33). The spoon's "ornate / tendrils of ivy" evoke at once materiality and immateriality, the organic and the inorganic, the living and the dead, just as the shovel did in Gay's earlier collection (33). This poem's many participial forms: "fingering" the spoon, "sampling" a sweet potato biscuit, "stirring," "knowing," "laughing and sipping coffee" suggest ongoing vitality and sensuality (the mornings Gay feeds Belton, perhaps), with the most intense and moving participials coming after this metapoetic moment: "I swore when I got into this poem I would convert/this sorrow into some kind of honey with the little musics" (40). Gay/the speaker was aiming, then, for "soul sounds," for aesthetic-sonic access to a dear friend six years after his passing.

The poem delivers those soul sounds through a combination of many iambs and a somewhat lesser number of trochees, lending it the tone of a conversation between intimates punctuated by reflections both painful and joyful. For example, the trochee "musics," insists that we pause (as does "Love" in "Bringing the Shovel Down" and in "Again") to consider the musicality of the poem itself as well as the appropriateness of intertwining music and poetry for this particular content, namely a terrible, violent loss coupled with a loving and living friendship. (Here we can see Gay wrestling with the same questions of poetic ethics that Brown explored in "Shovel.") And yet the speaker then immediately insists on the limitations of their poetry, saying that they "can't even make a metaphor" (though of course they *can* with the spoon) and concluding, "That's not the point" (40).

The "point," followed by one of the very few periods in the poem, is, ironically, not a simple end-stop, or an endpoint, or a singular metaphor or image (like, say, a wheelbarrow or plums). It's not about a present or simple past but an eternal afterlife: "After Don was murdered I dreamt of him,/hugging him and saying *you have to go now*" (40; emphasis in original). Poem and poet struggle with the fact that Belton had to *go* in *this* way, despite the fact that he had been, up to that point, a "survivor, a "53-year-old gay black man," "to which we did a little dance/listing the myriad bullets he'd dodged" (39). Among those bullets were HIV/AIDS and the fact that, in Rankine's words, "as a black person you can be killed for simply being black"[24]—or, in Wilderson's stark phrasing, "We were shot for breathing while Black."[25] At first, Gay's speaker seems to accept, even insist upon, his friend's passing: "again and again, *you have to go*" (41; emphasis in original). The phrase "again and again" suggests the perpetuity of Black loss and of Black mourning, very much in keeping with Rankine's insight and with Christina Sharpe's model of "Black immanent and imminent death."[26] But then the speaker delivers their clearest representation of the afterlife, in which the participles mingle with present, past, and future tenses so as to once again emphasize love and connectedness in a process that Ahad-Legardy describes as a "nostalgic retribution [that] encompasses a range of desires meant to assuage feelings of loss, trauma, and injury in the present":[27]

cinching his coat tight by the lapels,
for which Don peered at me again with those sad eyes,

or through me, or *into* me,
the way my dead do sometimes,

looking straight into their homes,
which hopefully have flowers

in a vase on a big wooden table,
and a comfortable chair or two,

and huge windows through which light
pours to wash clean and make a touch less awful

what forever otherwise will hurt. (41)

The rich combination of tenses in these lines expresses the speaker's being "coeval with the dead," to return to Hartman's words, with the eternity that marks the afterlife unfolding alongside their own life and being marked by shared immateriality ("through me, or *into* me") and materiality (flowers; big wooden table). A "touch," likewise, suggests at once tactility and brevity, materiality and temporality, such that imagining an afterlife mitigates but does not erase the pain of grief, which stands alone in the end.

This vivid representation of the afterlife in "Spoon" locates us in what Tracy K. Smith might term the "Realm of Shades," the title of a block poem in her 2018 collection, *Wade in the Water*.[28] Smith's poem renders a post-apocalyptic world, a kind of quasi-material afterlife, like Gay's, where window shades—"We . . . hung windows with sheets that broadcast our secrets after dark" (13)—both conceal and reveal a place where the ghost-shades of Hades anagrammatically "shade" into one another. In just the same way, light and dark comingle and blend through those "sheets," whether they are made of cloth or of the paper on which the poems are printed, allowing them to then divulge the poet's "secrets." Ultimately, "Realm of Shades" offers a far bleaker vision of an afterlife than does "Spoon," and that vision matches Smith's bleak representation of a present life: "There was still a here, but that's not where we were," a "here" that lacks substance and meaning: "clouds that harbored nothing."

It may not be coincidental that Smith's more pessimistic collection, *Wade in the Water*, was published after the 2016 US presidential election. Ross Gay, Tracy K. Smith, Claudia Rankine, and Danez Smith all published landmark works during the Obama administrations and the first Trump administration. In every case, the more recent works, from 2018 (*Wade in the Water*) and 2020

(*Be Holding*, *Just Us*, and *Homie*), are markedly less joyful than the poets' earlier collections had been (*Life on Mars*, *Catalog of Unabashed Gratitude*, *The Book of Delights*, and *Don't Call Us Dead*). This includes even *Citizen* (2014), which could hardly be termed joyful in any sustained way yet was followed by the still-grimmer *Just Us*. These differences in the collections across time reflect the fact that Levine's "sociopolitical institutions" became measurably more violent and hostile toward Black people, other people of color, and LGBTQIA+ people in the United States after November 2016, and of course far more so after November 2024. In the case of "Realm of Shades," not only its imagery but even its block prose poem form—highly unusual for Smith's poetry, which almost always includes line breaks and initial capitalization of each line—suggests a weightier and far less sanguine view than did Smith's earlier exploration of the afterlife in her 2011 collection *Life on Mars*.

I use the terms "vision" and "view" intentionally in order to honor the ekphrastic qualities of "Realm of Shades." The poem's emphasis on darkness and light and, more generally, visual elements is not incidental. Before the publication of *Wade in the Water*, the poem appeared in a 2017 edited collection of ekphrastic poems by Black poets, titled *Bearden's Odyssey* and inspired by artist Romare Bearden's *Black Odyssey* sequence of collages.[29] Smith is writing in response specifically to the collage titled *Realm of Shades*, which depicts Odysseus in the underworld, with all the characters Black (see figure 2). Ekphrasis, as a mediating poetic form between written and visual art, what Jarkko Toikkanen concisely terms an "intermedial experience,"[30] suits a poetics of the afterlife, which itself is mediating between the world of the living and the world of the dead.

Not surprisingly, Ross Gay, too, regularly makes use of ekphrasis, as in "Spoon," and as in the beautiful poem "Burial," also from *Catalog of Unabashed Gratitude* (11–14). In "Burial," the shovel is necessarily present yet remains implicit, just as the word "shovel" disappears after Brown's title, such that poem = shovel. In both poems, shovels and metapoetics work in concert. The "Burial" in Gay's title refers to the speaker's burying some of his father's ashes, as fertilizer, along with "two bare root plum trees" (once again, Williams and "This Is Just to Say" come to mind). The speaker takes

> . . . the jar
> which has become
> my father's house,
> and lonely for him and hoping to coax him back
> for my mother as much as me,

Figure 2
Romare Bearden, *Realm of Shades*. Original artwork 1977.

Courtesy of DC Moore Gallery, New York.

> poured some of him in the planting holes
> and he dove in glad for the robust air (11)

Here again, Gay is colliding with and challenging the terms and values of modernist American poetry, in this case Wallace Stevens's likewise ekphrastic poem, "Anecdote of a Jar."[31] In "Burial," we see a jar that, unlike Stevens's famous "jar in Tennessee," doesn't "take dominion everywhere," but rather enables a comingling of speaker, jar, and environment, with the jar and what it contains integral parts of a "robust" natural cycle.

As Gay's speaker is burying ashes from the jar and the trees together, a "slight gust" sends some of the ashes into his "nose and mouth," though "mostly" his father "disappeared/into the minor yawns in the earth/into which I placed the trees" (11–12). His father thus continues to live in him (literally!) and in an earth that is at once personified and paralleled with the speaker's own open mouth, so that "roots" of multiple sorts are buried/planted, "like shawls or jungle gyms, like/hookahs or the arms of ancestors" (12). This radical conceit of roots (this is actually a redundancy, given that the word "radical" comes from the Latin *radicalis*, for "of or forming the root")[32] in combination with these equally radical and deeply visual-material and human similes, revisits and reworks—perhaps a better word would be *transplants*—the most paradigmatic of all ekphrastic poems, Keats's "Ode on a Grecian Urn." Gay becomes not a "Sylvan historian" of a static or eternal art work, but a *garden* historian, holding "jar"/urn of ashes while marveling at the "magic dust our bodies become," which "casts spells on the roots" (11).

This joy in Black magic and Black roots exemplifies what Ahad-Legardy might term "a politics of pleasure," which she associates specifically with a "black feminist imperative" (9). Just so, "Burial" also supplants the gender politics of "Grecian Urn" as described in James Heffernan's classic study of ekphrasis, in which he argues that "figures sculpted on the womblike urn that is called an unravished bride refuse to cooperate with a male narrative of desire and consummation"[33]—that is, less euphemistically, rape.[34] By contrast, Gay's poem, lacking what Heffernan terms the "commonly gendered antagonism" he associates with ekphrasis,[35] offers us a speaker who remains fully sympathetic with others and who lacks the desire for "control" that Heffernan associates with the form. Gay's speaker opens the urn "for my mother as much as me" (11), similar to how the spoon in "Spoon" signified sympathetic connection with Belton. In both cases, ekphrasis expresses connection rather than control, rather like Tracy K. Smith's ekphrastic "connection" to Bearden. As Stephen Best has observed, "A communitarian impulse runs deep within black studies."[36]

These two poets' shared "impulse" toward ekphrastic connectivity challenges yet another classic analysis of ekphrasis, namely that of W. J. T. Mitchell, who argues that "our ambivalence about ekphrasis . . . is grounded in our ambivalence about other people" (163). Gay's poetry expresses nothing like ambivalence regarding either. Rather than being "stationed between two 'othernesses,'" as Mitchell would have it (164), ekphrasis *connects* in Gay's and in Tracy K. Smith's poetry; it never expresses "dominion." In "Burial," for instance, in place of Keats's famous concluding couplet, "Beauty is truth, truth beauty,—that is all/Ye know on earth, and all ye need to know," in "Burial," *earth itself*—unlike the broken earth in Brown's "Shovel"—sustains beauty and becomes the site of "conjuring," evoking a specifically Black cultural practice that is familial and cyclic, and therefore immortal. To adapt Quashie's description of a different Gay poem, in "Burial," "There is something of the magic of alive being in the poem" (127). Where Brown worries in "Shovel" about the aesthetic burying and forgetting of others, for Gay, poetry can *conjure* his father.

"Burial" evolves into a sustained memory of his father's "sweetness," a recurrent term and concept in the poem, like "honey" in "Spoon." In fact, the repetition of several key terms in "Burial," including "roots," "dust," "father," "air," "mouth," and "sweet" suggests a loose sestina form, a formal quality that in turn points, once again, both to meaning and to Gay's revision of received poetic forms. ("Bringing the Shovel Down," too, works as a kind of loose sestina, with the terms "love," "story," "night," "dream," "boy," and "stars" repeating throughout.) As writer Marilyn Krysl has observed, the "sestina's repeating form is designed to discover what is buried deepest in us."[37] In "Burial," the plums' sweetness maps directly onto his father's sweetness, lending his father an afterlife, actually an *un*burial, via poetry-writing and planting and their intersection. Naturally, then, "sweet" appears as the very last word in the poem: "when he knew he could make you happy / just by being a little silly / and sweet" (*Catalog of Unabashed Gratitude*, 14). These lines hearken back to a line earlier in "Burial" about the speaker's memory of his father's final moments, when his mother said to his dying father, "*it's ok, it's ok, you can go honey*," such that the sweetness of honey-love and the pain of loss meld with the sweetness of plums and the sweetness of his father in an eternal organic cycle (14).

Like Gay writing of his father and of Don Belton in *Catalog of Unabashed Gratitude*, Tracy K. Smith in *Life on Mars* *un*buries by writing elegiacally yet often joyfully in the wake of the 2008 death of her father, an avionics engineer who had worked on the Hubble telescope. The collection spins out from both that loss and her father's career.[38] As poet Joel Brouwer observes, "Smith's father was a scientist who worked on the Hubble's development, and in her elegies mourning his death, outer space serves both as a metaphor for the unknowable zone into which her father has vanished and as a way of expressing the hope that his existence hasn't ceased, merely changed."[39] *Life on Mars* comprises four parts, and the first part takes on what might be termed an individual "body's question" as well as "extremely large" (here I am alluding to Extremely Large Telescopes, or ELTs) questions (ELQs) about those "unknowable zones": What is the nature of the universe? Is there a god? If so, what is the nature of god? What will the future be like? What is the soul? What happens after we die? These six recurring questions establish the collection as a kind of "meta-sestina," with each part exploring those questions from a different perspective, as if testing various hypotheses in order to "discover what is buried deepest in us."

The second section considers how the local, the personal, and the familial lead us to pose the questions, particularly the question of "It," also a recurrent term that stands in the collection for the ineffability and mystery of our being, and our place in the universe, and the universe *it*self. These questions are *epic* in scale. It makes perfect sense, then, that Smith wrote in response to an African American visual version of epic in her poem "Realm of Shades," namely Bearden's representation of Odysseus in the underworld in his collage *Realm of Shades*, because her work is itself epic, perhaps most clearly so in *Life on Mars*, with its exploration of the afterlife/underworld and the joys and trials of Black people and other people of color on individual, familial, national, and international scales.

The third section is large-scale, zooming out from the individual and the familial to an explicit political engagement with the question of how we might sustain an ethics of care in the face of violence and racism inflicted upon others. For instance, this section's content includes American soldiers' torture of prisoners at Abu Ghraib that came to light in 2004 and the murders of Raul Flores and Brisenia Ylianna Flores in 2009 by the Minutemen American Defense, an American white supremacist vigilante group. In keeping with Caroline Levine's argument that "attending to the affordances of form opens up *a generalizable understanding of political power*" (7; emphasis in original), it is no coincidence that the section includes some of the most conventionally formal of the collection's poems. For example, a villanelle, "Solstice," links—via the repetition that characterizes the form—the gassing of geese at JFK airport with right-wing anti-immigration policies and talking points. And a near-sestina/near-villanelle, "Ransom," concerns Somali pirates and racist media coverage of them. After this large-scale content, the fourth section of the collection zooms back in, like a telescope or a microscope, on the local and personal, including Smith's own family, suggesting that, as the slogan goes, the personal is the political, but also that the universal is the personal is the political.

The section most consistently and explicitly concerned with the afterlife, however, is the second one. It operates at once on a relatively small (familial) and an extremely large (epic) scale. It includes just two poems. The first, "The Speed of Belief" (27–33), is dedicated to her father, and it works as a kind of synecdoche for *Life on Mars* as a whole, including the title's allusion to the 1977 David Bowie instrumental song, "Speed of Life," in that Bowie emerges as the collection's most sustained presence—except for, perhaps, the poet's parents. Written "*In memoriam, Floyd William Smith* 1935–2008," "The Speed of Belief" speculates about the answers to the collection's ELQs. Spanning seven pages (each of which could stand alone as a separate poem) and encompassing multiple metaphors and conceits, along with a variety of stanzaic and metrical forms, the poem's formal qualities match the scale and complexity of both the questions and the range of forms that unite and energize the collection as a whole. For instance, by way of provisional answers to one of the ELQs, a single-page section of the poem imagines her father's after-death experiences, which include meeting her mother, who had passed on fourteen years earlier:

> Probably he spun out of himself
> And landed squarely in that there, his new
> Body capable, lean, vibrating at the speed
> Of belief. She was probably waiting
> In the light everyone describes,
> Gesturing for him to come. . . .
> They told us not to go
> Tipping tables looking for them. Not even
> To visit their bodies in the ground. They are
> Sometimes maybe what calls out
> To people stuck in some impossible hell.
> The ones who later recall, "I heard a voice
> Saying *Go* and finally, as if by magic, I was able
> Simply to go." (30)

Echoing Gay's "go" in "Spoon," this poem, with its "go," explicitly considers the afterlife. "They" who have died, who have *gone*, do not want those left alive to seek connection with them (as in a séance) in what might be termed "inside of time," to adapt the parlance of the earlier "Shadow Poem" from *The Body's Question*. Those still alive are *not* to "go," with the enjambment of the seventh line above "tipping" us back into the world of the living, rather like the hinging "Love" in both "Bringing the Shovel Down" and "Again," and like Brown's "sweet music" in "Shovel."

Unlike Smith's "Shadow Poem" from *The Body's Question* and "Realm of Shades" from *Wade in the Water*, this part of "The Speed of Belief" is more conventional in form and therefore more representative of her poetry. A quasi-sonnet of fourteen lines, the poem seems to be lyrically measuring the time between the deaths of her parents (fourteen years). The line-length and meter are somewhat consistent with a sonnet, too, with several 9- and 10- and 11-syllable lines, some with mostly iambs (line 2) or mostly trochees (lines 1, 4, 5). As if heeding Harriet Wilson's declaration that she was "forced to some experiment"[40] with her writing, Smith stretches the received form of the sonnet, just as the poem stretches time, matching Michelle M. Wright's notion of "epiphenomenal time."[41] "The Speed of Belief," once again like Gay's

"Spoon," combines tenses: simple past ("spun," "heard"), past progressive ("was . . . waiting"), and present ("describes," "are") in the poetic equivalent of looking through a telescope, which always entails looking both into space and back in time. This telescopic process establishes a radical coeval-ness of places, persons, and times, as in her father's encountering her mother in an afterlife imagined and rendered by the poet in the present (and in the future, as each new reader encounters the poem).

In her 2015 memoir, *Ordinary Light*, Smith writes about her mother's illness and death from colon cancer in 1994.[42] Having traveled home from college that year to be with her, Smith closely observes her mother's decline, drawing—and drawing back—the shades to share this intimate experience with her readers. In a chapter titled "Another Dialect of the Soul," she describes how, under the influence of medications, her mother "began talking to someone in a low voice" (perhaps these are soul sounds). It was "as if," Smith observes, "she could see through this world to the next, to the places where ghosts and angels sit and walk and gesture unseen among us" (318). Smith then asks her mother, "Who is there with you?" Her mother's reply: "There are two angels sitting here, Tracy, and one of them just told me you are going to become a writer" (318). This passage about her mother's imminent passing combines time frames and tenses just as Ross Gay did in "Spoon" and as Smith herself did in "The Speed of Belief."

Smith recounts, populates, and animates this 1994 experience in her poem "The Angels" from *Wade in the Water* (6–7), a collection published in 2018, three years after the memoir *Ordinary Light*. "The Angels" tells of the speaker's encounter with two angels, who "slung themselves across chairs / Once in my motel room. . . . / . . . Emissaries / For something I needed to see" (6). The first stanza's many s's and g's ("slung," "chairs," "grizzled," "gear," "emissaries," "something," "see") deliver a song-like sibilance along with a hard consonance. Together, they produce an almost-anagrammatic consideration of the concept and term of "angels." As with shades/hades in "Realm of Shades," here we have angels, arranged and rearranged from multiple angles, who induce in us precisely the kinds of intertwined yet seemingly divergent feelings we have when we witness a loved one's passing: the harshness of "panic" and the loveliness of "fearsome grace" (6). The speaker "needed to see" these angels, "emissaries" of the afterlife and of her own mother, in order to perceive and document their "toil," "one scaled perfectly to eternity. / And still, they come, telling us / Through the ages not to fear" (6). Of course, "scaled" carries multiple meanings, including, among others, scales of measurement, scales of proportion and perspective, hierarchical scales that require ascent, and musical scales—with this last sort of scale perhaps most crucial for the poem's meaning. Throughout, its content depends on all the senses, but hearing and sound most of all, especially Black sound's quality of, in Anthony Reed's words, being "a medium of transformative energy" that in this instance tries to teach us not to fear death as finality.[43]

In the last stanza of "The Angels," Smith explicitly connects the poem to what she heard and saw upon her mother's passing as she had described it in her memoir, *Ordinary Light*:

My mother sat whispering with it
At the end of her life
While all the rooms of our house
Filled up with night. (7)

These four verse lines, as Nersessian says of the enjambment in Wordsworth's "The Prelude," "are the lines to which you pay attention, not just because they seem to be unloading a thought so passionate it won't break for endstops but also because that passion seems to promise something so revelatory, [so] intimate" (174). Within the intimate domestic space of "our house," ordinary light shades into night (much like mourning shaded into mornings in "Prayer") in "The Angels," one of Smith's most Dickinsonian poems. In *Ordinary Light*, Smith herself points to Emily Dickinson's poetry as "revelatory," writing of her fifth-grade experience reading and memorizing "I'm Nobody! Who are you?" describing it as "a poem whose meter had worked upon me quickly," and whose "rhyme scheme cemented, for me, a new sense of inevitability" (144–45). It is logical, then, that we, along with the speaker, can sense the "funeral" passing in the poet's brain (as well as in her mother's) in this poem. The speaker can "see" the angels in the first stanza, "sense" them in the second, smell them in the third—"To think of how they smelled, what / Comes to mind is rum and gasoline" (6)—"glimpse" them in the fourth, and *hear* them in the climactic fifth stanza: "Whose very voices cause faint souls to quake," a perfect iambic pentameter line near-riotous in its combination of senses and sensations (6). At the same time, the enjambed "it" in the last stanza ("My mother sat whispering with it / At the end of her life") recalls Smith's intense and sustained—always lyrical and often sonic—consideration of "It" throughout *Life on Mars*.

In *Life on Mars*, Smith's "It" is consistently filtered through the musical in a sonic equivalent of ekphrasis, "the verbal representation of [aural] experience," to adapt W. J. T. Mitchell's concise definition of poetic ekphrasis and its relation to "visual experience" (154). Perhaps a neologism such as "ektechne" (or "ektechnê," or "ekmousikē," or "ekmūsica") best expresses this concept. By blending the poetic and the musical through ektechne, then,

Smith takes advantage of sound-and-print's combined, synergistic "transformative energy," to again use Reed's words, in order to deliver her poetics of the afterlife.

From the start, *Life on Mars* depends on music. The collection is named for a poem within it; both take their titles from the 1971 David Bowie song "Life on Mars." Somewhat similar to Smith's *Life on Mars*, with its painful though familiar content (the loss of a loved one) expressed via rich lyrical form, Bowie's song delivers lyrics about typically American social and cultural experiences in their quotidian nature and their vacuity—"the film is a saddening bore"—their disappointment and isolation—"her friend is nowhere to be seen"—and their violence—"Take a look at the lawman / Beating up the wrong guy"—via a soaring melody.[44] Bowie's chorus twice poses a question about escaping this world and creating alternative, presumably better, worlds: "Is there life on Mars?" Ultimately, though, Smith's *Life on Mars* comes off as far more optimistic about both this life and the afterlife, at least in three of its four sections, than does Bowie's song. The title itself answers Bowie's question in the positive. Thus, in that much more positive register, Smith's version of "Life on Mars" theorizes, via her own family (rather like Harriet Jacobs does in *Incidents*), in Commander's words, a "fantastic, radical epistemological modality through which Afro-Atlantic identity can be lived across time and space."[45]

For instance, the poem "Don't You Wonder Sometimes," from the first (the ELQs-posing) section (19–21), also takes its title from Bowie's work, namely the first line from his 1977 song "Sound and Vision," a particularly fitting title given Smith's combined use of the ektechnic and the ekphrastic throughout the collection. "Sound and Vision" is ekphrastic, too; the lyrics mediate on "blue, blue electric blue / that's the colour of my room."[46] (Smith's "Realm of Shades" may also be alluding to "Sound and Vision": "Blue, blue / Pale blinds drawn all day / Nothing to do, nothing to say.") Smith's "Don't You Wonder Sometimes," however, turns out, once again, to be far more optimistic than the song, in part because of the presence of Bowie himself in *Life on Mars*. The poem imagines "It" as, "Not God, exactly," but "Some thin-hipped glittering Bowie-being" (19). As the poem unfolds, the distinction between this-world science and next-world souls melts away, as Bowie becomes an avatar of the first law of thermodynamics and of the afterlife, "Saying nothing is lost, that everything lives on waiting only / To be wanted back badly enough?" (19).

Bowie's spirit presides over much of the collection, standing in and for "It," such that his 2016 death lends even greater power and poignancy to the poetic speaker's imagining in "Don't You Wonder Sometimes" what this wanting "badly enough" could mean for her, after the deaths of her parents:

> Would I put on my coat and return to the kitchen where my
> Mother and father sit waiting, dinner keeping warm on the stove?
> Bowie will never die. Nothing will come for him in his sleep
> Or charging through his veins. And he'll never grow old. . . . (19)

At least in Smith's book, Bowie never does grow old; for him, "Time never stops" (20). He is "coy as Christ," yet he "is among us," savior-like and elusive but also omnipresent, much like the ELQs and It themselves (19, 20). The Bowie of *Life on Mars*, particularly in "Don't You Wonder Sometimes," emerges as a kind of nonbinary, benevolent Zeus (if such a thing were possible), complete with lightning bolts (see figure 3). Through its inclusion of lyrics from the chorus of Bowie's 1993 song "Bleed Like a Craze, Dad," the poem's last stanza imagines Bowie supplying something like a wise, clear, and godly answer to the ELQs: He sends "a thought like SHINE / SHINE SHINE SHINE SHINE / Straight to your mind" (21).[47] His final message to "everything," in the poem's short, italicized final line: "*Go ahead*" (italics in original). In keeping with the repetitions of "go" in Gay's work and in Smith's other work, "go ahead" here signifies both continuing to live and passing on, both of which lie within the purview of the gods. These lines point, too, to our desire to believe in a power that can command our living and our dying while being assured that "nothing is lost" in the process. We are stardust / We are golden: we shine regardless.[48]

The poem "The Universe Is a House Party," also in the book's first section (13), works as a companion poem for "Don't You Wonder Sometimes." After its initial words, "The universe is expanding," it imagines a universe with "bass throbbing" and "With radio waves from a generation ago / Drifting to the edge of what doesn't end," in the process sounding a great deal like "Bleed Like a Craze, Dad." Just as in this ektechnical metaphor of the universe/house party, Bowie's song begins with a familiar-sounding, beautiful, and rising major-key piano arpeggio only to move abruptly to a key change and then to the universe's "throbbing bass" (and drums), followed by a soaring chorus of "shine, shine, shine, shine." As Bowie expert Chris O'Leary notes, the song begins with "a little dancing phrase on high keys," what O'Leary terms a "parody of a Debussy prelude," "which gets diverted and broken down by the guitar kicking in."[49] Whereas O'Leary considers the song a somewhat failed patchwork, "a set of rough mixes that Bowie's considering using for some other song,"[50] "Bleed Like a Craze, Dad" actually works perfectly and wholly to express a messy Smithian house party in which, as the poem's first line says, "The universe is expanding" to contain "postcards / And panties, bottles with lipstick on the rim, / Orphan socks and napkins dried into knots" (13).

Figure 3
David Bowie, *Aladdin Sane*. Album cover.

In other words, both poem and song offer tidy and familiar, even clichéd, introductory motifs (expanding universe and Debussy-like intro) followed by inventive messes. Both offer studies of component parts and experiences that may arrive disjointed, like an arpeggio, but that are nonetheless intimately positioned next to one another, combined and recombined to create beauty. As another Bowie expert, Nicholas Pegg, remarks, "Bleed Like a Craze, Dad" is a "kaleidoscopic reshuffle of Bowie's past over which he delivers a quickfire rap, referring at one point to 'where the dead man walks,' reminding us that his habit of self-recycling is an ongoing process."[51] "The Universe is a House

Party," too, scopically recycles, following its list of detritus with "everyone thudding around drunk," and "We grind lenses to an impossible strength / Point them toward the future" (13). Although it would be more accurate to say that ELT lenses are pointed toward the past, this line does make sense given the broader meaning of the poem, which concerns a simultaneity of times, places, sounds, and sights, along with a sustained blurring of the distinction between living and dead, as in Bowie's lyric "Party on the dead" from "Bleed Like a Craze, Dad." Bowie's voice shines above all the disparate elements of his song, presiding over it much as he presides over Smith's book; even the piano motif returns at the end of the song, rather like an end-stopped line in a poem. In the same way, after nine couplets without a period, Smith's "House Party" ends with a period, a single end-stopped verse line—"Of course, it's ours. If it's anyone's, it's ours" (13). Here "it" signifies both the earth and the expanding universe of the poem's first line. As the poet's and the singer's shared "sound and vision" suggest, *Life on Mars* takes Bowie as its eternal musical "It," thereby performing/writing a shining music of the spheres, a universal house party, through Smith's sustained blending of ektechne and ekphrasis.

If Tracy K. Smith is spinning out a classical Pythagorean concept in *Life on Mars*—the music of the spheres—Danez Smith, in their exploration of Black queerness, HIV-positivity, and historical and present-day murders of Black people in *Don't Call Us Dead* (2017), is spinning out the medieval concept of *media vita in morte sumus*—in the midst of life, we are in death. For Danez Smith, Black queer men and nonbinary Black people bear, in Hartman's words, the "burdened individuality" that is necessarily produced by sociopolitical "norms that preclude substantive equality."[52] In this collection, as Levine contends, form enables a "*generalizable understanding of political power*" (7) of precisely that burdening sociopolitical sort. Yet form also helps produce the Black and queer "affective resistance," to use Ahad-Legardy's words (36), that Danez Smith celebrates in *Don't Call Us Dead*. Thus, logically, in their poetics of death-in-life and the afterlife, Danez Smith, like Ross Gay, Jericho Brown, and Tracy K. Smith, revels in an astonishing array of forms, including extensive enjambment, rhyme, couplets, block poems, innovative orthography (for example, in "Litany with Blood All Over" with its pooling of the word "blood" at the bottom of the page, 51–52), epistrophe (in "elegy with pixels & cum," 48), and even a crown of sonnets titled, appropriately enough, "crown" (56–59). In sum, the collection exemplifies what I termed at the outset of this chapter the conspicuous formalism of a contemporary Black poetics of the afterlife.

That formalism is especially evident in the poem "Recklessly," which functions in *Don't Call Us Dead* a bit like "The Speed of Belief" does in *Life on*

Mars, as a synecdoche for the collection's content and for its wide range of poetic forms. "Recklessly" is dedicated to Michael L. Johnson, a gay Black college athlete who was alleged to have knowingly infected white male sexual partners with HIV. Johnson was tried in 2015 and "convicted on multiple felony counts, including recklessly infecting another with H.I.V."[53] Like Gay's "Burial," "Recklessly" works as a kind of loose sestina, with "cell," "recklessly," "white," "blue(s)," "blood," and "boy" simmering throughout the seven-page poem and its varying stanzaic forms, adding up to a poem "designed to discover what is buried deepest in us," as Krysl put it. "Recklessly" also offers stunning rhymes and repetitions that bring somewhat distant lines together, as in the first four lines: "the bloodprison leads to prison/jail doubles as quarantine/chest to chest, men are silent/you're under arrest, under a **spell**" (41, emphasis added). These initial lines are followed by "but you don't know my name/don't ask, don't **tell**" in lines 15 and 16, which are followed by "i got the **cell** count blues/inside a **cell**: a man/inside his cells" in lines 19 and 20 (41, emphasis added). The neologism "bloodprison," the double-meaning "cells," and the rhymes and repetitions, taken together, link sex with death, blood cells with prison cells, and HIV positivity with incarceration and anti-Black racist oppression and violence. As a result, Danez Smith's poems in *Don't Call Us Dead* become primarily about—and *for*—perpetually at-risk Black boys and men, particularly those who are queer, including nonbinary queer Black people like Smith themself. Still, even if all these at-risk Black people are *while in life also in the midst of death*, they are also united in a heavenly solidarity—and that is so right from the very start of the collection, actually even *before* its first poem.

Don't Call Us Dead, from its cover on, suspends Black men in air, either hovering between life and death or inhabiting an up-there afterlife—perhaps a heaven, but certainly a world far more beautiful than this one. The cover consists of a gorgeous image, created by sculptor, photographer, and filmmaker Shikeith, that depicts a partly earthbound naked Black man with one foot off the ground, so seemingly about to rise, holding hands with another naked Black man aloft with a balloon in his and (see figure 4). Shikeith included the image in a 2014 art installation that he titled with a J. M. Barrie quotation, "The Moment You Doubt You Can Fly, You Cease Forever to Be Able to Do It," but also with the alternative title, "Somewhere over the ____." Installation materials included: "Soil, Figurative Sculpture, Wooden Chair, Audio, Wall Collage, Single Channel Video, Balloon."[54] In one striking sculpture also included in the installation, soil partly covers an at once buried and unburied sculpture of a naked Black man, with a balloon secured near his head (see figure 5). The poems in *Don't Call Us Dead* join with the cover art

Figure 4
Danez Smith, *Don't Call Us Dead*. Book cover.

Figure 5
Shikeith Installation, "The Moment You Doubt You Can Fly, You Cease Forever to Be Able to Do It."
Reproduced by permission of the artist.

to create large-scale ekphrasis, with Smith's recurring images of soil and dirt and earth, of burial and unburial—and of suspension—matching Shikeith's own recurring visual tropes.

The first poem in *Don't Call Us Dead* immediately solidifies this ekphrastic relationship. Titled "summer somewhere," it lends the collection its title: "please, don't call/us dead, call us alive someplace better" (3). Accessing that "better place" requires a rebirth into an afterlife where, unlike Trayvon Martin, Black boys "go out for sweets & come back," and where "there's no language/for *officer* or *law*, no color to call *white*" (3). This afterlife accommodates and values a Blackness so thoroughgoing that "if snow fell, it'd fall black" (3). An utter absence of white and whiteness, such that there are no words for it, stands as a logical prerequisite for a (Black) "sanctuary," a heaven, where "nothing is a gun," and where there are no police (8). In other words, sanctuary requires scientific and social *abolition*, a complete reversal both of Newton's universal law of gravity and of Levine's "sociopolitical institutions." Both are equally weighty in the world of *Don't Call Us Dead*.

Not surprisingly, then, reversal is deeply embedded not only in the images but also in the forms of "summer somewhere." Somewhat like Gay's "Spoon," Smith's title flows directly into the first stanza; taken together, title and first line form a chiasmus:

> **summer, somewhere**
>
> somewhere, a sun. below, boys, brown
> as rye play the dozens & ball, jump
>
> in the air & stay there. boys become new
> moons . . . (3)

The reversal inherent in chiasmus is encapsulated in a devastating line from much later in the poem: "sometimes we unfuneral a boy," a boy signified in the poem's first lines by the homophonic sun/son. To undead the son, forever in the air (like the sun), requires poetic reversal of both gravity and grave realities, linking the universal and the personal, as in *Life on Mars*. The lyricism and sibilance of these initial lines establish the natural beauty ("sun" *and* "moons") of the "we" that Smith's couplets "hold." To put this another way, in *Don't Call Us Dead*, naturally beautiful Black men and boys are eternally "spooned" in an up-there afterlife after they have lived together in a this-life that "spoons" them, that holds them together in both glorious queer sexualities and in "Black immanent and imminent death," to again use Sharpe's words (13). Or, as Quashie puts it, they are held together in the knowledge that "blackness, terror, and death are synonyms in the world" (146). To extend the imagery of the cover, they are perpetually at risk of falling, for the balloons also imply a lethal sound; they can burst with a bang. Just so, Shikeith has said that the balloon, a recurrent image in his dreams, is a "signifier and symbol in my work across photograph, film, and now sculpture" that carries two meanings in his art as in his psyche: In his dreams, either he reached for the balloon only to "fall to my death," or he "grabbed it and floated away."[55]

Smith's title "summer somewhere" seems to fill in Shikeith's alternate title, "Somewhere over the ______," with "summer," so that the balloon never bursts. In this poem, Black men float away into the afterlife, even if other kinds of suspension had been lethal in this-life. Thus, its title recalls Spiritualists' term for the afterlife, the Summerland, while the poem itself evokes the same sort of peaceful and idyllic afterlife that Spiritualists had imagined in the nineteenth century. But Smith's version of that afterlife is strictly for Black boys and men—most definitely not for the "predominantly middle-class [white] Anglo-Americans" who dominated the Spiritualist movement.[56] Once again, form helps build that Black, gun-free "sanctuary" located "up there."

An epic-scale twenty-page poem of nearly all couplets, "summer somewhere" collectivizes and elevates Black boys into their very own Summerland. Couplets suit this content, for, as Gay has said of his own use of the form, "it holds the *we*."[57] Smith's "we" (a word that appears twenty-two times in "summer somewhere") refers to Black boys and men, coupled during life and again after death, cross-temporally, whether they died from lynching—"we plucked brothers from branches"—or gun violence—"clutching wicked metals"—or HIV/AIDS—"through their own blood" (5). All are "*gone*" (emphasis in original), regardless of the particular historical and cultural contexts that produced their passing. Danez Smith, in their poetics of a Black afterlife, thus joins Tracy K. Smith and Ross Gay in a collective poetic conjugation of "to go."

For brothers who have not "gone," who remain in this life, the (body's) question then arises: Where and how to find those who have gone on to the Summerland? Just as for the other poets, for Danez Smith and for Shikeith, they must be un-buried. To adapt Wilderson's words, this is a poetic project of "unearthing and exposing."[58] It makes perfect sense, then, that "summer somewhere," like Gay's "Burial" and Brown's "Shovel" (after its title, that is), includes an implicit shovel: "we dig/a new one from the ground" (4). With these lines, Smith joins the speaker in "Shovel," to "dig and dig and dig," but in this case they dig not to bury/reveal the dead, but rather to create "a new reborn boy" (4). So here again we encounter reversal in Smith's project, as they unbury the once-dead but now hyper-alive, as the redundancy of "new" and "reborn" suggests.

After "summer somewhere," the entire collection unfolds as a process of un-dying, that is, living in an afterlife that Tracy K. Smith might term "outside of time" or, in Danez Smith's own terms, up in the air. This suspension in air, like the tropes of shovel and balloon, carries the intertwined joyful and terrible meanings that resonate throughout a contemporary Black poetics of the afterlife. As religious studies scholar Ashon T. Crawley puts this, "It is this joyful disposition, the practice of black social life, that makes black folks targets of various modalities and intensities of violence."[59] For example, Ross Gay's epic, ninety-five-page poem *Be Holding* (2020),[60] made up entirely of couplets (with the exception of the very last line), spins out from one glorious moment of suspension, namely the mid-air dunking of basketball legend Dr. J, who is in "emphatic and exquisite flight" (10) when a defender, Kareem Abdul-Jabbar, tries to stop him, with hands like

> a silver maple's branches
>   creaking and swaying

in a hurricane,
for Doc was amongst the trees

as we call the big men
like Kareem, *the trees,* (11)

As these eerie tree images imply, *Be Holding,* like "summer somewhere," is equally concerned with the suspension of lynching and the suspension of justice as it is with the genius and beauty of Black men who are able to stay up in the air, to defy gravity. In a particularly stunning passage, the poem renders the perspective of a tree forced to lynch:

with which the tree makes a kind of choir
moaning, *I'm sorry,*

twisting its roots in the molder
with what they've been made to do, (19)

In keeping with the broader, post-2016 shift in tone among all these poets' published collections, *Be Holding* focuses more on *having gone,* on death and dying—that is, the "bullets" *not* dodged—than do Gay's previous poetry collections. In a 2022 interview, Gay spoke about the Afropessimist origins of his title:

> This book used to be called "Flight." It was called "Flight" until I read *In the Wake* by Christina Sharpe. Now, it's true that the title change was also informed by Moten and Harney's *The Undercommons* and by a lot of other kinds of conversations, too. But reading Sharpe made me ask, "What is flight when there is nowhere to go?" And when I say, "There's nowhere to go," what I'm saying is, "We're not escaping the turmoil or tumult of history. We are not going to escape this."[61]

Like Sharpe with her exploration of all the possible meanings of "wake," Gay in *Be Holding* explores "holding" as a basketball foul, as an embrace, as an enslavers' ship hold—and as beholding and as being beholden. This is not to say that such less unabashedly grateful moments are absent in Gay's earlier, seemingly more Afro-Optimistic work. For example, "Spoon" recounts Belton's "terrifying" dream of being in a graveyard and being lifted away toward death, "floating/into the air," with the speaker "imagining a rope/cinched to his waist by which Don might be tethered/to this world" (37, 38). These lines produce a kind of dire mirror image of the cover of *Don't Call Us Dead,* which might be termed an Afro-Optimistic and Black queer rendering of the concept of suspense, of being held in the air and staying there. Together Gay's and Smith's mirrored images match poet Terrance Hayes's remarkable verse line: "One rope pulls a body down / And into earth, the other pulls up & after stars."[62] Ultimately, all these collections might be termed "both/and," as pulling-down and pulling-up, falling and rising, poetry, that at the same time centers Quashie's "aliveness." As Ross Gay remarked of *Be Holding*, "One of the things the poem is trying to wonder about and understand is Black life. Death is a feature of life, but, nevertheless, my interest is in Black *life*."[63]

Don't Call Us Dead is, likewise, perhaps primarily interested in Black *life*. And again like *Life on Mars*, *Don't Call Us Dead* relies regularly on the musical to express that life, Quashie's Black "aliveness," as well as Danez Smith's own version of the afterlife, an alternative space-time specifically for Black men and boys. In other words, as did Tracy K. Smith, Danez Smith relies on both ekphrasis and ektechne. For instance, the line "jump / in the air & stay there" (3) alludes to a 2010 song by Erykah Badu (a collaboration with Lil Wayne) of the same title, a song that in turn samples the lyric and the tune—although significantly not the on-the-one funk rhythm—of the P-Funk All-Stars' 1983 song "Hydraulic Pump." As *Pitchfork* writes, P-Funk's song "levitates over drums, harpsichord stabs, and scratchy vinyl swipes."[64] "Jump in the Air and Stay There" is, literally and figuratively, a "kaleidoscopic reshuffle," to reuse Pegg's description of Bowie's "Bleed Like a Craze, Dad." The video for "Jump in the Air and Stay There" consists almost entirely of kaleidoscopic images of Badu and Lil Wayne, while the music is a "reshuffling," a reprocessing of P-Funk's song in what *Pitchfork* terms Badu's "spacey rendering."[65] Levitation into some kind of sonic or literal space thus unites all three works: Smith's poem "summer somewhere," Badu's "Jump in the Air and Stay There," and P-Funk's "Hydraulic Pump."

However, the syncopated rhythms in Badu's version render it far more compatible than "Hydraulic Pump" would be with "summer somewhere," making it a logical intertext for Danez Smith in terms of both form and meaning. "Jump Up in the Air and Stay There" sounds almost like an African American prison or chain gang or work song, with a booming drum intro followed by heavy beats on the two and four supplied by hand-claps (granted, some syncopated work songs put the drum beat or clap on just the four).[66] Of course, musical syncopation and poetic syncopation differ, with poetry's version corresponding to the beat/accent on the one, that is, a trochee, rather than on the two, an iamb. Therefore, the song's syncopation (beats on two and four) corresponds to the poem's trochaic (beat on one) "summer" and "somewhere." The poem's sampling of the song's lyrics is likewise trochaic: "jump in" and "stay there." The ampersand in Smith's line that includes "in the air & stay there," visually at least, eliminates the unstressed "and" in much the way that

Badu's brief "n" ("jump in the air 'n' stay there") sonically abbreviates the "and." Both soft-pedal a potential iamb such that Badu's syncopations and Smith's trochees become sonic-visual counterparts in a reversal of conventional rhythmic forms. These sonic forms in turn echo the reversal of meaning that chiasmus produces literarily or rhetorically. As Henry Louis Gates Jr. has famously argued, chiasmus is the slave's trope, a "repetition and reversal" that permits a "slave-object" to write themselves "into a human-subject."[67] Poem and song stay in the air, defying the power of the awful kinds of gravity that would make a person into an object, the weight, in Hartman's words, of "the crushing effects of racism,"[68] particularly the relentless rhythms of forced labor and of the carceral state, in order to "unfuneral," to lift Black people up to the Summerland. As Badu sings, "I know you want to, reach to the higher level / Much further from the devil, until you feel the weather."[69]

As with its early engagement with being "up in the air" on its cover, *Don't Call Us Dead* engages with music even *before* its first poem. After cover and title, copyright, and dedication pages, the collection begins with two epigraphs that locate it precisely in the space between life and afterlife. The first, "If I die, I'm a legend," also connects Smith's poetic project to music from the outset. A line from hip hop/rap artist Drake's 2015 song "Legend," its verb-tense play places the singer "in the midst of death" while suggesting that he may be immortal (always in the midst of life, too), rather like Bowie in *Life on Mars*. "Legend" also places Drake/the singer among other Black men who may kill him but who themselves are also at risk: "They can't live this long / You don't know where you're gonna go."[70] Like Drake, Smith locates their poems amidst Black men who may well be the cause of their death, although they are lovers and sexual partners rather than rivals or enemies as in "Legend." Regardless, any one of them may "go" at any time and in any location, a knowledge that sounds and resounds throughout the world of hip hop, as I explore in the following chapter. In any case, here Smith, along with Drake, contributes to the collective conjugation project within a contemporary Black poetics of the afterlife, drawing on both Black musical and poetic traditions as they do so.

The second epigraph in *Don't Call Us Dead*, "he who wore death discourages any plague," comes from Sonia Sanchez's 1997 book *Does Your House Have Lions?* This intertextual relationship works at both sonic and poetic-formal levels to connect Danez Smith's poetry to the afterlife and to the spaces and sounds between this world and the next. Sanchez's is an epic poem, filtered through the voices of family members and ancestors, about trauma and tragic loss for Black people—from the Middle Passage to the assassination of Malcom X, to Sanchez's brother's 1981 death from AIDS. Near the end of the book, Sanchez represents her brother's voice at his dying, his soul sounds:

brother's voice
i am going out of my cell
i am ready

brother's voice
hold me with air
breathe me with air[71]

Smith's wordplay with "cell" in "Recklessly" is clearly paying homage to these stanzas in Sanchez's poem. And in echoing Sanchez, Smith doubts that a queer Black man or nonbinary person will escape any cell; they will not be able to dodge the "myriad bullets" Belton had "dodged," at least for fifty-three years, in Gay's "Spoon." Smith takes up this image of the bullet in "every day is a funeral & a miracle": "they sent a boy / when the bullet missed," and "I survived yesterday, spent it / ducking bullets, some / flying toward me & some / trying to rip their way out" (66). The alliteration of boy and bullet emphasizes the mapping of HIV onto police murders of Black men, or, as the speaker puts it quite plainly: "little / cops running inside / my veins" (65). What the speaker-poet *does* have to lift him up, in this life-midst-death, is what "my n**," a poem from Smith's 2020 collection *Homie*, calls "the heaven of now," together with his beloved Black men, his "n***as."[72]

To return to the image that began this chapter, in *Don't Call Us Dead*, "heaven," a Black afterlife, is signified, once again, by the shovel, even in a still-alive present. In "everyday a funeral & a miracle," in the speaker's nightmares their mother is "shoveling dirt down my throat," and "if i try to get up, she brings the shovel down / saying i miss you so much, my sweetest boy" (64). Like the deadly gravity that takes over when Shikeith's balloon bursts, here the shovel pushes down rather than pulls up. Or, as I argued at the beginning of this chapter, Smith's lines signify the connections and the ruptures, the love and violence in a Black poetics of the afterlife, in this case a specifically Black queer afterlife. The shovel appears, too, in Smith's poem "seroconversion," wherein "the god of shovels visits the god of soil" (38). This alliance signifies the deep, magical internality of sex between "two boys": "one / boy reaches his bare hand inside the other, pulls / out a parade of fantastic beasts: lions with house / fly wings, fish who thrive in boiling water, horses / who've learned to sleep while running" (38). These images also underscore the metamorphosis of magical sex into the potentially lethal illness of the poem's title, indeed to their interconnectedness. Seroconversion refers to the period during which HIV antibodies develop and become detectable through a blood test, a threshold state, paralleling the poem's exploration of the intense vitality of Black queer sex that can also bring out "little ruby tongues" of an infection (38). Soil and shovels thus represent vital and deep passions that are at once natural/organic and fantastic/magical at the same time that they also represent mortality and the afterlife: a burial first in another and then in a grave.

Yet there is a subtler shovel, a metapoetic one, at work in *Don't Call Us Dead* through its intertextuality with Sonia Sanchez's work. Yet there is a subtler shovel, a metapoetic one, at work in *Don't Call Us Dead* through Smith's homage to Sonia Sanchez. The "shovel," more specifically the "Golden Shovel," is a poetic form invented by Terrance Hayes in his own homage to Gwendolyn Brooks. Poet and former *Poetry* editor Don Share offers this helpful definition of the form:

> The last words of each line in a Golden Shovel poem are, in order, words from a line or lines taken often, but not invariably, from a Brooks poem. The results of this technique can be quite different in subject, tone, and texture from the source poem, depending upon the ingenuity and imagination of the poet who undertakes to compose one. As Robert Lee Brewer has pointed out, such a poem is part cento, part erasure. But don't let the word "erasure" mislead you. A poem in this form adds something even where it subtracts; the sum isn't necessarily greater than the parts, but in keeping with the spirit of paying tribute, it is more than equal to them.[73]

The original golden shovel, Hayes's poem titled "The Golden Shovel," honors Brooks's well-known poem "We Real Cool," which begins with the line, "The Pool Players. / Seven at the Golden Shovel."[74] Hayes's "The Golden Shovel" sustains the intertextual relationship with "We Real Cool" throughout and includes, for example, the following stanzas:

> He'd been defending his ma, trying to be a man. We
> stood in the road, and my father talked about jazz,
>
> how sometimes a tune is born of outrage. By June
> the boy would be locked upstate. That night we
>
> got down on our knees in my room. *If I should die*
> *before I wake,* Da said to me, *it will be too soon.*[75]

that are in conversation with this stanza from "We Real Cool":

> Jazz June. We
> Die soon.

All these stanzas concern untimely, yet foreseeable, death shared among a "we," or what Hayes terms Brooks's "insistent 'we.'"[76] Hayes's intertextual, highly relational form, his "tribute to Gwendolyn Brooks,"[77] suggests that there is an even greater weight being carried by the shovel. It signifies not only a collective burying/unburying imaged and sounded by the poets in this chapter but a still broader and deeper relationship among all these poets and their works—and between them and Black poets who have passed on before them.

Through this highly connective Black poetics of the afterlife, they are unearthing Quashie's aliveness in community, a connectedness so powerful that it successfully and thoroughly mediates between two apparently competing schools of thought, Afropessimism and Afro-Optimism—so powerful, in fact, that it can mediate between the living and the dead. This, then, is poetry that both engages with and *is* theory, as perhaps best exemplified by the metapoetic moments in the poems. What results is what we might term a meta-metapoetics uniting poets, poems, and poetic forms. If Ross Gay's "Burial" and Danez Smith's "Recklessly" work as loose sestinas, and Tracy K. Smith's *Life on Mars* works as a kind of meta-sestina, then there emerges an even grander sestina of *form* they have collectively "designed to discover what is buried deepest in us." The images of shovel/balloon, enjambment/suspension, ekphrasis, ektechne, the couplet, and the sestina itself—these six key formal elements repeat again and again across the work of Ross Gay, Jericho Brown, Tracy K. Smith, Danez Smith, and Terrance Hayes. Poets and poems together lend new life to received poetic forms and establish new ones to create a contemporary Black poetics of the afterlife that is *scaled perfectly to eternity*.

In the following chapter, I turn to hip hop and sorrow songs as art forms that, likewise, are scaled perfectly to eternity both formally and lyrically. For artists such as Kendrick Lamar, Notorious B.I.G., and Tupac Shakur, the afterlife becomes an ever-present possibility even as it offers the means to imagine another, better kind of world for the living: a way of levitating.

4

"Wade in the Water"

Hip Hop and Sorrow Songs

It is a commonplace that a great deal of hip hop music deals with death. Many hip hop artists, especially during the 1990s, have been preoccupied with their impending deaths or with their transition from this life to the afterlife. Given their all too often violent deaths, many have indeed been made to "wade to heaven through swamps of blood," as nineteenth-century Spiritualist Paschal Beverly Randolph put it.[1] Alternatively, they are always already dwelling in the "Realm of Shades," as poet Tracy K. Smith wrote in her 2018 poetry collection *Wade in the Water*.[2] To give a recent and powerful example of the idea of hip hop as being inextricable from Black mortality, Anthony Pinn in his brilliant 2024 book, *Deathlife: Hip Hop Thanatological Narrations of Blackness*, coined the titular term "deathlife" to describe how Black people actually stand for death for white Americans. Hip hop, in Pinn's view, offers "one of the more graphic narrations" of a history of Blackness in the United States that maps directly onto "a history of demise."[3] Yet there remains so much to say about how hip hop works, not only to narrate Black mortality in the context of a death-dealing American whiteness, as in Pinn's analysis, but also about how it manages "to take death back from death itself," to adapt Kevin Young's stunning words about poetry."[4]

In the following, I argue that hip hop—with its almost compulsive repetition of the ways that the artist, along with their community, must "wade to heaven through swamps of blood"—belongs within a long history of Spiritualism and within the equally long tradition of representation of an agential afterlife in African American literature and music that we have seen throughout this book. At least since the late 1980s, hip hop has demonstrated the same preoccupations with death and the afterlife that we saw in Randolph's writings

(Chapter 1) and in narratives by formerly enslaved persons (Chapter 2). In other words, yes, death-in-life matters a great deal for hip hop's meaning and power, but a lyrical and performative life-after-death matters just as much, if not more. Or, in the rather cynical words of the late and great Greg Tate, "In the Age of Death the only thing that matters is whether the dead keep appearing to entertain the living."[5]

Hip hop has long sounded back to us Karla Holloway's stark words about the "character" of Black experiences in and of the United States: "our daily lives are a complicated matter of color and death."[6] Holloway's version of Black death-in-life comes through audibly and clearly in the gangsta hip hop of the 1990s. Thus, Pinn's insight that for Kendrick Lamar, especially on *DAMN*, "death and life bleed into each other to become expression" applies equally well to the works of Tupac Shakur and Biggie Smalls, to name just two of the many 1990s hip hop artists preoccupied with death.[7] Of course, the fear of "going under" tracks back as far Grandmaster Flash's 1982 "The Message." Its last verse ends with the lines, "But now your eyes sing the sad, sad song / Of how you lived so fast and died so young."[8] Building on this foundation, 1990s hip hop regularly engages with death but also with the afterlife, as in the song "Book of Life" from Common's 1994 album *Resurrection*, which begins: "I got so much trouble on my mind / So I take time out my day to pray and I say / Now lay me down to sleep, hoping that I keep my soul."[9] Here, prayer is set alongside a perpetually implicit and thoroughly expected death, with the singer hoping either to live to see another day or at least to enter a heavenly afterlife with soul intact. Fittingly, then, "Book of Life" offers a patchwork of samples of biblical passages—for example, "As I walk down the road of existence," recalling the 23rd Psalm—along with samples of earlier rap and hip hop—for example, "It's like a jungle sometimes it makes me wonder / How I keep from going under, I ponder," quoting "The Message."[10] That the "road of existence" replaces the "valley of the shadow of death" underscores the fact that the artist understands that he dwells, even while in this real life, in Smith's (and Bearden's) "realm of shades" (see figure 2). Such lyrics signify that in hip hop, as Pinn has argued elsewhere, "there remains here an important tension, a battle between existential realities and religious sensibilities."[11]

Such a tension is not at all new in a Black American literary or musical tradition. We can, for instance, hear a similar tension in sorrow songs/spirituals. As Pinn explains, we can draw a strong religious and critical through line from spirituals to rap and hip hop. As he puts it, "Through the spirit of the spirituals and the blues came a variety of musical forms with creative alterations of existing styles and with sensitivity to the existential circumstances of their creators. There should be no wondering, then, about the birth of rap music as a vital—and often troubled and troubling—mode of musical expression."[12] In hip hop, this shared "spirit" with spirituals corresponds to "soul" in the most literal terms—that is, what of us lives on in the afterlife. As Common intones in "Book of Life": "So now I sing the new negro spiritual / It goes, get up stand up, stand up for your rights / Get up stand up, don't give up the fight." Common's proclaiming this song's status as a "new spiritual" in combination with his sampling of Bob Marley, Public Enemy ("I got so much trouble in my mind"), and Grandmaster Flash, "Book of Life" effectively establishes a long musical genealogy of the soul, and therefore of the afterlife, and a clearly agential, even activist, one, in rap and hip hop.

In their shared theorization of death and the afterlife, all these musics—sorrow songs/spirituals, the earliest rap, and hip hop from the 1990s to today—offer at once spiritual and material modes of self-construction and of hope—or, in some songs, of paranoia and despair. In Ralph C. Watkins's words, rap and hip hop artists are thereby "constructing a theology," one that contends consistently with an expectation of mortality and yet just as consistently longs, as in "Book of Life," for immortality and for a better world, a paradise.[13] If there is a "Gangsta's Paradise" then, as Kevin Young argues, for a "hip-hop artist [like Coolio in 1995], the funereal suffuses the ecstatic."[14] In fact, hip hop artists have focused so often on an expectation of mortality followed by a potentially ecstatic entrance into the afterlife that this double thematic could be said to characterize the art form; certainly, this is true of hip hop from the 1990s to the present. Notorious B.I.G.'s 1994 album *Ready to Die* placed next to his 1997 album *Life After Death* perhaps best encapsulates those twin preoccupations of death and the afterlife, especially given that *Life After Death* was released just two weeks after his murder. The serial deaths of hip hop artists (and Black men more broadly) thereby become foreseeable, with the result that to be a "Mortal Man," to cite Kendrick Lamar's song title from *To Pimp a Butterfly*, means, for Black men, to live always on the cusp of death and thus *im*mortality.

Both Notorious B.I.G./Biggie Smalls and Lamar, along with many other hip hop artists, are thus sounding out what Abdul R. JanMohamed terms "the death-bound-subject," that is, "the subject who is formed, from infancy on, by the imminent and ubiquitous threat of death."[15] And this "death-bound" hip hop subject is by no means a strictly West Coast and East Coast (or West Coast versus East Coast) phenomenon. The Geto Boys, a Houston hip hop group, helped inaugurate this death thematic, along with the genre of horrorcore rap, with their 1991 hit, "Mind Playing Tricks on Me." This song connects justified fears regarding imminent death with historical violences against Black men, as in the lyrics "At night I can't sleep, I toss and turn / Candle sticks in the dark, visions of bodies being burned," only to return, seemingly compulsively, to personal "paranoia": "But late at night, somethin ain't right/ I feel I'm being tailed by the same sucker's head lights." The Geto Boys in their spiritual register, unlike Tupac Shakur (as we shall see), are not at all confident that heaven awaits them: "Every sunday morning I'm in service/Prayin' for forgiveness/And trying to find an exit out of the business/I know the lord is looking at me."[16] This is decidedly not an ecstatic expression of the funereal. Even Lamar at times partakes of such paranoia and despair. As one of the lines of "Mortal Man" asks: "Would you know where the sermon is if I died in this next line?"[17] Will his audience honor Lamar's legacy and his message not just ahead of but also after his perpetually imminent death? While he seems not at all sure about the answer to his questions, he does seem quite sure about the ever-present possibility of his death, just like Biggie, 2Pac, the Geto Boys, and Grandmaster Flash.

We might expect, then—as we saw in the introduction with Danez Smith's *Homie* and in Chapter 3 with Danez Smith's *Don't Call Us Dead* and Jericho Brown's "Shovel"—that hip hop would document and honor the solidarity, the community, the consolation, and even the love, that a shared imminence of death can produce.[18] And yet Biggie Small's *Life After Death*, on the one hand, depends on sustained collaboration with other artists and, on the other, expresses deep enmity toward other Black men. This enmity seems to support Pinn's lament that "when not at its best, rap music provides a celebration of radical individualism and nihilism over against community and hope."[19] Yet even as he advances beefs with other artists, Notorious B.I.G. taps R. Kelly, the LOX, Jay-Z, Mase, Diddy/Puff Daddy, Too $hort, and Darryl McDaniels of Run D.M.C., along with Angela Winbush and Lil' Kim, among others, to contribute to *Life After Death*. We should not underestimate the community-building that such creative projects both depend on and promote, a bit like Janelle Monáe's Wondaland and Parliament-Funkadelic's loose collective that I considered in Chapter 1. As Tricia Rose observed of rap videos in her classic 1994 study of hip hop, *Black Noise*, "The emergence of the rap music video has also opened up a previously nonexistent creative arena for black visual artists," thereby enabling creative Black communities; in much the same way, many, many hip hop albums build remarkably expansive communities.[20] Or, as Pinn compellingly argues in *Deathlife*, "rap artists" often express "a tension between the individual and frameworks of communality played out through/in the fragility of life."[21]

Biggie Smalls, for one, often chose to emphasize only certain communalities, however. For example, the lyrics on *Life After Death* advance well-known coastal (and other) rivalries within hip hop, taking particular aim at Tupac

Shakur, who had been shot to death in September 1996, the year before the release of *Life After Death.* Just as Rose observes, albeit in a somewhat different context, "Rap music conjures and razes in the same stroke."[22] In "The Long Kiss Goodnight," a cut on *Life After Death*, Notorious B.I.G. conjures Shakur just to sustain his beef with him, to raze/raise him even after Shakur has taken up residence in the afterlife, whether in heaven or in hell: "bleed-in'" lovely, wit'chyo, spirit above me / Or beneath me, ya whole life ya live sneaky / Now ya rest eternally, sleepy, ya burn when ya creep me / Rest where the worms and the weak be.[23] These lyrics construct a masculinity that rejects weakness, yet they do not then associate that weakness definitively with either heaven or hell. This ambivalence and its implied question—"Will the strong gangsta ascend to heaven or descend to hell?"—emerge out of a complex hip hop theology that, in Margarita Simon Guillory's words, is "holding in tension categories of the sacred and profane."[24] It is in this spirit that Master P asks in his 1997 song "Is There a Heaven 4 a Gangsta?"[25] What counts as weak, what counts as strength, what counts as sin, what will be rewarded in this life, what will be rewarded in the afterlife—all these questions remain subject to speculation and theorization within hip hop theology.

That theology is not built upon a strictly Christian framework, despite the frequent appearance of biblical passages, especially the 23rd psalm, in hip hop lyrics. Hip hop's version of the afterlife, as I argued at the outset, often appears more akin to Paschal Beverly Randolph's Spiritualist sense of the afterlife, particularly as he represented it in *Dealings with the Dead*, than to a traditional Christian heaven or hell. Thus, André Key rightly argues that hip hop "has long housed multiple faith traditions,"[26] including, among others, Christianity, Islam,[27] and, I would add here, *Spiritualism*. Key compellingly likens this blending of faiths to perhaps the fundamental musical technique of hip hop, terming it "an extension of the sampling modality."[28] Sam Kestenbaum notes that Lamar in particular regularly samples multiple systems of faith and belief; as he puts it, "Lamar has integrated myriad religious and metaphysical materials into his own idiosyncratic worldview."[29] And though hip hop may regularly "sample" Spiritualism, it does so perhaps most famously in Kendrick Lamar's 2013 *GQ* interview regarding a visit he received from the spirit of Tupac Shakur:

> I was coming from a late studio session, sleeping on Mom's couch. I'm 26 now [Shakur was 25 when he died]—it wasn't that long ago. I remember being tired, tripping from the studio, lying down, and falling into a deep sleep and seeing a vision of Pac talking to me. Weirdest shit ever. I'm not huge on superstition and all that shit. That's what

> made it so crazy. It can make you go nuts. Hearing somebody that you looked up to for years saying, "Don't let the music die." Hearing it clear as day. Clear as day. Like he's right there. Just a silhouette.[30]

Neither the music nor Shakur himself has died, it would seem; rather, he returns to guide Lamar. Similarly, in *Dealings with the Dead,* as we saw in Chapter 1, the narrator (a version of Randolph himself) receives reports from his dead friend Cynthia about her experiences of the afterlife, beginning with her hearing the sound of bells as she enters the spirit world. Lamar and Tupac Shakur, like so many others in the hip hop world, likewise lyrically and sonically document their "dealings with the dead." As Tricia Rose has argued, "Rap's primary force is sonic, and the distinctive, systematic use of rhythm and sound, especially the use of repetition and musical breaks, are part of a rich history of New World black traditions and practices."[31]

For hip hop artists the afterlife offers yet another *technology*—like records and videos, like repetition and breaks, and like sampling and scratching—through which they can document and pull meaning from their communications with the dead. These technologies work in tandem to "resurrect," following Rose's formulation of a "techno-black syncretism" that she associates with sampling.[32] For example, both Lamar's recorded "interview" of Tupac Shakur in his 2015 "Mortal Man" and Snoop Dogg's holographic representation of Tupac at Coachella in 2012 rely on modern and contemporary sonic and visual technologies to resurrect Shakur.[33] According to Alex Weheliye, when new "technologies of orality and musicality," like phonographic recording, "were no longer tied to the immediate presence of human subjects," what results is not "a complete disappearance of the human" but rather a "resounding through new styles of technological folding."[34] It is through these technological "foldings," including the afterlife itself, that Lamar and Snoop have "rematerialized the human source."[35]

It is no coincidence that Spiritualists believed in spirit photography and spirit recordings; these, too, were technological means to resurrect, to connect to the afterlife, to rematerialize the dead. In other words, each new expressive and representational technology offers a new opportunity to engage with the dead. As Molly McGarry argues, "At least metaphorically, the photograph was a form of technology that could stop time and confer a form of immortality by which the living could be held indefinitely before the eye."[36] So it follows logically that, as Monica R. Miller explains, for Lamar, "The production of black meaning must begin with the spiritual domain," and he turns quite often to Shakur for that production. In other words, he is keeping Tupac indefinitely before his eye—and his ear.[37] That indefinite quality depends on the complex temporality of the afterlife as Lamar represents it; in Joseph R. Winters's words, "Kendrick alludes to a temporal hole, or a puncture in time, which indicates both an interruption into seamless conceptions of time as well as an opening toward alternative possibilities."[38]

Tupac Shakur, as one who has been repeatedly rematerialized, becomes at once object, subject, and agent of these syncretic hip hop technologies of the afterlife that in turn serve to "open up toward alternative possibilities" outside conventional linear time. As Winters has argued, "Tupac returns, or remains alive, through remembrance, mourning, mimesis, and homage," such that his music "inhabits the boundary between life and death."[39] Certainly, no hip hop artist more clearly and obviously theorized death and the afterlife than did Shakur. As Michael Eric Dyson notes in his magisterial biographical portrait of Shakur, "Always obsessed with death, Tupac seemed to forecast—and by his actions, nearly guarantee—his demise with frightening intensity."[40] This "second sight" comes through clearly in his works "I Wonder If Heaven Got a Ghetto" (both song and video were posthumously released in 1997) and "So Many Tears" (1995). Shakur has of course consistently been the subject/object of intensive efforts at resurrection, including Biggie Smalls's, Lamar's, Snoop Dogg's, and, in 2024, Drake's. Similarly, the posthumous biographical film *Tupac: Resurrection* consists almost entirely of Shakur's own words, remixed and repurposed to create a screenplay that continues on, even after it documents his death, with nearly three minutes of his reflections on his own life. His last words in the film: "Inside of you, I will be reborn."[41]

Shakur himself repeatedly imagined a solely Black afterlife, for example in the song "I Wonder If Heaven Got a Ghetto." The posthumous video for this song, directed by Lionel C. Martin, relies on the camera to stand in for Shakur's viewpoint as he enters a heaven filled with famous Black angels.[42] For another example, Shakur represented a remarkably agential afterlife in the song and video "I Ain't Mad at Cha" (1996), thereby connecting his work, and hip hop more broadly, to the empowering versions of the afterlife represented in *Dealings with the Dead* (Chapter 1) and in narratives by the formerly enslaved (Chapter 2). Juan M. Floyd-Thomas rightly argues, then, that "Tupac was instrumental in transforming hip-hop's politicized representations into quite literally a matter of life and death,"[43] and, I would argue, of the afterlife. For example, in the video for "I Ain't Mad at Cha," filmed May 15, 1996, just four months before his death (and released five days after it), Tupac, dressed in a white suit, returns from an all-Black and musical afterlife to visit and offer forgiveness and advice to his still-living "homie" and to his girlfriend, his white-clad figure glowing in an unearthly and angelic way, although he remains invisible to those who are still alive.[44] And yet his friend does see and retrieve the money Shakur's spirit leaves at his feet and seems to use it for condolence gifts for those mourning Shakur's passing, his partner and child. As Anthony Pinn succinctly puts it, the "dead are disembodied but impactful."[45] The song ends with a prayer delivered by a now-living Shakur anticipating his impending death (which took place less than four months after the video was recorded): "Father forgive us for livin' while all my homies stuck in prison . . . Picture us inside a ghetto heaven, a place to rest." In this song at least, unlike in "The Long Kiss Goodnight" with Notorious B.I.G. sustaining his beefs beyond death, Shakur constructs an afterlife that advances a broad Black solidarity that is musical/sonic as well as individual/emotional and collective/political. Unlike like both Shakur and Lamar, Biggie has no one to guide his spirit; his is a bleak passage into the afterlife, with death his only caller in "Suicidal Thoughts." By contrast, the heaven in the video for "I Ain't Mad at Cha" is peopled by actors representing the angels of Miles Davis, Billie Holiday, and Louis Armstrong, along with many other giants, all Black, of the music and entertainment world. Not only that, but Tupac is joined in heaven by Danny Boy, a collaborator and friend in real life, who sings the chorus with him.

This message of Black collectivity and political-activist sensibility comes through even more clearly in the lyrics of "I Wonder If Heaven Got a Ghetto." They include: "Here on Earth, tell me what's a black life worth," and "Ask Rodney, LaTasha, and many more."[46] Shakur goes on to "wonder what it takes to make this/One better place," with "better place," of course, a colloquial term for heaven.[47] Cassandra D. Chaney, one of the few scholars to have given sustained consideration to the afterlife (or, in her argument, heaven) in hip hop, argues that "essentially, Black males in Hip Hop create a spiritual connection to heaven and present heaven as an alternative to earth that is welcoming, loving, and eternal."[48] I agree up to a point; however, just as I have argued regarding formerly enslaved persons' narrative representations of the afterlife, Shakur constructs the afterlife *not* strictly as an escape but rather as a powerful and useful next-world model for what could (and should) actually be in this-world, taking advantage of heaven's "eternal," transtemporal nature. Shakur thereby creates, as did Douglass and Jacobs, Jameson's "*bold* spiritualism that posits the inseparability of an imagined future and an embodied present."[49] Or, as Winters has convincingly argued, both "sorrow and hope," and both mourning and "a yearning for a better world," are embedded in the very structure and the meaning of both hip hop and spirituals.[50] In Winters's words, "We continue to discover traces of these rhythmic cries [of spirituals] in hip-hop music."[51]

Notorious B.I.G.'s "Suicidal Thoughts" (1994), by contrast, offers a highly personal, individual, and grim, even nihilistic, opposite number to "I Wonder

If Heaven Got a Ghetto." He intones: "When I die, fuck it, I wanna go to hell / Cause I'm a piece of shit, it ain't hard to fucking tell / It don't make sense, going to heaven with the goodie-goodies / Dressed in white,"[52] as if explicitly rejecting the white-clad, angelic version of the afterlife in the "I Ain't Mad at Cha" video, while highlighting the differences in life experiences, family, and social class between himself and Shakur. In fact, over and against Shakur's Black collective/Afro-Optimistic version of the afterlife, Biggie offers an Afropessimistic one, wherein all he can see is sustained misery for his isolated soul. In just this way, Biggie seems to both anticipate and reject the premise of the posthumous 1997 video *I Wonder If Heaven Got a Ghetto*, in which a newly dead Tupac joins Jimi Hendrix and Black Panthers riding on a bus for his trip to heaven, where folks warmly welcome Tupac and call him by name upon his arrival.[53] For Biggie, the key name-call comes in the form of a phone call from death itself: "I swear to God I feel like death is fucking calling me." Of course, the murders of Tupac Shakur and Biggie Smalls, ironically and tragically, helped put to rest the regional beef. Imani Perry explains that "after the deaths of Tupac and Biggie, regional dis records largely disappeared, and collaborations between artists from various regions began to flourish."[54] Both become martyrs then, messianic figures who, after their deaths, serve as sources of healing and community.

This is not to argue that either Smalls or "Suicidal Thoughts" lacks political commitment. Rather like Wright's quite clearly political *Native Son*, the song begins with a literal wake-up call.[55] In the song, *Native Son*'s alarm clock becomes a telephone call, namely the suicidal Biggie Smalls's call to a friend, a role performed by Puff Daddy, for help. Puff Daddy answers: "Hello, aw shit n***a, what the fuck time is it." *Native Son* and "Suicidal Thoughts," both aware that there is little time left, drive inexorably and swiftly toward death: the execution of Bigger Thomas and the suicide of Biggie. The very form of "Suicidal Thoughts" expresses that drive. Its relentless flow and its ending—with the sounds of a gunshot, a body falling, and a heartbeat slowing until it stops—match Biggie's line: "the stress is building up." Both despite and because of the lyrical and sonic suspense in the song, its ending becomes inevitable, in fact fully predictable. As a result, Tupac Shakur, Biggie Smalls, and Bigger Thomas all embody JanMohamed's "death-bound subject."

In one of his last interviews before his own March 9, 1997, death, Biggie—quite literally a "death-bound" subject as of a February 24, 1997, BET interview—finally laid his beef with Shakur to rest.[56] He reports that he was "shocked" to hear that Tupac had died. No longer the "weak" Pac of "The Long Kiss Goodnight," in the interview Biggie says, "Pac is a strong dude," so strong that Biggie expected he would "pull through this one again." He concludes: "I mean, even though we was going through our drama I would never wish death on nobody.You know what I'm sayin'? Because there ain't no coming back from that."[57] If, arguably, Tupac has been resurrected a bit more intensively and consistently on into the present than has Biggie, that may be at least in part because of Shakur's construction of an agential afterlife over and against Biggie's pessimistic sense that "there ain't no coming back" from death.[58] To imagine oneself in an afterlife that provides a site of Black collectivity and love, as in "I Wonder If Heaven Got a Ghetto" and "I Ain't Mad at Cha" may also be to invite one's own repeated resurrection on behalf of those who long for Black connection and solidarity in this living life, particularly in the face of past and ongoing trauma.

Clearly, Shakur remains "disembodied but impactful" for Kendrick Lamar, in particular, who regularly documents Shakur's influence on him in his interviews and through his music. Perhaps the clearest and most powerful example of Shakur's impact on Lamar's work remains the stunning "Mortal Man" on the 2015 masterpiece, *To Pimp a Butterfly*. "Mortal Man," for Pinn, is "a narrative of death that is always and already also a narrative about life."[59] Yet the song depends upon and dwells in the afterlife just as much as, if not more than, it does in present-day living life. The song begins with the ghost of Nelson Mandela and ends with the "ghost" of Tupac Shakur, whom Lamar resurrects via an "interview" between himself and preexisting samples from the recorded voice of Shakur, in order to deliver what hip hop scholar Todd Craig terms "the rhetoric of sonic and visual uplift."[60] Or, in Greg Tate's spectacular description, in "Mortal Man," Lamar "conjures up" a "studio-rigged beyond-the-grave convo with 2Pac."[61] Like the balloon lifting two Black men heavenward (see figure 5, artist Shikeith's image reproduced on the cover of Danez Smith's *Don't Call Us Dead*), "Mortal Man" turns on multiple uplifting connections between living and dead Black men that happen in a liminal and intermedial space, one that is not of this living world but that can nevertheless help make that world better. Here again, we see (and hear) an agential afterlife. As Tate aptly observed, Lamar's album delivers "radical Black politics and for-real Black music."[62]

Formally, the song enacts just such a politics, one that offers the possibility of for-real connections among Black men through and across time. It begins with a repeated double chorus in the first four verses/stanzas; this doubling formally echoes the lyrics' blending of times, of life and the afterlife. The first part of the chorus begins with the dynamic and propulsive line, "the ghost of Mandela, hope my flows they propel it," suggesting that Lamar aims to have his own delivery/performance and poetic lyrics sustain, through form, the spirit and activism of Mandela, thereby honoring his enduring legacy—that is, the impact of both his life and his afterlife.[63] The second part asks, "When shit hit the fan, is you still a fan?" connecting Mandela's afterlife with the eventuality of Lamar's own entrance into it. In a form somewhat unusual for hip hop, the double chorus disappears once the song shifts to a long bridge verse that imagines solidarity among living Black men: "Just because you wore a different gang color than mine's / Doesn't mean I can't respect you as a black man / Forgetting all the pain and hurt we caused each other in these streets / If I respect you, we unify and stop the enemy from killing us." After this verse, which clearly echoes "I Ain't Mad at Cha," Lamar moves to his interview with Shakur, sampling prior Shakur interviews to produce a seamless interchange between them; we even hear the sound of a high-five, sounding and sealing their connection. Tupac Shakur thereby functions as a kind of presiding and uniting spirit, but this time, unlike in the video of "I Ain't Mad at Cha," that spirit remains fully present, both visible and audible for Lamar throughout his career.

Lamar's 2022 album, *Mr. Morale & the Big Steppers*, advances his spiritual quest and his construction of an afterlife, both lyrically and technologically, within an overall project of healing for himself while working toward stronger connections among Black people. The most obvious connection-making appears in the long and truly extraordinary roster of collaborators on the album, including songwriters, MCs, musicians, singers, and producers. The first cut on the album alone, "United in Grief," gives writing credit to (in this order) Jake Kosich of Beach Noise, Johnny Kosich, Kendrick Lamar, Matt Schaefer, Sounwave, Duval Timothy, J. Pounds, M. Spears, Sam Dew, and Timothy Maxey, and it gives production credit to OKLAMA, Sounwave, J.LBS, Duval Timothy, Beach Noise, and Timothy Maxey. The lyrics, too, speak to connection. The very title of "United in Grief" suggests that loss and trauma are precisely what, at least initially, serve to bring Lamar's Black community together; this is a kind of Black nationalism based on mourning, a United Black States of Sorrow. On the other hand, near the end of the song, Lamar calls out, "I grieve different," seemingly focused on himself, alone and apart.[64] But the immediate response, repeated twice: "Everybody grieves different." This line registers both lyrically and sonically, with its slower tempo and lower register, as a somber correction of Lamar's individualism. Or, perhaps more precisely, it functions as a reminder to allow for and express a wider perspective that ought to be—and in this instance is—layered onto the individual therapeutic experiences that the album is recounting.

The multiform quality of the music in "United in Grief" reinforces this lyrical combination of collectivity *and* individualism emerging out of death and yet living on after death. As composer Vivek Maddala, in a brilliant formal analysis of the song puts it, "United in Grief," like the album as a whole, "represents a kind of sonic alchemy—blurring, transforming, and combining unusual harmonic modes, clever chord progressions, modal interchange, and innovative rap flows into a new, enthralling kind of amalgam."[65] For example, the song begins with a choral invocation, made up of layers of Sam Dew's singing, that sounds more like Gregorian chant than rap: "I hope you find some peace of mind in this lifetime . . . I hope you find some paradise," with a glorious tempo change and a literally "up" note sounded on the last syllable of "paradise." "What happens next," Maddala enthuses, is "unexpected and theatrical," namely "staccato piano chords" that signal the shift from collective to individual, from prayer to therapy session, with Lamar's partner, Whitney Alford, interjecting to enjoin him to "tell the truth." "I've been goin' through something," he answers. This combination self and self-in-relation expresses the possibility of paradise on earth both for Lamar himself and for other Black people—at least once healing has taken place. Or, in Chance the Rapper's ecstatic words, "Wear your halo like a hat, that's like the latest fashion/I got angels all around me they keep me surrounded."[66]

Lamar's 2022 album, *Mr. Morale & the Big Steppers*, likewise insists upon the transcendent, surrounding power of his connections to those who have passed on and have entered the afterlife, particularly other Black men. As Lamar sings in "N95": "All my descendants, they come in my sleep and say I am too real (Huh, facts)."[67] He even refers to himself as a "spirit medium" on "Rich Spirit."[68] And in the video *The Heart Part 5*, he opens up Winters's "alternative possibilities" by using AI to transform his own face first into the faces of living Black men—O. J. Simpson (who was still alive at the time), Kanye West, Jussie Smollett, and Will Smith—and, finally, into faces of two famous Black men who died tragically—Kobe Bryant, the L.A. Lakers basketball star who died in a helicopter crash in 2020, and Nipsey Hussle, the South Central L.A. hip hop artist and activist who was murdered in 2019.[69] Here Lamar appears willing to embody, to channel as a medium, Black men broadly—in all their complexities, their flaws, and their greatness—whether they reside in this world or the next, via a technology that permits the "sampling" of the faces of both the living and the dead.

Granted, positioning Lamar as an agent for solidarity among Black men or for union among hip hop artists becomes a bit less plausible given his beef with Drake that exploded into the hip hop world and beyond in the spring of 2024.[70] As the beef unfolded, Drake became the latest to resurrect Tupac Shakur when he dropped "Taylor Made Freestyle" in his social media on April 19, 2024. Perhaps most provocatively, the song included AI versions of 2Pac's and Snoop Dogg's voices. Shakur's estate responded with a threat of legal action, with the result that Drake removed the song from the platforms Instagram and X.[71] Drake's reproduction of Tupac's voice was clearly designed to bait and to wound Lamar, given his well-known and cherished spiritual (and Spiritualist) connection to Shakur.[72] Adding Snoop to the mix helped spark a beef that ultimately grew well beyond the two, leading to a new regional one—this time not between West Coast and East Coast but between Canada and the US (or "Us") and, more specifically, California.

Lamar swiftly retaliated with his own songs, fanning that spark, especially with the definitive beef winner, "Not Like Us," released May 4, 2024. The song, from title on, renders Drake an outsider. The very first line "Psst, I see dead people" sets us up to understand that "Not Like Us" is going to bury Drake without praising him.[73] Gone is the Lamar who embraced such a wide range of Black figures, like Smollett and the highly controversial Kodak Black, whom Lamar tapped to collaborate on "Silent Hill" on *Mr. Morale*.[74] But ironically, Lamar's positioning Drake in "Not Like Us" as a "colonizer" serves as a classic example of producing unity among factions by means of a common enemy. Kendrick's Juneteenth 2024 concert in Inglewood, California, was a throughgoing performance and elaboration of the line from "Not Like Us": "You think the Bay gon' let you disrespect Pac, n***a?"[75] With this concert, then, Lamar resurrects Tupac yet again. With his "all eyes on me," another lyric in "Not Like Us," Lamar brings Shakur and his "All Eyez on Me" right onto the stage with him, if not holographically, then in other ways. The concert's last number before the encore was the 1995 Shakur classic, "California Love," with Dr. Dre himself joining Lamar for the performance (Dre performed on Shakur's 1995 version and appeared in the video for it). Immediately afterward, Lamar ended the concert with *five* repetitions of "Not Like Us."

This increasingly intense encore inspired West Coast solidarity in much the same way that Shakur's "California Love" had. In "California Love," for Shakur, "it's all good from Diego to the Bay."[76] He wants to "serenade the streets of L.A. / From Oakland to Sac-town, the Bay Area and back down," ending the song with the lyric "West Coast," elevating the solidarity of the entire region over any rivalries within it: "California knows how to party."[77] Lamar reenacts that same kind of regional unity on stage on Juneteenth, beginning his encore by saying to the audience, "Oh, you ain't gonna let nobody disrespect the West Coast, huh?" and "Oh, you ain't gonna let nobody imitate our legends, huh?" (obviously referring to Drake's AI-generated Tupac voice). He then launched into his first performance of "Not Like Us," bringing scores of Black people onto the stage with him over the course of four more performances of the song, including other hip hop artists, gang members, and athletes. During a "group pic" after the last of the five, Lamar declares, "This is Unity at its finest . . . Unity from each side of motherfucking L.A., Crips, Bloods," returning once again to Shakur and the lyrics of "California Love." But Lamar knows that those on stage are unified by grief as well as by enmity toward Drake. As the group assembles for the photo, he says, "We done lost a lot of, lot of homies to this music shit, a lot of homies to this street shit." Those on stage are *united in grief*, with Shakur presiding over that unity from the afterlife, as if all are saying together and to one another, "I Ain't Mad at Cha." In the end, of one thing we can be sure: Whatever new musical, performative, or representational technologies may emerge, they most definitely will be used to resurrect Tupac Shakur.

By contrast, poet Nikki Giovanni used one of the oldest of literary-representational forms to speak to and of the dead in order to resurrect Shakur—elegy. As Jahan Ramazani observes in his classic study of elegy, "The elegiac and self-elegiac genres" have been "codified since antiquity."[78] And, as Emily Rutter and colleagues point out, "Black writers have long been drawn" to the genre of elegy, while also "adapt[ing] it to the sociohistorical and cultural circumstances that distinguish the experiences of African Americans in a white-supremacist nation," underscoring the sustained collective and political power of the elegy for Black writers.[79] At once personal, collective, and political, Giovanni's 1997 poem "All Eyez on U" stands both as a famous and moving elegy for "2Pac" and as a counterpart to Shakur's self-elegiac 1996 album, *All Eyez on Me*.[80] Giovanni's title and poem are clearly offering a response to Shakur's call on that album; the last to be released before his death, it includes "I Ain't Mad At Cha" and "Heaven Ain't Hard 2 Find." In Giovanni's poem, a distraught and mourning speaker is "unable to comprehend why/2 Pac is not with us" (62).

Giovanni's deep engagement with Shakur and his passing matches her aesthetic and political agenda across time. Like the Black Panthers joining Tupac on the ride to heaven in the video *I Wonder If Heaven Got a Ghetto*, Nikki Giovanni blends time periods and activisms in this poem even as she herself, until her passing in 2024, provided a living link between the Black activisms of the 1960s (and therefore Tupac's parents, both members of the Black Panther Party) and contemporary Black activisms and musics. In "All Eyez on U," the speaker names yet another poet whose career and activism, like Giovanni's, extend from the '60s to the present: "Sonia Sanchez said when she learned of his passing she walked all day/walking the beautiful warrior home to our ancestors" (64).[81] Like Shakur, Giovanni and Sanchez have engaged in their writings with death as it is intertwined with activism and with matters of Black mortality and immortality, thereby taking full advantage of the complex temporality of the afterlife in order to envision a better place, a "beautiful warrior home." For example, in her 1997 book, *Does Your House Have Lions?* Sanchez connects her brother's death from HIV/AIDS to Malcolm X's assassination (see Chapter 3). Just so, in Giovanni's poem, Shakur joins the roster of great passed/past Black leaders and martyrs, with the poetic speaker rejecting the rivalries within hip hop (as if anticipating and decrying the Lamar-Drake beef) as any kind of index of his significance and impact:

> . . . what a beautiful boy to lose
> not me never me I do not believe east coast west coast I saw
> them murder Emmett Till I saw them murder Malcolm X I saw
> them murder Martin Luther King I witnessed them shooting
> Rap Brown I saw them beat LeRoi Jones I saw them fill their jails (63)

Yet at the same time that it mourns and rages, the poem also understands the power of Tupac in the afterlife:

> but he did not go away as Malcolm did not go away as Emmett
> Till will not go away your shooting him will not take him from us
> his spirit will fill our hearts his courage will strengthen us for the
> challenge his truth will straighten our backbones (63)

Here, the speaker identifies him with eternal natural forces, "as clear as a mountain stream as defining as a "lightning strike" (62), poised to impact this earth even, and perhaps especially, in and from his disembodied state in the afterlife.

Just as Giovanni provided a living link among the 1960s–'70s, the 1990s, and the contemporary, she forged a strong musical-historical link between hip hop (particularly gangsta rap of the 1990s, as in the poem "All Eyez on U") and older musics by means of her sustained engagement with sorrow songs/ spirituals. For instance, in 2022, Giovanni and jazz saxophonist Javon Jackson collaborated to produce an album titled *The Gospel According to Nikki Giovanni*. The record features nine of Giovanni's favorite hymns/sorrow songs, set to jazz, including a remarkable version of "Wade in the Water," the highlight of the album.[82] A 7:44-minute cool-jazz quartet interpretation, it features Jackson's singing saxophone, McClenty Hunter on drums, Jeremy Manasia on piano, and David Williams on bass, in what music critic J. D. Considine describes in his *Downbeat* review of the album as "a down-tempo, hard-bop approach."[83] Beginning at 3:30, over the music, Nikki Giovanni delivers a spoken-word version of her beloved 1975 free-verse poem, "A Very Simple Wish."[84] The poem's first two stanzas present domestic images of cabin and stew that seem to offer a form of healing for "all the lonely / people" and "the leftover folk" (218). But in the fourth stanza, the poem documents violence within Black communities:

i'm always surprised
that it's easier to stick
a gun in someone's face
or a knife in someone's back
than to touch skin to skin (218)

However, the version on *The Gospel According to Nikki Giovanni* does not include this bleak fourth stanza, as if the poet wishes to bracket the trauma stemming from the direct violence that had taken the life of Tupac and so many others as of 2022. Yet the album version does include the next three stanzas from the original poem, which despair of healing for Black people, collectively, in the United States. These stanzas include the lines: "i should imagine we shall lose our souls" and "i wonder why we don't love . . . people who look like us" (219). Yet in its final stanzas the poem returns to the possibility of collective healing via a return to the poem's initial domestic imagery, with Giovanni intoning, "i want to make a quilt," and concluding: "i've a mind to build a new world / want to play" (219). The last line stands alone, working as both a statement of desire by the speaker and as a question and invitation to others. The poem combines, then, the registers of despair and hope, suggesting that through art, created and performed collectively, a "new world" becomes possible. The collaboration between Giovanni and Jackson enacts precisely that sort of collaboration, that sort of joint "play." And there is rich, and useful, meaning in their choice to set this particular poem to the particular sorrow song "Wade in the Water."

"Wade in the Water"—with its many, many recorded versions, and of course with its origin as a collectively created and performed sorrow song long before the advent of recording technology—works as a musical-temporal index to the sounds, musical styles, and politics of each era in which it has been performed. These many iterations of the song range from the Sunset Four Jubilee Singers' 1925 recording (the oldest known recorded version of the song), to Fannie Lou Hamer's 1964 and The Staples Singers' 1967 versions (embedded in the Civil Rights Movement), to Sweet Honey in the Rock's 1988 Carnegie Hall live version (made especially poignant by Bernice Johnson Reagon's 2024 passing), to the Fisk Jubilee Singers' 1993 version, to The Blind Boys of Alabama's blues-inflected 2002 version, and to Nikki Giovanni's 2022 version, to name just a handful of recordings of the song. "Wade in the Water" thereby both possesses and expresses several forms of afterlife, both literal and symbolic. Perhaps most obviously, its lyrics refer to escape via water, offering a coded message to those escaping enslavement about how to elude enslavers and their posses' dogs; but the song also offers a meditation on crossing the river Jordan and the river Styx to achieve deliverance into this-life freedom and a sermon about crossing those same rivers into the freedom and potentialities of the afterlife. As Joseph Winters observes, "In many of the sorrow songs, we hear references to Jordan/the Promised Land, a symbol of earthly freedom and a vision of a reunion with God in the afterlife."[85] Yet the song also reverberates with the cultural afterlife of a traditional piece of music so very often performed and recorded in so many varied musical settings in ways that call on a Black collective, across eras, to act in the *now*. "Wade in the Water" is, above all, an *imperative*.

In one of its most remarkable recent afterlives, "Wade in the Water" was recorded by the hip hop/bluegrass band Gangstagrass for their 2015 album titled *American Music*.[86] A collaboration among the American band Gangstagrass (made up of producer and vocalist Rench, hip hop artists/MCs R-Son and Dolio the Sleuth, banjo player Dan Whitener, and fiddler B. E. Farrow), the Canadian soul/blues band Samantha Martin & Delta Sugar, and Liquid (Steve Hawley of the Canadian hip hop/rock band Bran Van 300), this richly layered version of "Wade in the Water" combines traditional performance and lyrics with new lyrics and hip hop stylings. In fact, Gangstagrass actually exceeds the sampling of spirituals of an artist like Common by intermixing traditional stanzas with their own explicitly political lyrics. For example, after Samantha Martin & Delta Sugar sing the traditional lyrics of "Wade in the Water" as a chorus over banjo- and fiddle-driven bluegrass with a hip hop backbeat behind it, Liquid raps a verse that includes these lyrics: "Time is spent, we all pay rent / I see the stars like the bars and they're still getting bent," delivering a national-material critique of a US prison industrial complex. He continues: "Wade in the water watch the systems turn rust / The machines that crushed us return to dust," expanding the meaning of escape via water to signify a kind of collective Luddite-like resistance to the contemporary machinations of capitalism, perhaps including AI. After more traditional choruses, Dolio the Sleuth enters with a rap that underscores the continuities between escaping enslavement and resisting contemporary oppressions: "By the cover of night, use the stars as my beacon / Keeping the plan on the hush as we're speaking / Sneaking off the plantation this evening." Echoing the command in Toomer's "Cotton Song," "lets not wait for it" (see introduction), Dolio continues, "(Let's go!) It [freedom] will never come if we don't take it / The chains we break while we make our escape quick." His conclusion: "That's why we wade through the water on purpose . . . generating turbulence."

This is truly, as the album's title promises, *American Music*, in that it recombines in sometimes startling ways at least three original American musics: sorrow songs/spirituals, bluegrass, and hip hop.[87] Of course, the very name of the band conveys this blending. This particular version of "Wade in the Water" blends historical periods beyond those obvious musical blendings, as well. For example, the term "hush" conveys the long history and the ongoing relevance of "hush harbor," a term signifying a space far away from white ears, a space where Black people could and can speak freely, from the days of enslavement on into the present.[88] "Speaking" free from chains leads to "generating turbulence," or, in other words, "troubling the waters" works as a metaphor for collective resistance even in the face of "certain death." Here again, life and the afterlife coincide in the imagination and creation of "a better life."

A similar cut, "O Death," appears on Gangstagrass's 2014 album *Broken Hearts and Stolen Money*.[89] As in their version of "Wade in the Water," in this song Gangstagrass blends a traditional folk tune, one from Appalachia, "Oh Death," with hip hop lyrics and performance. The song shifts from a traditional lyric, assigned to death itself, "Well I am death none can excel / I'll open the door to heaven and hell," to hip hop lyrics about "poor people . . . [b]earing scars of the past" who are "in search of that gate praying." The hip hop sections also offer an apocalyptic vision: "Lo and behold the pale horse / And the rider who decides the fate of one who made a failed choice / With a tail off behind it trails off in fire." Yet this apocalypse, like the word itself, connotes not only the end of the world but also *revelation* followed by an afterlife, by renewed possibility, for that fallen world[90]: "Praying heaven's coming, praying it doesn't come late / . . . When ash is always falling in death's rain / . . . Pull through together 'cause then they will rise." Here we return to the notion of elevation, the being up in the air that we saw in Chapter 3 in a contemporary Black poetics of the afterlife. As Kendrick Lamar chanted in "Untitled 07/2014–2016": "Levitate, levitate, levitate, levitate."[91]

Gangstagrass's song "Working on that Chain" from their 2020 album *No Time for Enemies* serves to connect all these motifs—apocalyptic events, death, the afterlife, and the potentialities and power of levitation—not only in many of their songs but also in *Soul Sounds* as a whole. Once again as in Toomer's "Cotton Song," "Working on that Chain" presents an activist present over and against the sonic backdrop of living a life in chains or working on a chain gang: "And I'm still out here working, working, working . . . Working on that chain." And yet the chain transforms over the course of the song, going from signifying a "prison" to signifying connections forged among people: "You can try to bring the world together / . . .When you give more than you gain / That's a hammer on the anvil / And a link upon the chain."

And it is to those who have died, have passed on, that the Gangstagrass performers turn for guidance about how to break oppressing chains in order to build loving ones in their place. Dolio sings: "Visions sent to me, let me

Figure 6
Artist once known, Alabama. *Untitled (Partial Log Cabin Quilt)*, 1940s.
Cotton. 80x76 inches.
Courtesy of High Museum of Art, Atlanta.
Purchase through funds provided by Collectors Evening 2017, 2017.199.

know the time's right / Ancestors showing me the errors in the hindsight / Spirits in the distance screaming at me 'Get your mind right' / Keep pushing and prepare for the divine rite.'"

These lyrics take us right back to the first stanza of Nikki Giovanni's "A Very Simple Wish" as spoken over "Wade in the Water":

i want to write an image
like a log-cabin quilt pattern
and stretch it across all the lonely
people who just don't fit in
  we might make a world
  if i do that

Like spirituals, quilts too carried coded messages for those escaping enslavement along the Underground Railroad, messages that continue to deliver powerful meanings now. As Jaqueline L. Tobin and Raymond G. Dobard have thoroughly documented, an "Underground Railroad Quilt Code" delivered data, via particular quilt patterns, to escaping enslaved people about how and where to travel safely to freedom.[92] For example, as one writer for the *Smithsonian Folklife Magazine* notes, the log-cabin quilt pattern means *"Seek shelter now, the people here are safe to speak with"*[93] (see figure 6). The chain of signification constructed by Lamar and other hip hop artists, including 2Pac and Biggie, in their lyrics and their flow can be likened to a quilt, with embedded messages delivered to friends and foes alike via extraordinarily intricate patterns. Just as with Anna Kornbluh's argument about the power of the form of the novel that I cited in Chapter 1, here I am arguing that Shakur's and Lamar's and Biggie's hip hop, sorrow songs, Black-created quilts, Giovanni's poetry, and the blended musics of Gangstagrass can all function as technologies of art and of craft[94] that, like the afterlife, offer "the special kind of thinking, the special kind of world making and world interpreting, that novels achieve," thereby "building new bridges for imaginative rebuilding."[95] This chain of meaning and building likewise takes us right back to Giovanni's last stanza in "A Very Simple Wish":

i want to make a quilt
of all the patches and find
one long strong pole
to lift it up

i've a mind to build
a new world

want to play

By tapping into the power and potentialities of the afterlife and the visions of ancestors, we too, may make a new world, a paradise on earth where it is safe to play, surrounded by angels.

Coda

One Better Place

Soul Sounds began with an argument for the power of the afterlife in African American literature and music and for the suitability of an interdisciplinary method, with sound studies primary, to support that argument. This methodology stemmed, in part, from sound studies scholars' insight that Spiritualists of the nineteenth century privileged the auditory over the visual, sound over sight, to paraphrase Jonathan Sterne.[1] Theirs was an afterlife filled with sound. However, as we saw in Chapter 3, in contemporary Black poets' renditions of the afterlife, sound and vision are not so readily distinguished or hierarchized. As I show in that chapter, ekphrasis and ektechne (my coinage for literary representations of sound and music) often work in concert to represent the afterlife. For example, Tracy K. Smith's poem "Don't You Wonder Sometimes," from the collection *Life on Mars*, is named for a Bowie song, and it offers sound imagery while also observing Bowie's appearance as a "thin-hipped glittering . . . being," all while elegizing Smith's parents as she *sees* them in the afterlife: "where my / Mother and father sit waiting, dinner keeping warm on the stove."[2]

This provisional undoing of the primacy of sound suggests the need for further scholarly engagement with the afterlife, what we might term a "new afterlife studies" that engages a full range of sensory approaches, aesthetic forms, and technologies that, in turn, can help identify and theorize new potentialities in the afterlife. Certainly, *Soul Sounds* identifies the afterlife, taken literally, as far more empowering and optimistic than Afropessimists' metaphoric "afterlives," understood as ongoing trauma from enslavement, even as it continues to value the critical insights of Afropessimism. The new afterlife studies might usefully extend that juxtaposition of Afropessimism and

Afro-Optimism. Other scholars could also investigate the power of tapping into time-spaces other than the afterlife in order to ameliorate what Anna Kornbluh has unflinchingly described as "our raging, dystopian hellscape of capitalist contradiction, climate catastrophe, and insurgent global fascism."[3] The afterlife, after all, does not provide the only means to access other potentially empowering times and places, including, perhaps counterintuitively, the past.

In *Rap on Race*, a 1971 book that documented conversations held between James Baldwin and Margaret Mead over the course of two days in 1970, the two agree that "mass production, the consumer society," in Baldwin's words, and particularly cars, are "things that menace us most."[4] Mead suggests one solution to that capitalist/climate change threat: "We should go back somewhere" (159). Baldwin immediately responds, "I don't want to go back anywhere. That isn't what I meant at all!" (159). Any return to the past holds no appeal for him, perhaps unsurprisingly. In her book *Afro-Nostalgia*, Badia Ahad-Legardy implicitly challenges Baldwin's response by questioning the commonplace notion that for Black Americans "no period can be culled to inspire good feelings in the present."[5] She argues that, on the contrary, "historical nostalgia is fully operative in contemporary black life" in ways that can instill pleasure, "joy, and thriving" (5, 4). Even as she insists on joy, Ahad-Legardy does not dismiss Afropessimism; rather, she positions her argument as a "complement to the dominant discourse of black trauma" (8). Nonetheless, markedly unlike Afropessimist scholars, she argues that "historical memory," at least when linked with a progressive agenda, offers a source of "recovery and redemption," particularly when filtered through "cultural production," through creative works (21).

Where Ahad-Legardy looks to nostalgia, I look to the afterlife as a social form that will enable us, in her words, "to build from it a future worth being nostalgic for" (165). Both models—nostalgia and the afterlife—depend on sustained access to other times and to nonlinear timelines. To return here to the introduction's discussion of Toomer and *Cane*, I argue that Barlow and other Toomer scholars have often overlooked Toomer's empowering representations of the afterlife and, in a related move, they have also been a bit too quick to dismiss *Cane*'s nostalgia. Barbara Foley, for example, argues that in *Cane* "even in the short lyrics and sketches redolent of romantic nostalgia, the repression of the history that hurts is incomplete."[6] Yet nostalgia naturally forms part of a preservation process that helps to secure familial and cultural traditions, just as Ahad-Legardy shows.

A preservation process likewise undergirds literary studies; the field honors and conserves texts across time. In a 2024 essay, "Tending the Tradition," Deborah E. McDowell describes her work of "devotion" as editor of the Beacon Black Women Writers Series, along with the tradition-building work of other Black women literary scholars in the 1980s: "Together we aspired to use our platforms not only to introduce to institutions of higher education the writers Morrison and others were editing, but also to revive those writers from earlier decades whose writings were now languishing in obscurity."[7] At essay's end, McDowell sums up this ongoing project of tending a Black women's literary tradition: "We devote ourselves to keeping it alive" (33). This sort of metaphorical "afterlife" is, contra both Saidiya Hartman and Kenneth Warren, both positive and enabling. At the same time, McDowell reminds us that recovery and preservation of a Black women's literary tradition, the ensuring of its afterlife, does in fact require indefatigable *work*. In her words, "We needed to remain ever on the alert for the fickle winds of academic change, ever watchful of the paradigm shifts and the sociopolitical arrangements that could re-subject the work to which we devoted our scholarly attention to threat or total extinction," in the context of "a general and historic devaluation of Black feminist intellectual activity" (30, 32). To preserve via creative work—as Jean Toomer does in *Cane* and as Harriet Jacobs does in *Incidents in the Life of a Slave Girl*—or to preserve via sustained, intensive, and collective scholarly work—as contemporary Black feminist literary scholars have done from the 1970s to the present—is to lend an afterlife to Black literary texts, to Black feminist theory, and to representations of diverse material experiences of Black people in the United States across time. Scholars and activists can center and access all of these *now* in order to imagine and work toward justice and equity. In other words, works of art and scholarship can help answer Tupac Shakur's question, "I wonder what it takes to make this / One better place."[8]

As I have argued throughout *Soul Sounds*, an agential afterlife, represented by artists and analyzed and preserved by scholars, provides us with aesthetic forms and imaginative possibilities through which to build a better present and a better future. Indeed, it is no coincidence that *Soul Sounds* emerged from my research on Afrofuturism. During a sabbatical initially focused on a born-digital Afrofuturism project, I had the realization that the afterlife is, in fact, a kind of future. I also realized that although the afterlife has been a prominent sustained motif within African American cultural history, it has been curiously neglected—or at least under-attended to—by literary scholars. This is not to say that the term itself has been neglected. On the contrary, as I mentioned in the introduction, numerous recent scholarly studies of African American literature, history, and culture depend on the words "afterlife" and "afterlives." To give just a handful of examples: a 2019 *American Literature* special issue on "the plantation, the postplantation, and the afterlives of slavery," an April 2021 *American Literary History* forum on "abolition's afterlives," and the work that inspired these: Saidiya Hartman's 2016 book, *Lose Your Mother*, in which she theorizes at length "the afterlife of slavery."[9] But all these studies, as important and compelling as they are, use the afterlife strictly as a metaphor, as shorthand to signify ongoing or haunting, and generally harmful, effects. This is so even when they are clearly considering literal Black loss, death, mourning, or mortality, as in Hartman's book. *Soul Sounds*, by contrast, has argued for the elevation and analysis of a distinctly nonmetaphorical afterlife. By taking the afterlife seriously, we may reveal its potential for social, political, aesthetic, and collective empowerment, while rightly honoring a belief held so strongly by so many.

As I also argued earlier in this book, the afterlife's complex temporality underlies its power. Unlike nostalgia, the afterlife does not rely on one temporal direction, namely looking backward. The afterlife has always been there, and it is and always will be there, temporally proximate. Only for those of us who are still alive does it lie in the future. *Soul Sounds* contends that this temporal layering, this *eternity*, offers us continuous access to other—possibly better—times and thus enables the reimagination and re-creation of our present, while neither requiring nor precluding a Christian understanding of the afterlife. The afterlife therefore works, up to a point at least, much as Fredric Jameson argues that science fiction works, by "transforming our own present into the determinate past of something yet to come," with all the political and material potentialities that positioning our present as the history of the future may hold.[10] But the afterlife actually exceeds Jameson's assessment of science fiction as politically efficacious, precisely because it is not limited by his contention that the present "is, after all, all that we have."[11] An understanding that the present is *not* all that we have underlies Afrofuturism and other futurist movements we readily view as progressive or liberatory.[12]

Soul Sounds also turns on the idea that, as James Baldwin says in *Rap on Race*, "We have to assume that we are responsible for the future of the world" (174). Alternatively, as Hortense Spillers puts it, scholars and artists must "replay not only *this* narrative but its *outcome* on the other side of disaster."[13] This book is intended to suggest at least one means that could help us get to the other side of disaster. Or, as Toni Morrison put it so movingly: "We speak, we write, we do language. That is how civilizations heal."[14] All the writers and musical artists in *Soul Sounds* understand the afterlife as being inseparable from this life, indeed continuous with it; therefore, it can offer healing, solace, and power in a time of seeming perpetual crisis. This book seeks, too, to acknowledge, appreciate, and embrace a specifically scholarly past as another means of taking responsibility for the future of the "world" of literary and cultural studies. Current African Americanist scholarship relies continuously, if not always explicitly, on the tradition-building work of Deborah E. McDowell, Hortense Spillers, Karla Holloway, William Andrews, Hazel Carby, Houston Baker Jr., and Henry Louis Gates Jr., among many other scholars. They created a kind of afterlife for eighteenth-, nineteenth-, and twentieth-century texts as, in the words of one of the peer reviewers of this book, a "counter to their own dire times." They publish and have published theory and scholarship that live on, as evidenced throughout *Soul Sounds* and particularly in Chapter 2. In the present, scholars of African American literature and culture can sustain the model these scholars built, lending their work an agential afterlife in our new "dire times." The academy will be a better place for it.

The project of making the academy, the nation, the world all "better places" has taken on greater significance, even urgency, for me as a result of the convergence of traumatic events in the years 2020 to 2026, particularly their disproportionate harm to Black people in the United States and most particularly in Minneapolis, where I have lived since 2004. This book argues that, in our present, the afterlife carries both deeply painful but also potentially healing meanings, given the contexts of unabating state-sponsored murders of Black people, unlawful detention and imprisonment of people of color and their allies, COVID-19 with its disproportionate effects on Black people and other people of color, and climate change with its likewise disproportionate harm to communities of color and poor communities (two communities that so often overlap)—and given, as I write this, the context of an in-progress fascist-authoritarian and white supremacist effort to crush our city, to torment and imprison immigrants and all people of color, and to punish, sometimes by death, legal observers and other community protectors. There is historical precedent for the afterlife as one recourse for change and as a source of solace in the face of converging deadly forces.

In the wake of the US Civil War and as a result of multiple cholera and tuberculosis epidemics in the United States, Americans turned to Spiritualism from the mid-1800s to the turn of the century in the hope of contacting departed loved ones. Several well-known nineteenth-century African American intellectuals delved into Spiritualism, including Paschal Beverly Randolph (the subject of my first chapter), Pauline Hopkins, and Harriet Wilson. Then, as now, communities with majority people of color and poor communities suffered disproportionately from epidemics and from other environmental, material, and social, not to mention governmental, ills. As a site of both pain and power, the afterlife may well reemerge in our present as a vehicle for imagining alternative realities and times. Even as belief in the afterlife may express and emerge out of rage or loss or grief (but at other times out of religious joy or rapture), that belief, whether Christian or not, holds out the possibility of once again holding our loved ones who have passed on, a possibility that becomes especially powerful for us when they died of COVID, or of murder by government forces in our streets, or in detention centers/concentration camps, with the awful result that, at their passing, we could not hold or mourn them as we needed to or as our customs dictated.

By way of conclusion, I return to the close-reading of "Georgia Dusk" that began this book. To this point in *Soul Sounds*, I have located in Toomer's poems in *Cane* (and in many other literary and musical works) the representation of a *literal* afterlife. However, I wish now to make space for more metaphorical forms of afterlife that likewise can enable us to make "one better place" in the here and now—in addition, that is, to the afterlife of literary texts established by a scholarly tradition. Turning again to "Georgia Dusk," I note that its fifth stanza extols another form of metaphorical afterlife and another form of tradition:

> Meanwhile, the men, with vestiges of pomp,
> Race memories of king and caravan,
> High-priests, an ostrich, and a juju-man,
> Go singing through the footpaths of the swamp.

Here the poetic speaker points to the musical expression and preservation of a former African glory, lending it an afterlife. That shared glorious past both goes before and lives alongside Christian glory: "dreams of Christ," as the last line says. Toomer's verse lines here call to mind the first chapter of W. E. B. Du Bois's *Souls of Black Folk*, "Of Our Spiritual Strivings," in which he writes: "The shadow of a mighty Negro past flits through the tale of Ethiopia the Shadowy and of Egypt the Sphinx. Through history, the powers of single black men flash here and there like falling stars, and die sometimes before the world has rightly gauged their brightness."[15] Du Bois returns to this image of Black male mortality and the eternal stars in the chapter "The Passing of the First-Born," in which he grieves the loss of his son:

> I held my face beside his little cheek, showed him the star-children and the twinkling lights as they began to flash, and stilled with an even-song the unvoiced terror of my life. . . . He died at eventide, when the sun lay like a brooding sorrow above the western hills, veiling its face; when the winds spoke not, and the trees, the great green trees he loved, stood motionless. I saw his breath beat quicker and

> quicker, pause, and then his little soul leapt like a star that travels in the night and left a world of darkness in its train. (209, 211)

In the elegiac chapter "Of Alexander Crummel," Du Bois writes similarly regarding Crummel:

> He sat one morning gazing toward the sea. He smiled and said, "The gate is rusty on the hinges." That night at star-rise a wind came moaning out of the west to blow the gate ajar, and then the soul I loved fled like a flame across the Seas, and in its seat sat Death. I wonder where he is to-day? I wonder if in that dim world beyond, as he came gliding in, there rose on some wan throne a King,—a dark and pierced Jew, who knows the writhings of the earthly damned, saying, as he laid those heart-wrung talents down, "Well done!" while round about the morning stars sat singing. (227)

These Du Boisian stars, like Toomer's "vestiges" and "race memories," signify the afterlife of a glorious African past and the inheritance it carries for Black Americans, and, as in hip hop, that inheritance stands alongside a Christian tradition. At the same time, Du Bois's "stars" embody and represent Black men who have passed on, like the more literal Black "stars" who appear in Tupac Shakur's *I Wonder If Heaven Got a Ghetto* or in Kendrick Lamar's *The Heart Part 5*.

Tracy K. Smith in *Life on Mars* offers a similarly literal, yet ironically also a more speculative (as well as a more gender-neutral and at times feminist), version of an afterlife populated by stars. In the extraordinary poem "My God, It's Full of Stars," a title that alludes to Stanley Kubrick's *2001: A Space Odyssey*, the speaker ponders the nature of god(s), death, and the afterlife: "Some like to imagine / A cosmic mother watching through a spray of stars, / Mouthing *yes, yes*, as we toddle toward the light."[16] We are all, in a sense, "toddling toward the light" to ultimately join those in the afterlife. Alternatively, we can make "the great error" that there is no afterlife, "believing we're alone, / That the others have come and gone—a momentary blip— / When all along, space might be choc-full of traffic, / Bursting at the seams with energy we neither feel / Nor see, flush against us . . ." (10). This energetic, crowded afterlife is unfolding right next to us, "flush" and "wide open," yet also "sealed tight, so nothing escapes. Not even time." We might not be able to enter that paradoxically wide-open yet sealed space until we have died, but in the meantime, we can access its timeless "frenzy of being" (10). For the speaker, this means that "I might be sitting now beside my father / As he raises a lit match to the bowl of his pipe / For the first time in the winter of 1959" (10). Even in an over-

Figure 7
"Hubble Spies a Glittering Gathering of Stars."
ESA/Hubble & NASA, R. Cohen.

whelming world, our loved ones who have passed on always shine as stars for us, while their traditions always remain available to us (see figure 7). We must do our best to hear, to see, and to feel, must *wade into*, a space "bursting at the seams with energy," tapping that energy to make this *one better place*. Then we, too, will "SHINE, SHINE, SHINE, SHINE."[17]

Acknowledgments

Many scholars, writers, artists, musicians, colleagues, friends, and family members made this book possible. My deepest thanks go to Professor Deborah E. McDowell, whose consummate scholarship and teaching have always offered both inspiration and aspiration. I am also profoundly grateful for the poetry of Ross Gay, Tracy K. Smith, Danez Smith, Jericho Brown, Claudia Rankine, and Terrance Hayes. I thank Shikeith both for his extraordinary art and for permission to use an image of it in the chapter on these poets' writings. And I will always be grateful for Janelle Monáe's work and presence on the planet (and perhaps beyond it).

I thank Michelle Wright, Xiomara Santamarina, Michael Prior, and Devin English for their invaluable readings of draft chapters. I also thank the anonymous readers for Fordham University Press; their insights improved this book considerably. Thanks, too, to the editorial and production staff at the press for literally making this book, and making it stronger. I am indebted to Richard Morrison for his steadfast commitment to my scholarship and his unparalleled work as an editor.

The roster of other scholars, writers, and musicians who have shaped my thought and this book is too lengthy for me to include here. But I would like particularly to honor Elizabeth Freeman, Nikki Giovanni, Dr. Barbara A. Holmes, and Bernice Johnson Reagon. Their work lives on, making this world one better place.

I continuously appreciate my colleagues and my students at Macalester College for their brilliance and commitment to intellectual community.

Finally, thank you to Eugene Shenk, my first and best reader.

Notes

Introduction: Let's Not Wait for the Afterlife

1. Jean Toomer, "Georgia Dusk," in *Cane* (1923), ed. Darwin T. Turner, Norton Critical Editions (New York: W. W. Norton, 1988), 15.

2. Daniel Barlow, "Literary Ethnomusicology and the Soundscape of Jean Toomer's *Cane*," *MELUS* 40, no. 1 (2014): 193. Further citations will be parenthetical in the text.

3. Here I am referring to and arguing against Kenneth W. Warren, *What Was African American Literature? The W. E. B. Du Bois Lectures* (Cambridge, MA: Harvard University Press, 2011), in which Warren argues that "if black writing is no longer expected to protest segregation or to serve as a metric in the onward advancement of the race, then it no longer exists as a literature" (113). Warren's argument has already been thoroughly critiqued by others, notably in Erica Edwards, "The Formidable Work of the Present, A Powerhouse of a Book," *Los Angeles Review of Books*, June 13, 2011; Marlon B. Ross, "Kenneth W. Warren's *What Was African American Literature?* A Review Essay," *Callaloo* 35, no. 3 (2012): 604–12; and Scott Selisker, "Review," *African American Review* 44, no. 4 (2011): 717–19. I do want to add to these adept analyses a focused challenge to Warren's notion that "African American literature was prospective rather than retrospective," meaning that it "was" more invested in achieving racial progress than in forging literary tradition (42). As I argue throughout *Soul Sounds*, such tidy, linear categories of time do not fit a tradition that returns again and again to representation of a transtemporal site of agency, the afterlife, that in turn enables both reflection and anticipation, prospection and retrospection. I cite Warren if only because his book garnered so much attention, including a series of pieces in *The Chronicle of Higher Education*, as Selisker notes (717).

4. Perhaps the fundamental error in Warren's argument regards his overlooking

the fact that scholarly work helps forge tradition, indeed can form part of a literary tradition. His harsh dismissal of Black academic memoir by "elites" in the 1980s and '90s reflects his reliance on a complete distinction between scholars and their writing and "literature" (122). His contention that "there is no broadly useful social end served by viewing contemporary black writing as a collective undertaking" stands as the antithesis of *Soul Sounds* (116).

5. Johannes Fabian, *Time and the Other: How Anthropology Makes Its Object* (1983; New York: Columbia University Press, 2002), 30.

6. Saidiya Hartman, "The Time of Slavery," *South Atlantic Quarterly* 101, no. 4 (2002): 759.

7. Hartman, "The Time of Slavery," 759.

8. Soyica Colbert, "How to Live Among What Is Dead," *Public Books* (January 18, 2022), accessed July 21, 2024, https://www.publicbooks.org/how-to-live-among-what-is-dead/?utm_source=PUBLIC+BOOKS+Newsletter&utm_campaign=6df22a8b18-EMAIL_CAMPAIGN_2022_1_24&utm_medium=email&utm_term=0_d048c39403-6df22a8b18-47239089&mc_cid=6df22a8b18.

9. Sampada Aranke, *Death's Futurity: The Visual Life of Black Power* (Durham, NC: Duke University Press, 2023), 15. See also Brent Hayes Edwards, "Other Afterlives," *PMLA* 138, no. 2 (2023): 233–40. Edwards offers an extended meditation on Hartman's term "afterlives," and although he nods to the "eschatological" nature of the afterlife, he returns quickly to the afterlife as a structural and metaphorical term for the ongoing effects of enslavement and of slavery.

10. Aranke, *Death's Futurity*, 20.

11. Frank B. Wilderson III, *Afropessimism* (New York: Liveright, 2020), 245.

12. Saidiya Hartman, *Scenes of Subjection: Terror, Slavery, and Self-Making in Nineteenth-Century America* (New York: Oxford University Press, 1997).

13. Joseph R. Winters, *The Disturbing Profane: Hip Hop, Blackness, and the Sacred* (Durham, NC: Duke University Press, 2025), 86. In keeping with my argument in *Soul Sounds*, Winters argues that "blackness and black people are not reducible to the white supremacist and colonial operations that converted Africans into property" (87). Winters, too, both embraces and challenges Afropessimistic thought, acknowledging the "death, loss, and anguish" as well as the "exaltation," "enjoyment," and "redemption" in sorrow songs and hip hop (33).

14. Fred Moten, *Black and Blur* (Durham, NC: Duke University Press, 2017), 2; Fred Moten, "The Case of Blackness," *Criticism* 50, no. 2 (2008): 180.

15. Hartman, *Scenes of Subjection*, 107.

16. Harriet Jacobs, *Incidents in the Life of a Slave Girl, Written by Herself* (1861; University of North Carolina: *Documenting the American South*), 267, https://docsouth.unc.edu/fpn/jacobs/jacobs.html.

17. Anna Kornbluh, "We Have Never Been Critical: Toward the Novel as Critique," *NOVEL: A Forum on Fiction* 50, no. 3 (2017): 398. See also Rita Felski, *The Limits of Critique* (Chicago: University of Chicago Press, 2015).

18. Toomer, "Georgia Dusk," 15.

19. Barbara Foley, "'In the Land of Cotton': Economics and Violence in Jean Toomer's *Cane*," *African American Review* 32, no. 2 (1998): 183; see 181–82 for an invaluable and thorough review of scholarship on *Cane*. Further citations will be parenthetical in the text. Reprint: Barbara Foley, "'In the Land of Cotton': Economics and Violence in Jean Toomer's *Cane*," *African American Review*, 5, no. 4 (2017): 987–1004.

20. Charles Chesnutt, *The Conjure Woman* (Boston: Houghton, Mifflin, 1899; *Documenting the American South*), "Po' Sandy," https://docsouth.unc.edu/southlit/chesnuttconjure/conjure.html#conjure36.

21. "DNA," Spotify, track 2 on Kendrick Lamar, *DAMN*, Aftermath/Interscope (Top Dawg Entertainment), 2017.

22. R. Murray Schafer, *The Tuning of the World: Toward a Theory of Soundscape Design* (Philadelphia: University of Pennsylvania Press, 1980), 7.

23. Foley, "In the Land of Cotton," 183, 184.

24. Jean Toomer, "Autobiographical Selection," in *Cane* (1923), ed. Darwin T. Turner, Norton Critical Editions (New York: W. W. Norton, 1988), 142.

25. I argue in the coda that neither a preservation project nor nostalgia precludes, and may actually enhance, a liberatory engagement with the present.

26. Foley, "In the Land of Cotton," 185.

27. Jean Toomer, "Cotton Song," in *Cane* (1923), ed. Darwin T. Turner, Norton Critical Editions (New York: W. W. Norton, 1988), 11.

28. H. William Rice, "Two Work Songs in Cane," *Black American Literature Forum* 23, no. 3 (1989): 595, *JSTOR*, https://doi.org/10.2307/2904209, accessed June 12, 2023.

29. Kevin Quashie, *Black Aliveness; or, A Poetics of Being* (Durham, NC: Duke University Press, 2021).

30. Chanté Joseph, "What Black Joy Means—And Why It's More Important Than Ever," *British Vogue*, July 29, 2020, https://www.vogue.co.uk/arts-and-lifestyle/article/what-is-black-joy. An equivalent mainstream representation of Afropessimism, published around the same time as Joseph's essay, appears in Frank B. Wilderson III, "Color Theory," *Harper's Magazine*, April 9, 2020, https://harpers.org/archive/2020/04/color-theory/.

31. Paschal Beverly Randolph, *After Death; or, Disembodied Man* (Boston: printed by the author, 1868; rpt. London: Forgotten Books, 2012), 9.

32. John Patrick Deveney, *Paschal Beverly Randolph: A Nineteenth-Century Black American Spiritualist, Rosicrucian, and Sex Magician* (Albany: State University of New York Press, 1997), 8–9.

33. Hartman, "The Time of Slavery," 760.

34. Mary T. Bassett, foreword to *The Pandemic Divide: How COVID Increased Inequality in America*, ed." Gwendolyn Wright, Lucas Hubbard, and William A. Darity (Durham, NC: Duke University Press, 2022), ix.

35. Victor LaValle, "Recognition," *New York Times Magazine*, "The Decameron Project," July 7, 2020 (1–15), https://www.nytimes.com/interactive/2020/07/07

/magazine/victor-lavalle-short-story.html. Further citations will be parenthetical in the text.

36. For further consideration of COVID-era fiction, see Katy Waldman, "What Covid Did to Fiction," *New Yorker*, June 10, 2024, https://www.newyorker.com/magazine/2024/06/17/what-covid-did-to-fiction.

37. Janelle Monáe, *Many Moons*, YouTube Video, posted April 4, 2009, 4:05–4:06, 4:12–4:13 https://youtu.be/EZyyORSHbaE?si=qK70HssIYjD3YzdL.

38. Monáe, *Many Moons*, 6:01–6:11.

39. Danez Smith, "For Andrew," in *Homie: Poems* (Minneapolis: Graywolf Press, 2020), 44. Further citations will be parenthetical in the text.

40. Danez Smith, "how many of us have them?" in *Homie*, 6.

41. Alexander G. Weheliye, *Phonographies: Grooves in Sonic Afro-Modernity* (Durham, NC: Duke University Press, 2005), 88, 89.

42. *Tupac: Resurrection*, dir. Lauren Lazin (Hollywood, CA; Paramount Pictures, 2003), DVD.

43. Kendrick Lamar, *The Heart Part 5*, directed by Dave Free & Kendrick Lamar, YouTube video posted May 8, 2022, https://youtu.be/uAPUkgeiFVY?si=ZTBWlBFMFenESeLP. Tupac Shakur, *I Wonder If Heaven Got a Ghetto*, YouTube video posted July 12, 2011, https://youtu.be/_fCoK2OVJAc?si=X6pnj1g5QuZM5qqI.

44. Paul Gilroy, "'Lost in Music': Wild Notes and Organized Sound," in *Sound and Literature*, ed. Anna Snaith (Cambridge, UK: Cambridge University Press, 2020), 171.

45. Schafer, *The Tuning of the World*, 7.

46. Mark M. Smith, *Listening to Nineteenth-Century America* (Chapel Hill: University of North Carolina Press, 2001), 2.

1. *Dealings with the Dead*: Paschal Beverly Randolph and Afrofuturism

1. Paschal Beverly Randolph, *Dealings with the Dead: The Human Soul, Its Migrations and Its Transmigrations, By the Rosicrucian* (Boston: printed by the author, 1861–62; rpt. London: Forgotten Books, 2012.

2. John Patrick Deveney, *Paschal Beverly Randolph: A Nineteenth-Century Black American Spiritualist, Rosicrucian, and Sex Magician* (Albany: State University of New York Press, 1997), 254.

3. Deveney, *Paschal Beverly Randolph*, 204–5.

4. Christine Ferguson, *Determined Spirits: Eugenics, Heredity and Racial Regeneration in Anglo-American Spiritualist Writing, 1848–1930* (Edinburgh: Edinburgh University Press, 2012), 114.

5. Alex W. Black, "'A New Enterprise in Our History': William Still, Conductor of *The Underground Rail Road* (1872)," *American Literary History* 32, no. 4: (2020): 670.

6. See Deveney, *Paschal Beverly Randolph*, 343–68, for extensive consideration of Randolph's publishing history.

7. Deveney has also identified a lost 1859 vampire novel, *Dhoula Bel, or the Magic Globe*, possibly an early version of *Ravalette*. See Deveney, *Paschal Beverly Randolph*, 443n29.

8. See Ferguson, *Determined Spirits*, 115–41. See also Lana Finley, "Paschal Beverly Randolph in the African American Community," in *Esotericism in African American Religious Experience*, ed. Stephen C. Finley, Margarita Simon Guillory, and Hugh R. Page Jr. (Leiden: Brill, 2014), 37–51. See also Russ Castronovo, *Necro Citizenship* (Durham, NC: Duke University Press, 2001), 167–68, 284–85n69, for brief consideration of *Dealings with the Dead* and, in an endnote, of Randolph.

9. Derrick R. Spires, "Genealogies of Black Modernities," *American Literary History* 32, no. 4 (2020): 611.

10. See Catherine Albanese, *A Republic of Mind and Spirit: A Cultural History of American Metaphysical Religion* (New Haven, CT: Yale University Press, 2007); Henrik Bogdan, "New Perspectives on Western Esotericism," *Nova Religio: The Journal of Alternative and Emergent Religions* 13, no. 3 (2010): 97–105; John B. Buescher, "'More Lurid Than Lucid': The Spiritualist Invention of the Word 'Sexism,'" *Journal of the American Academy of Religion* 70, no. 3 (2002): 561–92; John Patrick Deveney, "Paschal Beverly Randolph and Sexual Magic," in *Hidden Intercourse: Eros and Sexuality in the History of Western Esotericism*, ed. Wouter J. Hanegraaff and Jeffrey J. Kripal (Leiden: Brill, 2008), 355–67; John L. Jackson, "On Ethnographic Sincerity," *Current Anthropology* 51, no. S2 (2010): S279–87; Hugh B. Urban, "The Beast with Two Backs: Aleister Crowley, Sex Magic and the Exhaustion of Modernity," *Nova Religio: The Journal of Alternative and Emergent Religions* 7, no. 3 (2004): 7–25.

11. P. Gabrielle Foreman stands as virtually the only African Americanist literary scholar to have mentioned Randolph in print when she acknowledges him in an endnote as a "Black Spiritualist and author"; see Gabrielle P. Foreman, "The 'Christian Recorder,' Broken Families, and Educated Nations in Julia C. Collins's Civil War Novel *The Curse of Caste*," *African American Review* 40, no. 4 (2006): 715n11.

For exploration of the vigorous debates surrounding the designation of the first novel and the first woman-authored novel in the African American literary tradition, see William L. Andrews and Mitchell A. Kachun, editors' introduction to *The Curse of Caste; or, The Slave Bride* by Julia Collins (1865) (Oxford: Oxford University Press, 2006), xi–lxvi; P. Gabrielle Foreman and Reginald H. Pitts, introduction to *Our Nig; or, Sketches from the Life of a Free Black by Harriet Wilson* (1859) (New York: Penguin, 2005), xxiii–l; Xiomara Santamarina, "Fugitive Slave, Fugitive Novelist: *The Narrative of James Williams* (1838)," *American Literary History* 31, no. 1 (2019): 24–46; Dinitia Smith, "A Slave Story Is Rediscovered, and a Dispute Begins," *New York Times*, October 28, 2006, https://www.nytimes.com/2006/10/28/books/a-slave-story-is-rediscovered-and-a-dispute-begins.html; Rafia Zafar, "Of Print and Primogeniture; or, The Curse of Firsts," *African American Review* 40, no. 4 (2006): 619–21.

12. Yet inconsistency actually renders Randolph typical of many adherents to Spiritualism in the nineteenth-century United States and therefore representative of the movement. As Cathy Gutierrez points out, "The Spiritualist movement resisted centralized authority and intellectual coercion of any sort, making their writing ideologically inconsistent on certain points and obscuring longer term trends." See Cathy Gutierrez, *Plato's Ghost: Spiritualism in the American Renaissance* (Oxford: Oxford University Press, 2009), 9. See also Albanese, *A Republic of Mind and Spirit*, 245.

13. Eve Kosofsky Sedgwick, "Paranoid Reading and Reparative Reading; or, You're So Paranoid, You Probably Think This Essay Is About You," in *Touching Feeling* (Durham, NC: Duke University Press, 2002), 124–51.

14. Paschal Beverly Randolph, *Eulis! The History of Love: Its Wondrous Magic, Chemistry, Rules, Laws, Modes, Moods, and Rationale* (Toledo: printed by author, 1874; rpt. Toledo: Randolph Publishing Company, 1906), 39.

15. Finley, "Paschal Beverly Randolph in the African American Community," 37.

16. Here I am arguing against scholars of the Spiritualist movement who assert, as Robert S. Cox has done, that "African Americans showed relatively little interest in the spirits." See Robert S. Cox, *Body and Soul: A Sympathetic History of American Spiritualism* (Charlottesville: University of Virginia Press, 2003), 166. Molly McGarry makes a similar assertion; see Molly McGarry, *Ghosts of Futures Past: Spiritualism and the Cultural Politics of Nineteenth-Century America* (Berkeley: University of California Press, 2008), 19. Such assertions falter when we take into consideration that four of the most prominent African American intellectuals, writers, and activists of the nineteenth century, Randolph, Harriet Wilson, Pauline Hopkins, and Sojourner Truth, all contributed to the movement.

17. See Kali Tal, "That Just Kills Me: Black Militant Near-Future Fiction," *Social Text* 71, no. 2 (2002): 65–91, for discussion of other nineteenth-century antecedents for Afrofuturism.

18. See Brandon C. Ogbunu, "How Afrofuturism Can Help the World Mend," *Wired*, July 15, 2020, https://www.wired.com/story/how-afrofuturism-can-help-the-world-mend/#:~:text=A%20century%20later%2C%20as%20a,consider%20universes%20of%20better%20alternatives. Accessed August 1, 2024.

19. Anna Kornbluh, *The Order of Forms: Realism, Formalism, and Social Space* (Chicago: University of Chicago Press, 2019), 156.

20. Richard Iton, *In Search of the Black Fantastic: Politics and Popular Culture in the Post–Civil Rights Era* (New York: Oxford University Press, 2008), 287.

21. Hortense Spillers, "Moving on Down the Line: Variations on the African-American Sermon," in *Black, White, and in Color: Essays on American Literature and Culture* (1988; Chicago: University of Chicago Press, 2003), 276.

22. Daylanne K. English, "Review of *Woody Guthrie's Modern World Blues*, by Will Kaufman; *Beyond the Crossroads: The Devil and the Blues Tradition*, by Adam Gussow; *Conjuring Freedom: Music and Masculinity in the Civil War's 'Gospel Army,'* by Johari Jabir; and *The Great Woman Singer: Gender and Voice in Puerto Rican Music*, by Licia Fiol-Matta," *American Literature* 93, no. 4 (2021): 719.

23. Alain Corbin, *Village Bells: Sound and Meaning in the 19th-Century French Countryside* (New York: Columbia University Press, 1994), 98.

24. Richard Cullen Rath, *How Early America Sounded* (Ithaca, NY: Cornell University Press, 2003), 51.

25. Mark M. Smith, *Listening to Nineteenth-Century America* (Chapel Hill: University of North Carolina Press, 2001), 34.

26. Jonathan Sterne, "Hearing," in *Keywords in Sound*, ed. David Novak and Matt Sakakeeny (Durham, NC: Duke University Press, 2015), 67. Also see Leigh Eric Schmidt, *Hearing Things: Religion, Illusion, and the American Enlightenment* (Cambridge, MA: Harvard University Press, 2000), 6–8, 15–37.

27. Paschal Beverly Randolph, *Seership! The Magnetic Mirror. A Practical Guide to Those Who Aspire to Clairvoyance-Absolute. Original and Selected, from Various European and Asiatic Adepts* (Toledo, OH: printed by author 1870; rpt. Toledo, OH: K. C. Randolph, 1896), Internet Archive, https://archive.org/details/SeershipTheMagneticMirror, 60.

28. Bernard Fielding, "The Occult Lore of Bells," *Occult Review*, December 1918, 322.

29. Anonymous, "Ring Out the Old, Ring in the New," *Spiritual Magazine*, January 1, 1868, 1, http://www.iapsop.com/archive/materials/spiritual_magazine_uk/spiritual_magazine_s2_v3_n1_jan_1868.pdf. Further citations will be parenthetical in the text.

30. Edward White, "In the Joints of Their Toes," *Paris Review* (blog), November 4, 2016, https://www.theparisreview.org/blog/2016/11/04/in-the-joints-of-their-toes/. Of course, this is not to argue that there were no Spiritualist and mystical movements in the United States prior to 1848. A number of scholars have focused on such movements in the antebellum period; see Albanese, *Republic of Mind and Spirit*, Brett E. Carroll, *Spiritualism in Antebellum America* (Bloomington: Indiana University Press, 1997), and Schmidt, *Hearing Things*.

31. Reuben Briggs Davenport, *The Death-Blow to Spiritualism, Being the True Story of the Fox Sisters, as Revealed by the Authority of Margaret Fox Cane and Catherine Fox Jencken* (New York: G. W. Dillingham, 1888), 103, http://www.gutenberg.org/files/33506/33506-h/33506-h.htm.

32. See Albanese, *Republic of Mind and Spirit*; Ann Braude, *Radical Spirits: Spiritualism and Women's Rights in Nineteenth-Century America* (Boston: Beacon Press, 1989); Carroll, *Spiritualism in Antebellum America*; Cox, *Body and Soul*; Guttierez, *Plato's Ghost*; John J. Kucich, *Ghostly Communion: Cross-Cultural Spiritualism in Nineteenth-Century American Literature* (Hanover, NH: Dartmouth College Press, 2004); and McGarry, *Ghosts of Futures Past*.

33. See Albanese, *Republic of Mind and Spirit*.

34. See Braude, *Radical Spirits*, 1–2; and Richard A. Meckel, *Save the Babies: American Public Health Reform and the Prevention of Infant Mortality, 1850–1929*, 2nd ed. (Rochester, NY: University of Rochester Press, 2015).

35. David K. Nartonis, "The Rise of 19th-Century American Spiritualism, 1854–1873," *Journal for the Scientific Study of Religion* 49, no. 2 (2010): 362. Nartonis

offers a helpful and expansive discussion of the overdetermined rise of Spiritualism, grounding his study in period sources, namely "newspaper reports of Spiritualist activity" (363). He quantifies the newspaper coverage by city, identifying Boston (Randolph's primary location for his Spiritualist and sex magician work and Harriet Wilson's for her work as a medium) as having the most newspaper coverage of Spiritualist activities of any urban area in the United States during the second half of the nineteenth century.

36. McGarry, *Ghosts of Futures Past*, 6.

37. Deveney, *Paschal Beverly Randolph*, 9.

38. R. J. Ellis and Henry Louis Gates Jr. confirm that the death of Wilson's son inspired, at least in part, her turn toward Spiritualism. See R. J. Ellis and Henry Louis Gates Jr., "'Grievances at the Treatment She Received': Harriet E. Wilson's Spiritualist Career in Boston, 1868–1900," *American Literary History* 24, no. 2 (2012): 240.

39. See John Noble Wilford, "How Epidemics Shaped the Modern Metropolis," *New York Times*, April 15, 2008, http://www.nytimes.com/2008/04/15/science/15chol.html. Wilford reports that the epidemic "left 3,515 dead out of a population of 250,000." Also see Charles E. Rosenberg, *The Cholera Years: The United States in 1832, 1849, and 1866*, 2nd ed. (Chicago: University of Chicago Press, 1987).

40. Sari Altschuler and Priscilla Wald, "COVID-19: Pandemic Reading," *American Literature* 92, no. 4 (2020): 681.

41. Altschuler and Wald, "COVID-19: Pandemic Reading," 681–82.

42. David Walker, "The Humbug in American Religion Ritual Theories of Nineteenth-Century Spiritualism," *Religion and American Culture: A Journal of Interpretation* 23, no. 1 (2013): 41.

43. McGarry, *Ghosts of Futures Past*, 19.

44. Christine Ferguson, "Eugenics and the Afterlife: Lombroso, Doyle, and the Spiritualist Purification of the Race," *Journal of Victorian Culture* 12, no. 1 (2007): 64.

45. Randolph, *Dealings with the Dead*, 123, 28. Further citations will be parenthetical in the text.

46. Paschal Beverly Randolph, *After Death; or, Disembodied Man* (Boston: printed by the author, 1868; rpt. London: Forgotten Books, 2012), 53. Further citations will be parenthetical in the text.

47. See Therí Alyce Pickens, *Black Madness :: Mad Blackness* (Durham, NC: Duke University Press, 2019) for a brilliant analysis of, and challenge to, associations of Blackness with disability. For more on scholarly discussions and debates on Blackness and disability, see Therí Alyce Pickens, ed., "Blackness and Disability," Special issue, *African American Review* 50, no. 2 (2017); and Sami Schalk, *Bodyminds Reimagined: (Dis)ability, Race, and Gender in Black Women's Speculative Fiction* (Durham, NC: Duke University Press, 2018).

48. Perhaps not surprisingly, Spiritualism and racism were perfectly compatible, despite some links between the movement and abolitionism and other progressive movements. A number of historians of Spiritualism have pointed to white

Spiritualists' racist imagination and use of Indian spirit guides; see McGarry *Ghosts of Futures Past*, 66–93, for an excellent discussion of that practice. Other scholars have noted Spiritualists' widely held belief in a racially hierarchical afterlife; as Albanese, for one, tartly puts it, "Segregation in the spiritland was apparently the norm" (*Republic of Mind and Spirit*, 241).

49. Paschal Beverly Randolph. *The "Learned Pundit" and "Man with Two Souls": His Curious Life, Works, and Career. The Great Free-Love Trial. Randolph's Grand Defence. His Address to the Jury, and Mankind. The Verdict* (Boston: Randolph Publishing House, 1872), 18. Further citations will be parenthetical in the text.

50. Deveney, *Paschal Beverly Randolph*, 1, 4.

51. See Gene Andrew Jarrett, *Deans and Truants: Race and Realism in American Literature* (Philadelphia: University of Pennsylvania Press, 2007), 1–27.

52. Paschal Beverly Randolph, letter to the editor, *New Orleans Tribune*, December 8, 1864, 2. This letter is also quoted in Deveney, *Paschal Beverly Randolph*, 6, although misattributed there to the December 2, 1864, issue of the newspaper.

53. Anna Kornbluh, "We Have Never Been Critical: Toward the Novel as Critique," *Novel* 50, no. 3 (2017): 403.

54. Paschal Beverly Randolph, *Tom Clark and His Wife, Their Double Dreams and the Curious Things That Befell Them Therein; or, The Rosicrucian's Story* (New York: Sinclair Tousey, 1863; Project Gutenberg, 2011), Part I, para 1, https://www.gutenberg.org/cache/epub/35366/pg35366-images.html. Further citations will be parenthetical in the text.

55. See Smith, *Listening to Nineteenth-Century America*, 16, for a fine analysis of "aural sectionalism," that is, how sound underlay the establishment of Southern and Northern division and difference in the United States in the antebellum period.

56. Recent estimates of the numbers of Civil War dead have ranged from 620,000 to 750,000. See David J. Hacker, "A Census-Based Count of the Civil War Dead," *Civil War History* 57, no. 4 (2011): 306–47; Drew Gilpin Faust, "'The Dread Void of Uncertainty': Naming the Dead in the American Civil War," *Southern Cultures* 11, no. 2 (2005): 7–32; and Drew Gilpin Faust, *The Republic of Suffering* (New York: Alfred A. Knopf, 2008). For an interesting challenge to the notion of the exceptional toll on Americans of the numbers of Civil War dead, see Nicholas Marshall, "The Great Exaggeration: Death and the Civil War," *Journal of the Civil War Era* 4, no. 1 (2014): 3–27. Regardless of the particular impact of the Civil War, just as Marshall argues, "Civil War–era Americans regularly lost family members . . . and understood that the hand of death could reach out for them at any moment" (6). For statistics on COVID mortality in the United States, see World Health Organization COVID-19 Dashboard: https://data.who.int/dashboards/covid19/deaths?n=o.

57. David Walker, *Appeal to the Coloured Citizens of the World* (1829; New York: Hill and Wang, 1995), 3.

58. Albanese, *Republic of Mind and Spirit*, 15.

59. Michelle D. Commander, *Afro-Atlantic Flight: Speculative Returns and the Black Fantastic* (Durham, NC: Duke University Press, 2017), 6, 84, 91.

60. Sheila Rothman, *Living in the Shadow of Death: Tuberculosis and the Social Experience of Illness in American History* (New York: Basic, HarperCollins, 1994), 2.

61. Corbin, *Village Bells*, 121. For a succinct definition of the term "soundscape," see R. Murray Schafer, "The Soundscape," in *The Sound Studies Reader*, ed. Jonathan Sterne (London: Routledge, 2012), 101. Also see R. Murray Schafer, *The Soundscape: Our Sonic Environment and the Tuning of the World* (1977; Rochester, VT: Destiny Books, 1994) for a classic work of sound studies, wherein he introduces the influential term "soundscape." In the 2010s and 2020s, however, sound studies scholars have challenged Schafer's concept and term "soundscape." For two examples, see Andrew J. Eisenberg, "Space," in *Keywords in Sound*, ed. David Novak and Matt Sakakeeny (Durham, NC: Duke University Press, 2015), 197–99; and Marina Peterson, *Atmospheric Noise: The Indefinite Urbanism of Los Angeles* (Durham, NC: Duke University Press, 2021).

62. Charles Hirschkind, "Religion," in *Keywords in Sound*, ed. David Novak and Matt Sakakeeny (Durham, NC: Duke University Press, 2015), 169.

63. Julian Henriques, "Sonic Dominance and the Reggae Sound System Session," in *The Auditory Culture Reader*, ed. Michael Bull and Les Back (Oxford: Berg, 2003), 461. Emphasis in original.

64. Kodwo Eshun, *More Brilliant Than the Sun: Adventures in Sonic Fiction* (London: Quartet Books, 1998), 01[004]. Further citations will be parenthetical in the text.

65. Braude, *Radical Spirits*, 117–20.

66. Randolph's lifetime was characterized by the passage of a series of increasingly restrictive federal obscenity laws, beginning in the 1820s and culminating in the 1873 "Act of the Suppression of Trade in, and Circulation of, Obscene Literature and Articles of Immoral Use," commonly known as the Comstock Act. Randolph himself fell victim to these laws. Although much of Randolph's autobiography, *Curious Life*, consists of self-promotion, with a hefty portion of it given over to quotations of newspaper articles (some authentic and some fabricated) extolling Randolph's genius and eloquence, it also details his real 1872 arrest on charges of being in possession of obscene written materials, namely his own books and pamphlets, along with a subsequent, but purely imaginary, "free-love" trial. In actuality, Randolph was freed after two nights in jail because a judge determined that the reading matter that he possessed was not in fact obscene. See Deveney, *Paschal Beverly Randolph*, 198–99. It is almost beyond imagining that in the present there are radical anti-choice politicians and policy advocates who are working to revive and apply the Comstock Act. See Mabel Felix, Laurie Sobel, and Alina Salganicoff, "The Comstock Act: Implications Nationwide," KFF Website, April 15, 2024, https://www.kff.org/womens-health-policy/issue-brief/the-comstock-act-implications-for-abortion-care-nationwide/.

67. Hugh B. Urban, "'Magia Sexualis': Sex, Secrecy, and Liberation in Modern

Western Esotericism," *Journal of the American Academy of Religion* 72, no. 3 (2004): 696.

68. Randolph, *Seership!* 84.

69. Randolph, *Eulis!* 8, 203, 176. Further citations will be parenthetical in the text.

70. Harriet Wilson, preface to *Our Nig; or, Sketches from the Life of a Free Black, in a Two-Story White House, North* (1859; Project Gutenberg, 2011), https://www.gutenberg.org/ebooks/584.

71. Ferguson, "Eugenics and the Afterlife," 47.

72. Ann duCille, *The Coupling Convention: Sex, Text, and Tradition in Black Women's Fiction* (New York: Oxford University Press, 1993), 5.

73. DuCille, *The Coupling Convention*, 6.

74. Admittedly, Monáe has since disavowed the Afrofuturist label. See Michael Shulman, "Janelle Monáe Peels the Onion," *New Yorker*, January 8, 2023, https://www.newyorker.com/culture/the-new-yorker-interview/janelle-monae-peels-the-onion. In the interview, Monáe says, "I consider myself to be a 'presenturist.' That is a word that I made up: instead of a futurist, I'm a *present*urist. If I'm thinking about the future, I'm having anxiety. . . . This has been my lifework, as a futurist turned presenturist." Her most recent album *Age of Pleasure* bears out this sense of the present, and of enjoying that present, as paramount; see Janelle Monáe, *Age of Pleasure*, Wondaland Productions LLC (2023).

75. Janelle Monáe, "Screwed," on *Dirty Computer*, dir. Andrew Donoho and Chuck Lightning, prod. Janelle Monáe et al., April 27, 2018, YouTube video, 17:40–44, https://youtu.be/jdH2Sy-BlNE.

76. Quoted in Deveney, *Paschal Beverly Randolph*, 317.

77. Janelle Monáe, *Metropolis*, Bad Boy Records, 2008, liner notes.

78. Monáe, "Screwed," 17:58–18:29. This section is much like the end of her *Q.U.E.E.N* video, which also delivers a clear political and historical message; see Janelle Monáe, *Q.U.E.E.N.*, dir. Alan Ferguson, prod. David Kwon Kim, May 1, 2013, YouTube video, 5:13–6:01, https://youtu.be/tEddixS-UoU.

79. The term "misogynoir," meaning the particular form of misogyny experienced by Black women, was coined by Moya Bailey. See Moya Bailey, *Misogynoir Transformed: Black Women's Digital Resistance* (New York: New York University Press, 2021).

80. See Janelle Monáe, *Electric Lady*, Atlantic Corporation, 2015. See also Janelle Monáe, *Electric Lady*, dir. Alan Ferguson, YouTube video, July 30, 2014, https://youtu.be/LPFgBCUBMYk?si=hDshowQ-zdiXli2b.

81. See Zolan Kanno-Youngs, "US Watched George Floyd Protests in 15 Cities Using Aerial Surveillance," *New York Times*, June 19, 2020, https://www.nytimes.com/2020/06/19/us/politics/george-floyd-protests-surveillance.html.

82. Randolph, *Eulis!* 1906, 33.

83. Monáe, "Screwed," 24:45.

84. Monáe, "Screwed," 16:32–35.

85. José Esteban Muñoz, *Cruising Utopia: The Then and There of Queer Futurity* (New York: New York University Press, 2009), 11.

86. Monáe, "Screwed," 24:27–28.

87. Elizabeth Freeman, *Time Binds: Queer Temporalities, Queer Histories* (Durham, NC: Duke University Press, 2010), xii. Further citations will be parenthetical in the text.

88. I owe this insight entirely to my brilliant former student, Alexia Hall, who made this point at Macalester College on April 17, 2019.

89. Although I wrote this sentence considerably before the presidential campaign of summer 2024, "weird," as used by Minnesota Governor Tim Walz to describe Republicans' attacks on sexual, gender, and reproductive freedoms resonates with the distinction I am making here between Randolph's anti-queer, anti-transgender form of sex magic and Monáe's liberatory form of sex magic. See "Gov. Walz: 'People Like JD Vance Know Nothing about Small Town America,'" Joe Scarborough, Interview with Tim Walz, "Morning Joe," *MSNBC News*, July 23, 2024, YouTube Video, 2:57–2:58, https://youtu.be/tviViJqpgpY?si=4RXzVeIo7jK64oEA.

90. Carla L. Peterson, "Mapping Taste: Urban Modernities from the *Tatler* and *Spectator* to *Frederick Douglass's Paper*," *American Literary History* 32, no. 4 (2020): 703.

91. See "Colored Conventions National Convention of Colored Men Held in the City of Syracuse, New York, in 1864, October 4, 5, 6, and 7, 1864," *Colored Conventions Project*, P. Gabrielle Foreman et al., https://coloredconventions.org//. See also Deveney, *Paschal Beverly Randolph*, 156–57.

92. Deveney, *Paschal Beverly Randolph*, 309.

93. Kathryn Yusoff, *A Billion Black Anthropocenes or None* (Minneapolis: University of Minnesota Press, 2018), xii.

94. For just one example, see McGarry, *Ghosts of Futures Past*, Chapter 2, on white Spiritualists' fetishistic use of Native Americans. As McGarry explains, white Spiritualists "positioned Native Americans as a vital link between this world and the next, always poised to be the Indian guide who could bring Spiritualists through the veil" (66).

95. As Randolph wrote in *After Death*, "I turn with loathing and horror from the bare recollection even, of my 'mediumship'" (31). See also Deveney, *Paschal Beverly Randolph*, 92–99.

96. McGarry, *Ghosts of Futures Past*, 6.

97. Randolph, *Dealings with Dead*, 22.

98. Ytasha Womack, *Afrofuturism: The World of Black Sci-fi and Fantasy Culture* (Chicago: University of Chicago Press, 2013), 9.

99. Kodwo Eshun, "Further Considerations of Afrofuturism," *CR: The New Centennial Review* 3, no. 2 (2003): 289. Here Eshun, too, implicitly refutes Ken Warren's argument about African American literature.

100. Walter Benjamin, *The Arcades Project*, trans. Howard Eiland and Kevin McLaughlin (Cambridge, MA: Belknap Press of Harvard University Press, 1999), 462.

101. Parliament, "Mothership Connection/Starchild," track 2, on Parliament, *Mothership Connection*, Casablanca, 1975, album.

102. Moreover, a replica of the original 1970s mothership, actually used on stage in the 1990s, has been preserved for the future in its current location at the National Museum of African American History and Culture, https://nmaahc.si.edu/object/nmaahc_2011.83.1.1-.9.

103. Janelle Monáe, *Many Moons*, YouTube video, April 4, 2009, 6:04–6:07. https://youtu.be/EZyyORSHbaE.

104. Sun Ra's 1974 film, *Space Is the Place*, represents the selection process for those permitted to travel on a kind of mothership to escape the earth. See Sun Ra, *Space Is the Place*, dir. John Coney, YouTube video, posted by Steelworker Records (1977; October 14, 2022) 1:13:45–1:13:54, 1:15:40–1:16:38, https://youtu.be/owCPrIEliZc?si=DVJbXsoVxWfoHY5h.

105. Muñoz, *Cruising Utopia*, 185.

106. Such an argument is characteristic of the "temporal turn" in African American literary and cultural studies. See, for just a few excellent examples, Michelle M. Wright, *The Physics of Blackness: Beyond the Middle Passage Epistemology* (Minneapolis: University of Minnesota Press, 2015); Gregory Laski, *Untimely Democracy: The Politics of Progress After Slavery* (New York: Oxford University Press, 2018); and Anthony Reed, *Freedom Time: The Poetics and Politics of Black Experimental Writing* (Baltimore: Johns Hopkins University Press, 2014).

107. Walter Benjamin, *Illuminations: Essays and Reflections*, ed. Hannah Arendt, trans. Harry Zohn (1968; New York: Schocken Books, 1985), 261.

108. Alexander G. Weheliye, *Habeas Viscus: Racializing Assemblages, Biopolitics, and Black Feminist Theories of the Human* (Durham, NC: Duke University Press, 2014), 85.

109. See Fred Moten, *Black and Blur* (Durham, NC: Duke University Press, 2017).

110. Daylanne K. English and Alvin [now Ava] Kim, "Now We Want Our Funk Cut: Janelle Monáe's Neo-Afrofuturism," *American Studies* 52, no. 4 (2013): 218, 228.

111. Martin Luther King Jr., *Where Do We Go from Here: Chaos or Community?* (Boston: Beacon Press, 1967), 150.

112. Kara Keeling, *Queer Times, Black Futures* (New York: New York University Press, 2019), 213.

2. "Marvels of Inventiveness": Black Feminist Technologies of Time

1. For an exceptionally lucid and thorough account of the history and breadth of literary studies and time, see Theodore Martin, "Temporality and Literary Theory," *Oxford Research Encyclopedia of Literature*, December 22, 2016, https://doi.org/10.1093/acrefore/9780190201098.013.122.

2. Michelle M. Wright, *The Physics of Blackness: Beyond the Middle Passage Epistemology* (Minneapolis: University of Minnesota Press, 2015), 3–5.

3. Karla F. C. Holloway, "The Death of Culture," *Massachusetts Review* 40, no. 1 (Spring 1999): 34. CPT itself is an old term; the earliest usage in print I have located appears in 1898 in the African American newspaper *The Savannah Tribune* in an anonymous article: "We need not mention anything about the unpunctuality of the Negro. . . . Of course, we as a race are fast becoming independent; and among other things, have inaugurated our own time, known as Colored People Time, or CPT." See "Our Present Needs," *Savannah Tribune*, August 6, 1898, 2, *African American Newspapers 1827–1998*, Database.

4. For further analysis of the relationship between "difference" and "distinctiveness," see Daylanne K. English, "Race, Writing, and Time," in *Literature and Time*, ed. Thomas Allen (Cambridge: Cambridge University Press, 2018), 225–27. Also see Henry Louis Gates Jr., "Introduction: Writing 'Race' and the Difference It Makes," in *"Race," Writing, and Difference*, ed. Henry Louis Gates Jr. (Chicago: University of Chicago Press, 1986), 2.

5. Holloway, "Death of Culture," 39.

6. Hortense Spillers, "Mama's Baby, Papa's Maybe: An American Grammar Book," in *Black, White, and in Color: Essays on American Literature and Culture* (1987; Chicago: University of Chicago Press, 2003), 203.

7. Holmes writes: "My life is committed to the struggle for justice, the healing of the human spirit, and the art of relevant and radical creativity." See https://www.drbarbaraholmes.com/bio. Accessed July 27, 2022.

8. James H. Cone, A *Black Theology of Liberation, Fortieth Anniversary Edition* (1970; Maryknoll, NY: Orbis Books, 2010), 145.

9. Cone, A *Black Theology of Liberation*, 145.

10. As I explore in depth later, slave narratives model engagement with, and representation of, complex multiple temporalities for contemporary futurisms, including Afrofuturism, Indigenous Futurism, Arab Futurism, Chicanafuturism, Asian Futurism, "Crip Futurity" and other related movements. For definition and discussion of Crip Futurity, see Alison Kafer, *Feminist, Queer, Crip* (Bloomington: Indiana University Press, 2013); see especially 3, 20–47.

11. Homi Bhabha, *Location of Culture* (London: Routledge, 1991), 340. Further citations will be parenthetical in the text.

12. Harriet Jacobs, *Incidents in the Life of a Slave Girl, Written by Herself* (1861; University of North Carolina: *Documenting the American South*), 36, https://docsouth.unc.edu/fpn/jacobs/jacobs.html. Further citations will be parenthetical in the text.

13. Vincent W. Lloyd, *Religion of the Field Negro: On Black Secularism and Black Theology* (New York: Fordham University Press, 2017), 31.

14. Frederick Douglass, *Narrative of the Life of Frederick Douglass, an American Slave, Written by Himself* (1845; New York: Signet, 1968), 83. Further citations will be parenthetical in the text.

15. Frederick Douglass, *My Bondage and My Freedom* (1855; New York: Library of America, 1996), 286. Further citations will be parenthetical in the text.

16. Paul Gilroy, *The Black Atlantic: Modernity and Double Consciousness* (Cambridge, MA: Harvard University Press, 1993), 63. Further citations will be parenthetical in the text.

17. Russ Castronovo, *Necro Citizenship: Death, Eroticism, and the Public Sphere in the Nineteenth-Century United States* (Durham, NC: Duke University Press, 2001), 45.

18. Coleman adopts the terms "womanism" and "womanist" from Alice Walker's well-known nomenclature for a specifically Black feminism that supplants white women-focused feminism of the 1960s and 1970s. See Alice Walker, *In Search of Our Mother's Gardens* (1967; New York: Houghton Mifflin, 1983); see especially xi–xii and 81.

19. Monica A. Coleman, *Making a Way Out of No Way: A Womanist Theology* (Minneapolis: Fortress Press, 2008), 62–63. Further citations will be parenthetical in the text.

20. Fredric Jameson, "The End of Temporality," *Critical Inquiry* 29, no. 4 (2003): 713.

21. Giorgio Agamben, *The Time That Remains: A Commentary on the Letter to the Romans*, trans. Patricia Dailey (Stanford, CA: Stanford University Press, 2005), 62, emphasis in original. Further citations will be parenthetical in the text.

22. Saidiya Hartman, "The Time of Slavery," *South Atlantic Quarterly* 101, no. 4 (Fall 2002): 760, 759. Further citations will be parenthetical in the text.

23. My interdisciplinary analysis of race and time in this instance is in keeping with, and is indebted to, Wright's *Physics of Blackness*. I am also deeply indebted to my observational astronomer colleague at Macalester College, Professor John Cannon, for my understanding of spherical accretion and time. See also A. L. Maraschi Treves and M. Abramowicz, "Basic Elements of the Theory of Accretion," *Publications of the Astronomical Society of the Pacific* 100, no. 626 (April 1988): 427 51; and J. Frank, A. R. King, and D. J. Raine, *Accretion Power in Astrophysics*, 3rd ed. (Cambridge: Cambridge University Press, 2002).

24. See Katherine McKittrick, "The Last Place They Thought Of: Black Women's Geographies," in *Demonic Grounds* (Minneapolis: University of Minnesota Press, 2006), 37–63. As McKittrick argues, "The margin, then, is not straightforwardly metaphoric" (55).

25. See Georg Wilhelm Friedrich Hegel, *The Philosophy of History*, trans. John Sibree (New York: Cosimo, 2007), 99.

26. For a discussion of the reception history of slave narratives, see Mitch Kachun, "Slave Narratives and Historical Memory," in *The Oxford Handbook of the African American Slave Narrative*, ed. John Ernest (New York: Oxford University Press, 2014), 22–35.

27. Jacqueline Goldsby, "'I Disguised My Hand': Writing Versions of the Truth in Harriet Jacobs's *Incidents in the Life of a Slave Girl* and John Jacobs's 'A True

Tale of Slavery,'" in *Harriet Jacobs and Incidents in the Life of a Slave Girl: New Critical Essays*, ed. Deborah M. Garfield and Rafia Zafar (Cambridge: Cambridge University Press, 1996), 13. Further citations will be parenthetical in the text.

28. See Kachun, "Slave Narratives and Historical Memory," 30–31.

29. "Temporal" in this instance refers not to time, but rather, to the *OED*'s second definition for the term as:

> 2. Of or pertaining to time as the sphere of human life; terrestrial as opposed to heavenly; of man's present life as distinguished from a future existence; concerning or involving merely the material interests of this world; worldly, earthly. (Opposed to eternal or spiritual). *Oxford English Dictionary*, n.d, "temporal, *adj*." Accessed July 27, 2022, https://www.oed.com/dictionary/temporal_adj1?tab=meaning_and_use#18881873.

30. Barbara A. Holmes, "'We'll Make Us a World': A Post-Obama Politics of Embodied Creativity," in *Ain't I a Womanist, Too? Third Wave Womanist Religious Thought*, ed. Monica A. Coleman and Layli Maparyan (Minneapolis: Augsburg Fortress, 2013), 18, 9.

31. Jennifer Lynn Stoever, *The Sonic Color Line: Race and the Cultural Politics of Listening* (New York: New York University Press, 2016), 56. Further references will be parenthetical in the text.

32. Mendi + Keith Obadike, *Numbers Station 2 [Red Record]* excerpt, YouTube video, 0:12–19, April 21, 2016, https://youtu.be/Ww2vrBB9Gno.

33. Mendi + Keith Obadike, *Numbers Station 2 [Red Record]*, YouTube Video, April 21, 2016, https://youtu.be/Ww2vrBB9Gno.

34. Julie Beth Napolin, "Scenes of Subjection: Women's Voices Narrating Black Death," *Sounding Out!* (blog), December 9, 2016, https://soundstudiesblog.com/2016/12/19/scenes-of-subjection-womens-voices-narrating-black-death/.

35. Julie Beth Napolin, "b.O.s. 13.4 / *Numbers Station [Red Record]*," *ASAP Journal*, August 13, 2020. https://asapjournal.com/13-4-numbers-station-red-record-julie-beth-napolin/.

36. Mendi + Keith Obadike, *Untitled*, YouTube Video, 0:26–0:46, September 13, 2021, https://youtu.be/DkS-hHmVEq8.

37. "Napolin, "b.O.s. 13.4."

38. Napolin, "Scenes of Subjection."

39. Napolin, "Scenes of Subjection."

40. Napolin, "Scenes of Subjection."

41. See Catherine S. Ramírez, "Afrofuturism/Chicanafuturism," *Aztlán* 33, no. 1 (2008): 189.

42. Curtis Marez, *Farm Worker Futurism: Speculative Technologies of Resistance* (Minneapolis: University of Minnesota Press, 2016), 9.

43. Janelle Monáe, *Q.U.E.E.N.*, dir. Alan Ferguson, prod. David Kwon Kim, May 1, 2013, YouTube video, 5:28–5:38, https://youtu.be/tEddixS-UoU.

44. Janelle Monáe, *Electric Lady*, dir. Alan Ferguson, YouTube video, July 30, 2014, https://youtu.be/LPFgBCUBMYk.

45. Jenn Pelly, "Janelle Monáe's 'Electric Lady' Video Features T.I., Estelle, Esperanza Spalding, T-Boz, Her Mom," *Pitchfork*, July 30, 2014, https://pitchfork.com/news/56092-janelle-monaes-electric-lady-video-features-ti-estelle-esperanza-spalding-t-boz-her-mom/.

46. Hortense Spillers, "Moving on Down the Line: Variations on the African-American Sermon," in *Black, White, and in Color: Essays on American Literature and Culture* (1988; Chicago: University of Chicago Press, 2003), 252.

47. Spillers, "Moving on Down the Line," 276.

48. Janelle Monáe, *Dirty Computer*, dir. Andrew Donoho and Chuck Lightning, prod. Janelle Monáe et al., April 27, 2018, YouTube video, 44:32–45:50, https://youtu.be/jdH2Sy-BlNE.

49. Spillers, "Moving on Down the Line," 276.

50. Barbara A. Holmes, *Crisis Contemplation: Healing the Wounded Village* (Albuquerque, NM: CAC Publishing, 2021), 98.

3. "Scaled Perfectly to Eternity": A Contemporary Black Poetics

1. Ross Gay, *Bringing the Shovel Down* (Pittsburgh, PA: University of Pittsburgh Press, 2011). Further citations will be parenthetical in the text.

2. Ross Gay, *Catalog of Unabashed Gratitude* (Pittsburgh, PA: University of Pittsburgh Press, 2015). Further citations will be parenthetical in the text.

3. Ross Gay, *The Book of Delights* (Chapel Hill, NC: Algonquin Books of Chapel Hill, 2019). Further citations will be parenthetical in the text.

4. Jericho Brown, *The Tradition* (Port Townsend, WA: Copper Canyon Press, 2019). Further citations will be parenthetical in the text.

5. Danez Smith, *Don't Call Us Dead* (Minneapolis: Graywolf Press, 2017). Further citations will be parenthetical in the text.

6. Claudia Rankine, "The Condition of Black Life Is One of Mourning," *New York Times Magazine*, June 22, 2015, https://www.nytimes.com/2015/06/22/magazine/the-condition-of-black-life-is-one-of-mourning.html.

7. Caroline Levine, *Forms: Whole, Rhythm, Hierarchy, Network* (Princeton, NJ: Princeton University Press, 2015), 2. Further citations will be parenthetical in the text.

8. Daylanne K. English, *Unnatural Selections: Eugenics in American Modernism and the Harlem Renaissance* (Chapel Hill: University of North Carolina Press, 2003), 33.

9. Tracy K. Smith, *The Body's Question* (Minneapolis: Graywolf Press, 2003). Further citations will be parenthetical in the text.

10. Saidiya V. Hartman, *Scenes of Subjection: Terror, Slavery, and Self-Making in Nineteenth-Century America* (New York: Oxford University Press, 1997), 19–20.

11. Hartman, *Scenes of Subjection*, 19.

12. Kevin Quashie, *Black Aliveness; or, a Poetics of Being* (Durham, NC: Duke University Press, 2021), 132. Further citations will be parenthetical in the text.

13. Linda Gregerson, "The Poem That Changed My Life: Ross Gay's 'Bringing the Shovel Down,'" Poets.org, November 30, 2016, https://poets.org/text/poem-changed-my-life-ross-gays-bringing-shovel-down.

14. There has been, of course, a great deal of analysis of this poem in particular and of modernist poetics in general. For one of the most pertinent readings for my purposes, see Ann Fisher-Wirth, "The Allocations of Desire: 'This Is Just to Say' and Flossie Williams's 'Reply,'" *William Carlos Williams Review* 22, no. 2 (1996): 47–56, http://www.jstor.org/stable/24565314. Fisher-Wirth efficiently dispatches what remains one of the most influential analyses of the poem, namely Charles Altieri's, by focusing on Williams's wife's sardonic poetic reply to "This Is Just to Say." See Charles Altieri, "Presence and Reference in a Literary Text: The Example of Williams' 'This Is Just to Say,'" *Critical Inquiry* 3 (Spring 1979): 30–44.

15. Ross Gay, "Beholding Black Life: A Conversation with Ross Gay, Frank Guridy, and Deborah Paredez," interview by Frank Andre Guridy and Deborah Paredez, *Public Books*, June 1, 2022, https://www.publicbooks.org/beholding-black-life-a-conversation-with-ross-gay-frank-guridy-deborah-paredez/?utm_source=PUBLIC+BOOKS+Newsletter&utm_campaign=e5389b38c7-EMAIL_CAMPAIGN_2022_6_6&utm_medium=email&utm_term=0_d048c39403-e5389b38c7-47239089&mc_cid=e5389b38c7&mc_eid=78d37ce77a.

16. Brown, "Shovel," in *Tradition*, 36–37. Further citations will be parenthetical in the text.

17. Anahid Nersessian, *The Calamity Form: On Poetry and Social Life* (Chicago: University of Chicago Press, 2020), 175. Further citations will be parenthetical in the text.

18. Calvin L. Warren, *Ontological Terror: Blackness, Nihilism, and Emancipation* (Durham, NC: Duke University Press, 2018), 29. Strikeout in original.

19. As Hartman puts it, "As well, the 'time of slavery' negates the common-sense intuition of time as continuity or progression, then and now coexist; we are coeval with the dead." See Saidiya Hartman, "The Time of Slavery," *South Atlantic Quarterly* 101, no. 4 (2002): 759.

20. Badia Ahad-Legardy, *Afro-Nostalgia: Feeling Good in Contemporary Black Culture* (Urbana: University of Illinois Press, 2021), 3; Michelle D. Commander, *Afro-Atlantic Flight: Speculative Returns and the Black Fantastic* (Durham, NC: Duke University Press, 2017), 128.

21. And though the poem does not quite deliver terza rima, it does offer near rhymes and anagrams across stanzas, as in "earth," "ether" and "there," connecting the poem with a tradition of poets, from Dante to Adrienne Rich, who have deployed that form to write of various kinds of underworld and afterlife. See Adrienne Rich, "Terza Rima," in *Fox: Poems 1998–2000* (New York: W. W. Norton, 2001), 41–53; see especially Rich's allusion to Gramsci's ashes, 51.

22. Saidiya Hartman, *Lose Your Mother: A Journey Along the Atlantic Slave Route* (New York: Farrar, Straus and Giroux, 2016), 6.

23. Ross Gay and Aimee Nezhukumatathil, *Lace & Pyrite: Letters from Two Gardeners* (Union, NJ: Get Fresh Publishing, 2014), first quotation from the unpaginated introduction; second quotation on page 15.

24. Rankine, "The Condition of Black Life."

25. Frank Wilderson, "An Afropessimist on the Year Since George Floyd Was Murdered: Notes of a (Minneapolis) Native Son, *The Nation*, June 14/21, 2021, https://www.thenation.com/article/society/george-floyd-afropessimism/.

26. Christina Sharpe, *In the Wake: On Blackness and Being* (Durham, NC: Duke University Press, 2016), 13.

27. Ahad-Legardy, *Afro-Nostalgia*, 30. Further citations will be parenthetical in the text.

28. Tracy K. Smith, *Wade in the Water* (Minneapolis: Graywolf Press, 2018), 13. Further citations will be parenthetical in the text.

29. Tracy K. Smith, "Realm of Shades," in *Bearden's Odyssey: Poets Respond to the Art of Romare Bearden*, ed. Kwame Dawes and Matthew Shenoda (Evanston, IL: TriQuarterly Books/Northwestern University Press, 2017), 90.

30. Jarkko Toikkanen, "Intermedial Experience and Ekphrasis in Wordsworth's 'Slumber,'" *Partial Answers: Journal of Literature and the History of Ideas* 17, no. 1 (2019): 108, doi.10.1353/pan.2019.0006.

31. Wallace Stevens, "Anecdote of the Jar," *Poetry* 1 (October 1919): 8.

32. *Oxford English Dictionary*, n.d. "radical," adj. and n., accessed June 27, 2022. www.oed.com/view/Entry/157251.

33. James A. W. Heffernan, *Museum of Words: The Poetics of Ekphrasis from Homer to Ashbery* (Chicago: University of Chicago Press, 1993), 6. The argument of the book—neatly summed up on its last page: "the unending struggle between the image and the word" (189)—is particularly inapt for understanding ekphrasis in a contemporary Black poetics of the afterlife.

34. W. J. T. Mitchell concurs about what he terms "ekphrastic ambivalence toward the female figure." See W. J. T. Mitchell, *Picture Theory* (Chicago: University of Chicago Press, 1994), 170.

35. Heffernan, *Museum of Words*, 7.

36. Stephen Best, *None Like Us: Blackness, Belonging, Aesthetic Life* (Durham, NC: Duke University Press, 2018), 1.

37. Marilyn Krysl, introduction to *Obsession: Sestinas in the Twenty-First Century*, ed. Carolyn Beard Whitlow and Marilyn Krysl (Dartmouth, NH: Dartmouth College Press, 2014), xiv.

38. Tracy K. Smith, *Life on Mars: Poems* (Minneapolis: Graywolf Press, 2011). Citations will be parenthetical in the text.

39. Joel Brouwer, "Poems of Childhood, Grief and Deep Space," review of *Life on Mars*, by Tracy K. Smith, *New York Times*, August 26, 2011, https://www.nytimes.com/2011/08/28/books/review/life-on-mars-by-tracy-k-smith-book-review.html.

40. Harriet Wilson, preface to *Our Nig; or, Sketches from the Life of a Free Black* (1859; New York: Penguin, 2005), 3.

41. Michelle M. Wright, *The Physics of Blackness: Beyond the Middle Passage Epistemology* (Minneapolis: University of Minnesota Press, 2015), 3–5.

42. Tracy K. Smith, *Ordinary Light: A Memoir* (New York: Vintage Books, 2015). Further citations will be parenthetical in the text.

43. Anthony Reed, *Soundworks: Race, Sound, and Poetry in Production* (Durham, NC: Duke University Press, 2021), 38.

44. "Life on Mars," track 4 on David Bowie, *Hunky Dory*, RCA 1971.

45. Commander, *Afro-Atlantic Flight*, 6.

46. "Sound and Vision," track 4 on David Bowie, *Low*, RCA, 1977.

47. "Bleed Like a Craze, Dad," Spotify, track 5, David Bowie, *Buddha of Suburbia*, 1993, Jones/Tintoretto Entertainment Company/Parlophone Records remaster, 2021.

48. Joni Mitchell, "Woodstock," on *Ladies of the Canyon*, Warner Records, Inc., March 1, 1970.

49. Chris O'Leary, "Pushing Ahead of the Dame: David Bowie, Song by Song," *Bleed Like a Craze, Dad* (website), December 17, 2012, https://bowiesongs.wordpress.com/2012/12/17/bleed-like-a-craze-dad/. See also Chris O'Leary, *Ashes to Ashes; The Songs of David Bowie, 1976–2016* (London: Repeater Books, 2018), 362.

50. O'Leary, "Pushing Ahead of the Dame."

51. Nicholas Pegg, *The Complete David Bowie* (2016; London: Titan Books, 2000), 45.

52. Hartman, *Scenes of Subjection*, 122.

53. Emily S. Rueb, "He Emerged from Prison a Potent Symbol of H.I.V. Criminalization," *New York Times*, July 14, 2019, https://www.nytimes.com/2019/07/14/us/michael-johnson-hiv-prison.html. See also Kayla Drake, "Missouri Loosens Laws Criminalizing HIV Transmission After 30 Years of 'Faulty Assumptions,'" *NPR*, July 15, 2021, https://news.stlpublicradio.org/government-politics-issues/2021-07-15/missouri-updates-hiv-laws-criminalizing-transmission-for-the-first-time-in-over-30-years.

54. See Shikeith, *#Blackmendream*, film (2014), https://shikeith.com/blackmendream; Shikeith, "The moment you doubt whether you can fly, you cease forever to be able to do it," Art Installation (2014), https://shikeith.com/the-moment-you-doubt-whether-you-can-fly; and Shikeith, *Bio*, Artist's Website, https://shikeith.com/bio, accessed August 5, 2024. Page no longer available.

55. Joshua Tranen, "Dreaming About Balloons: An Interview with Shikeith Cathey," *Yale Daily News*, April 7, 2017, https://yaledailynews.com/blog/2017/04/07/dreaming-about-balloons-an-interview-with-shikeith-cathey/.

56. Molly McGarry, *Ghosts of Futures Past: Spiritualism and the Cultural Politics of Nineteenth-Century America* (Berkeley: University of California Press, 2008), 19.

57. Gay, "Beholding Black Life."

58. Frank B. Wilderson III, *Afropessimism* (New York: Liveright, 2020), 14.

59. Ashon T. Crawley, "Blackpentekintsugi Breath," in Shikeith, *Notes Towards Becoming a Spill* (New York: Aperture, 2022), 55.

60. Ross Gay, *Be Holding: A Poem* (Pittsburgh, PA: University of Pittsburgh Press, 2020). Further citations will be parenthetical in the text.

61. Gay, "Beholding Black Life."

62. Terrance Hayes, "Our Sermon Today Concerns the Dialectic," in *American Sonnets for My Past and Future Assassins* (New York: Penguin, 2018), 27.

63. Gay, "Beholding Black Life." Emphasis in original.

64. Anonymous review of *Jump in the Air and Stay There [ft. Lil Wayne and Bilal]*, by Erykah Badu, *Pitchfork*, February 2, 2010, https://pitchfork.com/reviews/tracks/11751-jump-in-the-air-and-stay-there-ft-lil-wayne-and-bilal/.

65. Erykah Badu, *Jump Up in the Air and Stay There*, YouTube video (Universal Motown Records, a division of UMG Recordings, Inc., March 29, 2010), https://youtu.be/TFS-ThoW8vM?si=SiUYzXnkvvnPqroX.

66. Listen, for an example, to Frank Jordan, "I'm Going to Leland," in *Field Recordings Vol. 4: Mississippi & Alabama (1934–1942)* (Document Records, 1998), https://search.alexanderstreet.com/view/work/398744, accessed August 5, 2024.

67. Henry Louis Gates Jr. *The Signifying Monkey: A Theory of African-American Literary Criticism* (New York: Oxford University Press, 1988), 172.

68. Hartman, *Lose Your Mother*, 165.

69. Badu, *Jump Up in the Air and Stay There.*

70. "Legend," Spotify, track 1 on Drake, *If You're Reading This It's Too Late*, Cash Money Records, 2015.

71. Sonia Sanchez, *Does Your House Have Lions?* (Boston: Beacon Press, 1997), 64–65.

72. Danez Smith, "My N**," in *Homie: Poems* (Minneapolis: Graywolf Press, 2020), 68.

73. Don Share, "Introduction: The Golden Shovel," *Poetry Magazine*, February 1, 2017, https://www.poetryfoundation.org/poetrymagazine/articles/92023/introduction-586e948ad9af8. Accessed August 22, 2022.

74. Gwendolyn Brooks, "We Real Cool," 1963, *Poetry Foundation*, https://www.poetryfoundation.org/poetrymagazine/poems/28112/we-real-cool/. Accessed September 5, 2025.

75. Terrance Hayes, "The Golden Shovel," in *Lighthead* (New York: Penguin Books, 2010), 7.

76. Terrance Hayes, foreword to *The Golden Shovel Anthology: New Poems Honoring Gwendolyn Brooks*, ed. Peter Kahn, Ravi Shankar, and Patricia Smith (Fayetteville: University of Arkansas Press, 2019), xxix.

77. Hayes, foreword to *The Golden Shovel Anthology*, xxvii.

4. "Wade in the Water": Hip Hop and Sorrow Songs

1. See Chapter 1 and Paschal Beverly Randolph, *Love and Its Hidden History: Also, The Master Passion; or The Curtain Raised on Woman, Love, And Marriage, Female Beauty: Its Attainment, Culture, and Retention, with Hints for the Increase of Woman's Power. A Book for Woman, Man, Wives, Husbands, and Lovers, Loving, the Unloved, and the Yearning Ones of the World* (Boston: Randolph and Company, 1870), 57.

2. See Chapter 3 and Tracy K. Smith, "Realm of Shades," in *Wade in the Water: Poems* (Minneapolis: Graywolf Press, 2018), 13.

3. Anthony B. Pinn, *Deathlife: Hip Hop and Thanatological Narrations of Blackness* (Durham, NC: Duke University Press, 2024), 2.

4. Kevin Young, *The Grey Album: On the Blackness of Blackness* (Minneapolis: Graywolf Press, 2012), 400.

5. Greg Tate, "Come Join the Zombie Parade: Deborah Grant," in *Flyboy 2: The Greg Tate Reader* (Durham, NC: Duke University Press, 2016), 223.

6. Anthony B. Pinn concurs. See Pinn, *Deathlife*, 6. See Karla F. C. Holloway, "The Death of Culture," *Massachusetts Review* 40, no. 1 (Spring 1999): 34. CPT itself is an old term; the earliest usage in print I have located dates from 1898 in the African American newspaper *The Savannah Tribune*; see "Our Present Needs," August 6, 1898, 2.

7. See Pinn, *Deathlife*, 91.

8. "The Message," Spotify, track 1 on *The Message*, Grandmaster Flash, The Furious Five, The Sugarhill Gang, *Rapper's Delight*, Warner's Music-X5 Music Group, 1982.

9. "Book of Life," Spotify, track 4 on Common, *Resurrection*, Relativity Records, 1994.

10. "Book of Life."

11. Anthony B. Pinn, "Introduction: Making a World with a Beat: Musical Expression's Relationship to Religious Identity and Experience," in *Noise and Spirit: The Religious and Spiritual Sensibilities of Rap Music*, ed. Anthony B. Pinn (New York: NYU Press, 2003),17.

12. Pinn, "Introduction: Making a World with a Beat," 12.

13. Ralph C. Watkins, "Rap, Religion, and New Realities: The Emergence of a Religious Discourse in Rap Music," in *Noise and Spirit: The Religious and Spiritual Sensibilities of Rap Music.*, ed. Anthony B. Pinn (New York: NYU Press, 2003), 186.

14. Young, *Grey Album*, 394. "Gangsta's Paradise," Spotify, track 2 on Coolio, *Gangsta's Paradise*, Tommy Boy Music, LLC, 1995.

15. Abdul R. JanMohamed, *The Death-Bound-Subject: Richard Wright's Archaeology of Death* (Durham, NC: Duke University Press, 2005), 2.

16. "Mind Playing Tricks on Me," Spotify, track 6 on Geto Boys, *We Can't Be Stopped*, Rap-a-Lot Records, 1991.

17. "Mortal Man," Spotify, track 16 on Kendrick Lamar, *To Pimp a Butterfly*, Aftermath/ Interscope (Top Dawg Entertainment), 2015.

18. I have made a similar argument elsewhere regarding the Black collectivity that emerges out of a shared expectation of death as represented in literary texts: "Death becomes not a process of 'individuation,' as Derrida would have it, but a process of collectivization, of community. This keen awareness of shared mortality—the predictability of one's people's death in and across time— is perhaps the most profound and stirring thematic thread in African American literature, and in African American history." Daylanne K. English, *Each Hour Redeem: Time and Justice in African American Literature* (Minneapolis: University of Minnesota Press, 2012), 144.

19. See Pinn, "Introduction: Making a World with a Beat," 14.

20. Tricia Rose, *Black Noise: Rap Music and Black Culture in Contemporary America* (Middletown, CT: Wesleyan University Press, 1994), 9.

21. Pinn, *Deathlife*, 10.

22. Rose, *Black Noise*, 65.

23. "Long Kiss Goodnight," Spotify, track 23 on Notorious B.I.G., *Life After Death*, 1997; Bad Boy Records, Inc., Remaster, 2014.

24. Margarita Simon Guillory, "Can I Be Both? Blackness and the Negotiation of Binary Categories in Kendrick Lamar's *Section.80*," in *Kendrick Lamar and the Making of Black Meaning*, ed. Christopher M. Driscoll, Anthony B. Pinn, and Monica R. Miller (London: Routledge, 2020), 35.

25. "Is There a Heaven for a Gangsta?" 1997, Spotify, track 17 on Master P., *The Best of Master P.*, Priority Records, 2005.

26. André E. Key, "Damnation, Identity, and Truth: Vocabularies of Suffering in Kendrick Lamar's *DAMN*," in *Kendrick Lamar and the Making of Black Meaning*, ed. Christopher M. Driscoll, Anthony B. Pinn, and Monica R. Miller (London: Routledge, 2020), 305.

27. To give just one particularly well-known example of the presence of Islam in hip hop, Daddy Kane's 1989 song "Young, Gifted and Black" begins with a recorded excerpt from a Louis Farrakhan sermon:

> So out of the mercy of Allah
> And the LAW, written in our nature
> We call an individual, into existence
> And when that individual, I make, NO apologies
> For what I'm about to say

and includes the lyric: "No pork on my fork, strictly fish on my fork," alluding to Nation of Islam and Islamic dietary restrictions. See "Young, Gifted, and Black," Spotify, track 5 on Big Daddy Kane, *It's a Big Daddy Thing*, Cold Chillin' Records/ Warner Records, Inc., 1989.

28. Key, "Damnation," 306.

29. Sam Kestenbaum, " "I'm an Israelite": Kendrick Lamar's Spiritual Search, Hebrew Israelite Religion, and the Politics of a Celebrity Encounter," in *Kendrick*

Lamar and the Making of Black Meaning, ed. Christopher M. Driscoll, Anthony B. Pinn, and Monica R. Miller (London: Routledge, 2020), 286. A line in the song "YAH" on Lamar's album *DAMN*—"I'm a Israelite, don't call me black no mo' / That word is only a color, it ain't facts no mo'"—ignited interest in and concern regarding his possible embrace of the Hebrew Israelite religion, a long-standing and heterogeneous Black American religious tradition that asserts that Black people are the direct descendants of the Israelites (though most Hebrew Israelites do not claim to be Jewish). See "YAH," Spotify, track 3 on Kendrick Lamar, *DAMN*, Aftermath/ Interscope (Top Dawg Entertainment), 2017. The religion has been quite controversial for a number of reasons, including its departures from traditional interpretations of scripture, lack of historical evidence for its central claim, and, in some sects, masculinism, antisemitism, or other extremist social views. Despite all that, if Lamar himself were a Hebrew Israelite, it would suggest that he is following alternative histories and timelines in ways that might be compatible with the alternative forms of temporality that I am exploring in *Soul Sounds*. However, in a 2017 *Rolling Stone* interview, when asked about that line from "YAH," Lamar claimed that it expresses not his own view but that of his cousin Carl Duckworth, who does belong to a Hebrew Israelite organization. Lamar responded, "Everything that I say on that record is from his [Carl's] perspective. That's always been my thing. Always listen to people's history and their background." See Brian Hiatt, "Kendrick Lamar: The Rolling Stone Interview," *Rolling Stone*, August 9, 2017, https://www.rollingstone.com/music/music-features/kendrick-lamar-the-rolling-stone-interview-199817/. At the very least, this interest in the Hebrew Israelites certainly supports Kestenbaum's point that Lamar incorporates many religious and metaphysical views "into his own idiosyncratic worldview." Similarly, Joseph R. Winters refers to Lamar as a "bricoleur" in his "drawing from . . . different [religious and spiritual] traditions and practices." See Joseph R. Winters, *The Disturbing Profane: Hip Hop, Blackness, and the Sacred* (Durham, NC: Duke University Press, 2025), 98.

30. Steve Marsh, "Kendrick Lamar: Rapper of the Year," *GQ*, November 12, 2013, https://www.gq.com/story/kendrick-lamar-men-of-the-year-rapper.

31. Rose, *Black Noise*, 64.

32. Rose, *Black Noise*, 96.

33. This performance included Dr. Dre, Kendrick Lamar (introduced by Dr. Dre), along with 50 Cent, Eminem, and others. Shakur was brought back to life via hologram directly following a performance of "California Love" by Snoop and Dr. Dre, a performance echoed in Lamar's Juneteenth 2024 concert.

34. Alexander G. Weheliye, *Phonographies: Grooves in Sonic Afro-Modernity* (Durham, NC: Duke University Press, 2005), 7.

35. Weheliye, *Phonographies*, 7.

36. Molly McGarry, *Ghosts of Futures Past: Spiritualism and the Cultural Politics of Nineteenth-Century America* (Berkeley: University of California Press, 2008), 107.

37. Monica R. Miller, "Can Dead Homies Speak? The Spirit and Flesh of Black Meaning," in *Kendrick Lamar and the Making of Black Meaning*, ed. Christopher

M. Driscoll, Anthony B. Pinn, and Monica R. Miller (London: Routledge, 2020), 161.

38. Joseph R. Winters, "Beyond Flight and Containment: Kendrick Lamar, Black Study, and an Ethics of the Wound," in *Kendrick Lamar and the Making of Black Meaning*, ed. Christopher M. Driscoll, Anthony B. Pinn, and Monica R. Miller (London: Routledge, 2020), 212.

39. Winters, *The Disturbing Profane*, 4.

40. Michael Eric Dyson, *Holler If You Hear Me: Searching for Tupac Shakur* (New York: Basic Civitas Books, 2001), 222. Alejandro Nava makes a similarly powerful observation: "Anyone familiar with Tupac will know that death was . . . a demonic force that bullied and inspired him at once. Not unlike Lorca, death creeped and prowled in the haunted corners of his mind and seemed to concentrate his thoughts like nothing else." See Alejandro Nava, *In Search of Soul: Hip Hop, Literature and Religion* (Oakland: University of California Press, 2017), 180.

41. *Tupac: Resurrection*, dir. by Lauren Lazin (Hollywood, CA: Paramount Pictures, 2003), DVD, 1:44:46–49.

42. *2-Pac—I Wonder If Heaven Got a Ghetto*, YouTube video, dir. Lionel C. Martin, September 21, 1997, https://youtu.be/XSh4z4RZX90?si=63lBEo8pTACCd6qN; Remastered 2011, https://youtu.be/_fCoK2OVJAc?si=1GbogJ7gS-Y6iFKw.

43. Juan M. Floyd-Thomas, "The Good, the m.A.A.d, and the Holy: Kendrick Lamar's Meditations on Sin and Moral Agency in the Post-Gangsta Era," in *Kendrick Lamar and the Making of Black Meaning*, ed. Christopher M. Driscoll, Anthony B. Pinn, and Monica R. Miller (London: Routledge, 2020), 85.

44. *I Ain't Mad at Cha*, featuring Danny Boy, YouTube video, Tupac Shakur, dir. Tupac Shakur and Kevin Swain (Been There, 1996), https://youtu.be/oXkKURgzYVY?si=jtUbBHMDQ-ZGVB22.

45. Pinn, *Deathlife*, 156.

46. "I Wonder If Heaven Got a Ghetto," Spotify, track 10, *R U Still Down [Remember Me]*, Interscope Records, 1997, 1:32–1:44.

47. *I Ain't Mad at Cha*, YouTube video, 2:45–2:47. Of course, we must acknowledge that Tupac did not consistently work toward Black solidarity or a "better place." He beefed with Biggie just as much as Biggie beefed with him, and sometimes in truly awful ways, as in "Hit 'Em Up," in which he coarsely body-shames Biggie and claims he slept with his wife. See "Hit 'Em Up," Spotify, featuring Outlawz, track 12 on 2Pac, *2Pac's Greatest Hits*, Deathrow Records/Interscope Records, 1998.

48. Cassandra D. Chaney, "'Is There a Heaven for a Gangsta?' Hip Hop, Spirituality, and Heaven," *Journal of Hip Hop Studies* 5, no. 1 (2018): 54. Chaney also supplies a very useful charting of the occurrences of heaven in men's hip hop songs (47–49).

49. Fredric Jameson, "The End of Temporality," *Critical Inquiry* 29, no. 4 (2003): 713.

50. Joseph Winters, "Contemporary Sorrow Songs: Traces of Mourning, Lament,

and Vulnerability in Hip Hop," *African American Review* 46, no. 1 (Spring 2013): 9, 11. See also Nava, *In Search of Soul*: "To insist that hip-hop is life-affirming and pleasurable does not, of course, deny its moments of pathos; the two experiences are artfully combined in hip-hop, making for wild juxtapositions. I'm reminded of Frederick Douglass's comments about the slave spirituals: 'They would sometimes sing the most pathetic sentiment in the most rapturous tone, and the most rapturous sentiment in the most pathetic tone'" (191).

51. Winters, "Contemporary Sorrow Songs," 14.

52. "Suicidal Thoughts," album, track 17 on Notorious B.I.G, *Ready to Die*, Bad Boy Records, 1994, 0:42–0:52.

53. *2-Pac—I Wonder If Heaven Got a Ghetto*, YouTube video, dir. Lionel C. Martin, September 21, 1997, remastered July 12, 2011, https://youtu.be/_fCoK2OVJAc?si=fH1-FZIRoBCyIaYe, 2:23–2:30, 2:45–3:32.

54. Imani Perry, *Prophets of the Hood: Politics and Poetics in Hip Hop* (Durham, NC: Duke University Press, 2004), 24.

55. "Suicidal Thoughts," 0:00–0:10. For a discussion of the significance of the alarm clock in *Native Son*, see English, *Each Hour Redeem*, 82–83.

56. Joe Clair, "Interview with Biggie Smalls," YouTube video, BET Networks, February 24, 1997, https://youtu.be/Rk6Bn3vsAsQ?si=oNoSPoHikcUndvlz, posted May 21, 2019.

This interview was also sampled in the song "Runnin' (Dying to Live)" in the Tupac bio-pic *Resurrection*.

57. Clair, "Interview with Biggie Smalls."

58. Of course, a more pragmatic cause may be that Tupac had recorded more music to sample from at the time of his death than had Biggie when he died. Not only that, but Biggie has in fact been "resurrected" quite a few times, as well. For example, both Timbaland and Nas used AI to re-create his voice, and Meta created a VR version of him. See Julian Mark, "AI Can Bring the Notorious B.I.G.'s Voice Back to Life. Should It?" *Washington Post*, May 10, 2023, https://www.washingtonpost.com/technology/2023/05/10/ai-voices-biggie/; Kristin Robinson, "How AI Brought Biggie Back from the Dead," *Billboard* May 11, 2023, https://www.billboard.com/pro/notorious-big-timbaland-ai-collab-raises-questions/; and Tanya Basu, "I Just Watched Biggie Smalls Perform 'Live' in the Metaverse," *MIT Technology Review*, December 16, 2022, https://www.technologyreview.com/2022/12/16/1065393/biggie-smalls-metaverse/.

59. Pinn, *Deathlife*, 74.

60. Todd Craig, "Open Season 2015: Hip-Hop's Responsibility in Civil Rights Lost," *Modern Language Studies* 45, no. 1 (Summer 2015): 52.

61. Greg Tate, "Review of Kendrick Lamar, *To Pimp a Butterfly*," *Rolling Stone*, March 19, 2015, https://www.rollingstone.com/music/music-album-reviews/to-pimp-a-butterfly-119818/.

62. Tate, "Review of Kendrick Lamar, *To Pimp a Butterfly*."

63. Lamar, "Mortal Man."

64. "United in Grief," Spotify, featuring Sam Dew, disc 1, track 1 on Kendrick Lamar, *Mr. Morale & The Big Steppers*, pgLang/Top Dawg, Entertainment/Aftermath/Interscope Records, May 13, 2022. O. J. Simpson died on April 10, 2024.

65. Vivek Maddala, "A Composer Breaks Down the Music Theory Behind Kendrick Lamar's 'United in Grief,'" *Stereogum* June 6, 2022, https://www.stereogum.com/2188951/a-composer-breaks-down-the-music-theory-behind-kendrick-lamars-united-in-grief/columns/in-theory/.

66. "Angels" (feat. saba), Tidal, track 8, Chance the Rapper, *Coloring Book*, May 12, 2016.

67. "N95," Spotify, disc 1, track 2, Kendrick Lamar, *Mr. Morale & the Big Steppers*, pgLang/Top Dawg, Entertainment/Aftermath/Interscope Records, Hobalt Music Publishing, Sony Music Publishing, May 13, 2022.

68. "Rich Spirit," Spotify, disc 1, track 7, Kendrick Lamar, *Mr. Morale & the Big Steppers*, pgLang/Top Dawg, Entertainment/Aftermath/Interscope Records, 2022.

69. "The Heart Part 5," Spotify, disc 3, track 1, Kendrick Lamar, *Mr. Morale & the Big Steppers*, pgLang/Top Dawg, Entertainment/Aftermath/Interscope Records, Sony Music Publishing, Warner Chappell Music, 2022. For the video, see *The Heart Part* 5, YouTube video, dir. Dave Free and Kendrick Lamar, pgLang / project3, May 8, 2022, https://youtu.be/uAPUkgeiFVY?si=ozRSn30N8UdjrnfT.

70. Joe Coscarelli, "Kendrick Lamar vs. Drake Beef Goes Nuclear: What to Know," *New York Times*, May 6, 2024, https://www.nytimes.com/2024/05/06/arts/music/kendrick-lamar-drake-explainer.html?smid=nytcore-android-share.

71. Matthew Strauss, "2Pac's Estate Threatens Drake with Legal Action over 'Taylor Made Freestyle,'" *Pitchfork* April 24, 2024, https://pitchfork.com/news/2pacs-estate-threatens-drake-with-legal-action-over-taylor-made-freestyle/. See also Angela Yang and Saba Hamedy, "Drake Pulls 'Taylor Made Freestyle' after Tupac Estate Threatens Action for Apparent Use of AI Voice," NBC News, April 26, 2024, https://www.nbcnews.com/pop-culture/pop-culture-news/drake-pulls-taylor-made-freestyle-tupac-estate-threatens-action-appare rcna149592.

72. Though interestingly, Lamar seems to put some distance between himself and Shakur as a presiding spirit in a lyric from "Savior": "Yeah, Tupac dead, gotta think for yourself," a line that seems to be directed to hip hop fans but perhaps also toward himself; see "Savior," Spotify, disc 2, track 4, Kendrick Lamar, *Mr. Morale & the Big Steppers*, pgLang/Top Dawg, Entertainment/Aftermath/Interscope Records, Concord Music Publishing, Pulse Publishing Administration, Sony Music Publishing, Universal Music, 2022.

73. "Not Like Us," Spotify, Kendrick Lamar, Kendrick Lamar/Interscope Records, May 4, 2024.

74. Kodak Black can be considered far more than just controversial, given his conviction for assault of a minor; see Althea Legaspi, "Kodak Black Pleads Guilty to First-Degree Assault and Battery in Sexual Misconduct Case," *Rolling Stone*, April 28, 2021, https://www.rollingstone.com/music/music-news/kodak-black-pleads-guilty -to-first-degree-assault-and-battery-in-sexual-misconduct-case-1162747/. See

"Silent Hill," featuring Kodak Black, Spotify, disc 2, track 3, Kendrick Lamar, *Mr. Morale & the Big Steppers*, pgLang/Top Dawg, Entertainment/Aftermath/Interscope Records, Kobalt Publishing, Sony Music Publishing, 2022.

75. "Juneteenth Concert," Kendrick Lamar, https://youtu.be/XuVGq4OdwnA?si=Z-ZjJ6y82QTza70G, accessed June 24, 2024. This video has since been removed from YouTube.

76. "California Love," Spotify, disc 1, track 6. 2Pac, *2Pac's Greatest Hits*, 1995; Dr. Dre. Death Row Records, 1998.

77. "California Love."

78. Jahan Ramazani, Introduction to *Yeats and the Poetry of Death: Elegy, Self-Elegy, and the Sublime* (New Haven, CT: Yale University Press, 1990), 5, https://doi.org/10.2307/j.ctt211qw4f.5. One could replace the name "Yeats" with "Shakur" and the genre "modern lyric" with "hip hop" throughout Ramazani's book and still produce consistent and useful meanings.

79. Emily Rutter et al., Introduction to *Revisiting the Elegy in the Black Lives Matter Era*, ed. Tiffany Austin, Sequoia Maner, Emily Rugh Rutter, and Darlene Anita Scott (New York: Routledge, 2020), 11.

80. Nikki Giovanni, "All Eyez on U," *Love Poems* (New York: William Morrow, 1997), 62–64. Further citations will be parenthetical in the text.

81. Of course, Sanchez, too, wrote a poetic elegy for Shakur. See Sonia Sanchez, "For Tupac Amaru Shakur," in *Like the Singing Coming Off the Drums* (Boston: Beacon Press, 1998), 118–23, and she dedicated this collection in "to Afemi and Tupac Amaru Shakur" (unpaginated dedication page).

82. "Wade in the Water," Spotify, featuring Nikki Giovanni, track 2, Javon Jackson, *The Gospel According to Nikki Giovanni*, Solid Jackson Records, February 17, 2022.

83. J. D. Considine, "Review of Javon Jackson, *The Gospel According to Nikki Giovanni*," *Downbeat*, March 2022, https://downbeat.com/reviews/detail/the-gospel-according-to-nikki-giovanni.

84. Nikki Giovanni, "A Very Simple Wish," in *The Collected Poetry of Nikki Giovanni 1968-1998* (New York: Harper Perennial, 2003), 218-19. Further citations will be parenthetical in the text.

85. Winters, "Contemporary Sorrow Songs," 11.

86. "Wade in the Water," Spotify, track 12 on Gangstagrass, *American Music*, Rench Audio, April 9, 2015. Also see Farah Stockman, "This Is the Music America Needs," *New York Times*, August 5, 2023, https://www.nytimes.com/2023/08/05/opinion/gangstagrass-music-america.html.

87. Gangstagrass's 2024 release, *The Blackest Thing on the Menu*, blends even more musics, with soul, funk, and R&B joining hip hop and bluegrass on the album. See *The Blackest Thing on the Menu*, Spotify, Album, Gangstagrass, Rench Audio, June 14, 2024.

88. The term "hush" here refers to a long tradition of "hush harbors," where enslaved Black people could gather, away from white ears and eyes, in what Suzanne E. Smith describes as "secluded, usually wooded, places near the slave

quarters where the enslaved could congregate for religious services and social gatherings." See Suzanne E. Smith, *To Serve the Living: Funeral Directors and the African American Way of Death* (Cambridge, MA: Harvard University Press, 2010), 25. As Vorris L. Nunley defines and theorizes the term:

> AAHHR [African American hush harbor rhetoric] remains a powerful aspect of African American rhetoric containing and conveying African American epistemes and rationalities central to African American life and culture and to what Black folks are puttin' down. Away from the disciplining gaze of whiteness. This rhetoric emerges from camouflaged spaces and places. . . . Enslaved and free African Americans referred to these spatialities as hush harbors. (Vorris L. Nunley, *Keepin' It Hushed* [Detroit, MI: Wayne State University Press, 2011], 3).

89. "O Death," Spotify, track 8 on Gangstagrass, *Broken Hearts and Stolen Money*, Rench Audio, 2014.

90. *Oxford English Dictionary*, "apocalypse, *(n.)*," accessed July 22, 2024, https://doi.org/10.1093/OED/4668314849.

91. "Untitled 07/2014–2016," Spotify, track 7, Kendrick Lamar, *Untitled, unmastered*, Aftermath/Interscope (Top Dawg Entertainment), 2016.

92. Jaqueline L. Tobin and Raymond G. Dobard, PhD, *Hidden in Plain View: A Secret Story of Quilts and the Underground Railroad* (New York: Doubleday, 2010), 21–23, 26, 33.

93. Marie Claire Bryant, "Underground Railroad Quilt Codes: What We Know, What We Believe, and What Inspires Us," *Smithsonian Center for Folklife and Cultural Heritage Magazine*, May 2, 2019, accessed June 18, 2024, https://folklife.si.edu/magazine/underground-railroad-quilt-codes.

94. For a powerful account of craft as practice and theory, see Amy E. Elkins, *Crafting Feminism: From Literary Modernism to the Multimedia Present* (New York: Oxford University Press, 2022); see especially the following passages on quilts and quilting: 12–13, 163–68, 228.

95. Anna Kornbluh, "We Have Never Been Critical: Toward the Novel as Critique," *Novel* 50, no. 3 (2017): 403.

Coda: One Better Place

1. Jonathan Sterne, "Hearing," in *Keywords in Sound*, ed. David Novak and Matt Sakakeeny (Durham, NC: Duke University Press, 2015), 67.

2. Tracy K. Smith, "Don't You Wonder Sometimes," in *Life on Mars* (Minneapolis: Graywolf Press, 2011), 19–21.

3. Anna Kornbluh, "We Have Never Been Critical: Toward the Novel as Critique," *Novel: A Forum on Fiction* 50, no. 3 (2017): 398–99.

4. See Margaret Mead and James Baldwin, A *Rap on Race* (Philadelphia: Lippincott, 1971), 158. Further citations will be parenthetical in the text.

5. Badia Ahad-Legardy, *Afro-Nostalgia: Feeling Good in Contemporary Black Culture* (Urbana: University of Illinois Press, 2021), 2. Further citations will be parenthetical in the text.

6. Barbra Foley, "Georgia on His Mind: Part 1 of Cane," in *Jean Toomer: Race, Repression, and Revolution* (Urbana: University of Illinois Press, 2014), 189. For another example, see Wesley Beal, "The Form and Politics of Networks in Jean Toomer's *Cane*," *American Literary History* 24, no. 4 (2012): 658–79. Beal argues that "the metaphorics of cane in this narrative of nostalgia and collective memory may well distort the very community it looks back to" (669).

7. Deborah E. McDowell, "Tending the Tradition: Gayl Jones and the Beacon Black Women Writers Series," *Palimpsest* 13, no. 2 (2024): 19. Further citations will be parenthetical in the text.

8. As he sings, "I wonder what it takes to make this / One better place." Tupac Shakur, "Changes," Spotify, featuring Talent, disc 2, track 5, 2Pac, *2Pac's Greatest Hits*, Deathrow Records/Interscope Records, 1998. 2Pac's holistic prescription in this song:

> We gotta make a change
> It's time for us as a people to start makin' some changes
> Let's change the way we eat
> Let's change the way we live
> And let's change the way we treat each other

9. See Saidiya Hartman, *Lose Your Mother: A Journey Along the Atlantic Slave Route* (New York: Farrar, Straus and Giroux, 2007); Gwen Bergner, "Introduction: The Plantation, the Postplantation, and the Afterlives of Slavery," *American Literature* 91, no. 3 (September 2019): 447–57; Jeffrey Insko, Michael Stancliff, Jeannine Marie DeLombard, Joy James, Brigitte Fielder, Jennifer C. James, and Teresa A. Goddu, "Abolition's Afterlives," *American Literary History* 5, no. 4 (Winter 2021): 1759–1824. See also Dana Luciano, "Forum: Afterlives of 19th-Century American Racism," *J19* 6, no. 1 (2018): 167–74; Rebecca Evans, "Geomemory and Genre Friction: Infrastructural Violence and Plantation Afterlives in Contemporary African American Novels," *American Literature* 93, no. 3 (2021): 455–72.

10. Fredric Jameson, "Progress versus Utopia; or, Can We Imagine the Future?" *Science Fiction Studies* 9, no. 2, Special Issue, *Utopia and Anti-Utopia* (July 1982): 152.

11. Jameson, "Progress versus Utopia," 151.

12. Granted, a similar understanding of the time of the afterlife underlies some quite reactionary versions of the afterlife, particularly among white evangelicals. For example, when Mississippi Governor Tate Reeves spoke on August 26, 2021, about COVID and COVID rates in his state, he said:

> I'm often asked by some of my friends on the other side of the aisle about COVID, and why does it seem like folks in Mississippi and maybe the mid-

South are a little less scared, shall we say. When we believe in eternal life—when you believe that living on this earth is but a blip on the screen—then you don't have to be so scared of things. (The Associated Press, "Tate Reeves: Christians Are 'Less Scared' of COVID Because of Their Belief in Eternal Life," Rpt. *WLBT News*, Jackson, Mississippi, August 30, 2021, https://www.wlbt.com/2021/08/31/tate-reeves-christians-are-less-scared-covid-because-their-belief-eternal-life/).

Reeves was promptly excoriated by liberals and progressives, particularly on twitter. But he is supplying useful information about mask and vaccination resistance and about apathy regarding climate change. Rather than reacting solely with contempt or anger to such beliefs, what if we paused and took them seriously and then considered them as a means to understand those who value eternal life over and above this earthly life, regardless of their race or political affiliation? We may also find that their willingness to die has a limit, particularly at a time when Medicaid and the Affordable Care Act are being at least partly dismantled. See also T. J. Mayfield, "Mississippi View of COVID-19 and Kidney Failure," *Clinical Journal of the American Society of Nephrology* 18, no. 5 (May 2023): 549–50, doi.10.2215/CJN.0000000000000151, Epub May 1, 2022, PMCID: PMC10371279. As Mayfield observes, "At the time of the [AP] article's release, Mississippi had the highest *per capita* rate of new coronavirus cases and deaths in the United States, followed by Florida, Tennessee, South Carolina, and Louisiana."

13. Hortense Spillers, "Moving on Down the Line: Variations on the African-American Sermon," 1988, in *Black, White, and in Color: Essays on American Literature and Culture* (Chicago: University of Chicago Press, 2003), 176.

14. Toni Morrison, "No Place for Self-Pity, No Room for Fear," *The Nation*, March 23, 2015, https://www.thenation.com/article/archive/no-place-self-pity-no-room-fear/.

15. W. E. B. Du Bois, *The Souls of Black Folk* (Chicago: A. C. McClurg, 1903; University of North Carolina: *Documenting the American South*), https://docsouth.unc.edu/church/duboissouls/dubois.html, 4. Further citations will be parenthetical in the text.

16. Tracy K. Smith, "My God, It's Full of Stars," in *Life on Mars* (Minneapolis: Graywolf Press, 2011), 8. Further citations will be parenthetical in the text.

17. Tracy K. Smith, "Don't You Wonder Sometimes," in *Life on Mars*, p. 21, lines 3–4.

Discography and Videography

Badu, Erykah. *Jump Up in the Air and Stay There*. YouTube Video. Universal Motown Records, March 29, 2010. https://youtu.be/TFS-ThoW8vM?si=SiUYzXnkvvnPqroX.
Big Daddy Kane. *It's a Big Daddy Thing*. Album. Cold Chillin' Records/Warner Records, Inc., 1989.
Bowie, David. *Buddha of Suburbia*. 1993. Album. Jones/Tintoretto Entertainment Company/Parlophone Records, Remaster, 2021.
Bowie, David. *Hunky Dory*. Album. RCA, 1971.
Bowie, David. *Low*. Album. RCA, 1977.
Chance the Rapper. *Coloring Book*. Mixtape. Apple Music, May 13, 2016.
Clair, Joe. *Interview with Biggie Smalls*. YouTube Video. BET Networks, February 24, 1997. Posted May 21, 2019. https://youtu.be/Rk6Bn3vsAsQ?si=0N0SP0HIkcUndvlz/.
Common. *Resurrection*. Album. Relativity Records, 1994.
Coolio. *Gangsta's Paradise*. Album. Tommy Boy Music, LLC, 1995.
Drake. *If You're Reading This It's Too Late*. Album. Cash Money Records, 2015.
Gangstagrass. *American Music*. Album. Rench Audio, April 9, 2015.
Gangstagrass. *The Blackest Thing on the Menu*. Album. Gangstagrass/Rench Audio, June 14, 2024.
Gangstagrass. *Broken Hearts and Stolen Money*. Album. Rench Audio, 2014.
Geto Boys. *We Can't Be Stopped*. Album. Rap-a-Lot Records, 1991.
Giovanni, Nikki, and Javon Jackson. *The Gospel According to Nikki Giovanni*. Album. Solid Jackson Records, 2022.
Grandmaster Flash, The Furious Five, The Sugarhill Gang. *The Message*. Album. Warner's Music-X5 Music Group, 1982.
Jordan, Frank. "I'm Going to Leland." *Field Recordings Vol. 4: Mississippi &*

Alabama (1934–1942). Recording. Document Records, 1998. https://search.alexanderstreet.com/view/work/398744. Accessed August 5, 2024.
Lamar, Kendrick. *DAMN*. Album. Top Dawg Entertainment, 2017.
Lamar, Kendrick. *The Heart Part 5*. YouTube Video. Directed by Dave Free and Kendrick Lamar, May 8, 2022. https://youtu.be/uAPUkgeiFVY?si=ozRSn30N8UdjrnfT.
Lamar, Kendrick. *Juneteenth Concert*. YouTube Video. https://youtu.be/XuVGq4OdwnA?si=Z-ZjJ6y82QTza70G. Accessed June 24, 2024 (video has since been removed from YouTube).
Lamar, Kendrick. *Mr. Morale & The Big Steppers*, pgLang/Top Dawg, Entertainment/Aftermath/Interscope Records, May 13, 2022.
Lamar, Kendrick. "Not Like Us." Recording. Kendrick Lamar/Interscope Records, May 4, 2024.
Lamar, Kendrick. *To Pimp a Butterfly*. Album. Aftermath/Interscope (Top Dawg Entertainment), 2015.
Lamar, Kendrick. *Untitled, unmastered*. Album. Aftermath/Interscope (Top Dawg Entertainment), 2016.
Master P. *The Best of Master P*. Album. Priority Records, 2005.
Mitchell, Joni. *Ladies of the Canyon*. Album. Warner Records, Inc., 1970.
Monáe, Janelle. *Age of Pleasure*. Album. Wondaland Productions LLC, 2023.
Monáe, Janelle. *Dirty Computer*. YouTube Video. Directed by Andrew Donoho and Chuck Lightning, April 27, 2018. https://youtu.be/jdH2Sy-BlNE.
Monáe, Janelle. *Electric Lady*. Album. Atlantic Corporation, 2015.
Monáe, Janelle. *Electric Lady*. YouTube Video. Directed by Alan Ferguson, July 30, 2014. https://youtu.be/LPFgBCUBMYk?si=hDshowQ-zdiXli2b.
Monáe, Janelle. *Many Moons*. YouTube Video. Directed by Alan Ferguson, April 4, 2009. https://youtu.be/EZyyORSHbaE?si=qK70HssIYjD3YzdL.
Monáe, Janelle. *Metropolis*. Album. Bad Boy Records, 2008.
Monáe, Janelle. *Q.U.E.E.N.* YouTube Video. Directed by Alan Ferguson, May 1, 2013. https://youtu.be/tEddixS-UoU?si=tO3HS3inqNrNElfS.
Notorious B.I.G. *Life After Death*, 1997. Album. Bad Boy Records, Inc., Remaster, 2014.
Notorious B.I.G. *Ready to Die*. Album. Bad Boy Records, 1994.
Obadike, Mendi + Keith. *Numbers Station 2 [Red Record]*. YouTube Video. April 21, 2016. https://youtu.be/Ww2vrBB9Gno.
Obadike, Mendi + Keith. *Untitled*. YouTube Video. September 13, 2021, https://youtu.be/DkS-hHmVEq8.
Parliament. *Mothership Connection*. Album. Casablanca, 1975.
P-Funk All Stars. *Urban Dancefloor Guerillas*. Album. Sony Music Entertainment, 1984.
Ra, Sun. *Space Is the Place*. Film/YouTube Video. Directed by John Coney, 1974. https://youtu.be/owCPrIEliZc?si=DVJbXsoVxWfoHY5h.

Shakur, Tupac (2Pac). *2Pac's Greatest Hits*, 1995; Death Row Records/Interscope Records, 1998.

Shakur, Tupac. *I Ain't Mad at Cha*. YouTube Video. Directed by Tupac Shakur and Kevin Swain, 1996. https://youtu.be/oXkKURgzYVY?si=jtUbBHMDQ-ZGVB22/.

Shakur, Tupac. *I Wonder If Heaven Got a Ghetto*. YouTube Video. Directed by Lionel C. Martin, September 21, 1997. https://youtu.be/XSh4z4RZX90?si=63lBE08pTACCd6qN. Remastered 2017, https://youtu.be/_fCoK2OVJAc?si=1GbogJ7gS-Y6iFKw.

Shakur, Tupac. *R U Still Down [Remember Me]*. Album. Interscope Records, 1997.

Shikeith. *#Blackmendream*. Film. Written and directed by Shikeith, 2014. https://shikeith.com/blackmendream.

2-Pac—I Wonder If Heaven Got a Ghetto. YouTube Video. Directed by Lionel C. Martin, September 21, 1997. Remastered July 12, 2011. https://youtu.be/_fCoK2OVJAc?si=fH1-FZIRoBCyIaYe.

Tupac: Resurrection. DVD. Directed by Lauren Lazin. Paramount Pictures, 2003.

Wonder, Stevie. *Songs in the Key of Life*. Album. Motown Records, a Division of UMG Recordings, Inc., 1976.

Bibliography

Agamben, Giorgio. *The Time That Remains: A Commentary on the Letter to the Romans*. Translated by Patricia Dailey. Stanford, CA: Stanford University Press, 2005.

Ahad-Legardy, Badia. *Afro-Nostalgia: Feeling Good in Contemporary Black Culture*. Urbana: University of Illinois Press, 2021.

Albanese, Catherine. *A Republic of Mind and Spirit: A Cultural History of American Metaphysical Religion*. New Haven, CT: Yale University Press, 2007.

Altieri, Charles. "Presence and Reference in a Literary Text: The Example of Williams' 'This Is Just to Say.'" *Critical Inquiry* 3 (Spring 1979): 30–44.

Altschuler, Sari, and Priscilla Wald. "COVID-19: Pandemic Reading." *American Literature* 92, no. 4 (2020): 681–88.

Andrews, William L., and Mitchell A. Kachun. "Editors' introduction to *The Curse of Caste; or, The Slave Bride* by Julia Collins (1865)," xi–lxvi. Oxford: Oxford University Press, 2006.

Anonymous. "Our Present Needs." *Savannah Tribune*, August 6, 1898. *African American Newspapers 1827–1998*. Accessed September 27, 2025.

Anonymous. Review of "Jump in the Air and Stay There," ft. Lil Wayne and Bilal, by Erykah Badu. *Pitchfork*, February 2, 2010. https://pitchfork.com/reviews/tracks/11751-jump-in-the-air-and-stay-there-ft-lil-wayne-and-bilal/.

Anonymous. "Ring Out the Old, Ring in the New." *Spiritual Magazine*, January 1, 1868, 1–4. http://www.iapsop.com/archive/materials/spiritual_magazine_uk/spiritual_magazine_s2_v3_n1_jan_1868.pdf.

Aranke, Sampada. *Death's Futurity: The Visual Life of Black Power*. Durham, NC: Duke University Press, 2023.

Associated Press. "Tate Reeves: Christians Are 'Less Scared' of COVID Because of Their Belief in Eternal Life." Rpt. *WLBT News*, August 30, 2021. https://www.wlbt

.com/2021/08/31/tate-reeves-christians-are-less-scared-covid-because-their-belief-eternal-life/.
Bailey, Moya. *Misogynoir Transformed: Black Women's Digital Resistance*. New York: New York University Press, 2021.
Barlow, Daniel. "Literary Ethnomusicology and the Soundscape of Jean Toomer's Cane." *MELUS* 40, no. 1 (2014): 192–211.
Bassett, Mary T. Foreword to *The Pandemic Divide: How COVID Increased Inequality in America*. Edited by Gwendolyn Wright, Lucas Hubbard, and William A. Darity, xi–xiii. Durham, NC: Duke University Press, 2022.
Basu, Tanya. "I Just Watched Biggie Smalls Perform 'Live' in the Metaverse." *MIT Technology Review*, December 16, 2022. https://www.technologyreview.com/2022/12/16/1065393/biggie-smalls-metaverse/.
Beal, Wesley. "The Form and Politics of Networks in Jean Toomer's *Cane*." *American Literary History* 24, no. 4 (2012): 658–79.
Benjamin, Walter. *The Arcades Project*. Translated by Howard Eiland and Kevin McLaughlin. Cambridge, MA: Belknap Press of Harvard University Press, 1999.
Benjamin, Walter. *Illuminations: Essays and Reflections*. 1968. Edited by Hannah Arendt. Translated by Harry Zohn. New York: Schocken Books, 1985.
Bergner, Gwen. "Introduction: The Plantation, the Postplantation, and the Afterlives of Slavery." *American Literature* 91, no. 3 (September 2019): 447–57.
Best, Stephen. *None Like Us: Blackness, Belonging, Aesthetic Life*. Durham, NC: Duke University Press, 2018.
Bhabha, Homi. *Location of Culture*. London: Routledge, 1991.
Black, Alex W. "'A New Enterprise in Our History': William Still, Conductor of *The Underground Rail Road* (1872)." *American Literary History* 32, no. 4 (2020): 668–90.
Bogdan, Henrik. "New Perspectives on Western Esotericism." *Nova Religio: The Journal of Alternative and Emergent Religion* 13, no. 3 (2010): 97–105.
Braude, Ann. *Radical Spirits: Spiritualism and Women's Rights in Nineteenth-Century America*. Boston: Beacon Press, 1989.
Brooks, Gwendolyn. "We Real Cool." 1963. *Poetry Foundation*. https://www.poetryfoundation.org/poetrymagazine/poems/28112/we-real-cool/. Accessed September 6, 2025.
Brouwer, Joel. "Poems of Childhood, Grief and Deep Space." Review of *Life on Mars*, by Tracy K. Smith. *New York Times*, August 26, 2011. https://www.nytimes.com/2011/08/28/books/review/life-on-mars-by-tracy-k-smith-book-review.html.
Brown, Jericho. *The Tradition*. Port Townsend, WA: Copper Canyon Press, 2019.
Bryant, Marie Claire. "Underground Railroad Quilt Codes: What We Know, What We Believe, and What Inspires Us." *Smithsonian Center for Folklife and Cultural Heritage Magazine*, May 2, 2019. https://folklife.si.edu/magazine/underground-railroad-quilt-codes. Accessed June 18, 2024.
Buescher, John B. "'More Lurid Than Lucid': The Spiritualist Invention of the

Word 'Sexism.'" *Journal of the American Academy of Religion* 70, no. 3 (2002): 561–92.

Carroll, Brett E. *Spiritualism in Antebellum America*. Bloomington: Indiana University Press, 1997.

Castronovo, Russ. *Necro Citizenship: Death, Eroticism, and the Public Sphere in the Nineteenth-Century United States*. Durham, NC: Duke University Press, 2001.

Chaney, Cassandra D. "'Is There a Heaven for a Gangsta?' Hip Hop, Spirituality, and Heaven." *Journal of Hip Hop Studies* 5, no. 1 (2018): 35–63.

Chesnutt, Charles. "Po' Sandy." In *The Conjure Woman*. Boston: Houghton, Mifflin, 1899. Reprint, *Documenting the American South*. https://docsouth.unc.edu/southlit/chesnuttconjure/conjure.html#conjure36.

Colbert, Soyica. "How to Live Among What Is Dead." *Public Books*, January 18, 2022. https://www.publicbooks.org/how-to-live-among-what-is-dead/?utm_source=PUBLIC+BOOKS+Newsletter&utm_campaign=6df22a8b18-EMAIL_CAMPAIGN_2022_1_24&utm_medium=email&utm_term=0_d048c39403–6df22a8b18–47239089&mc_cid=6df22a8b18. Accessed July 21, 2024.

Coleman, Monica A. *Making a Way Out of No Way: A Womanist Theology*. Minneapolis: Fortress Press, 2008.

Commander, Michelle D. *Afro-Atlantic Flight: Speculative Returns and the Black Fantastic*. Durham, NC: Duke University Press, 2017.

Cone, James H. *A Black Theology of Liberation, Fortieth Anniversary Edition*. 1970. Maryknoll, NY: Orbis Books, 2010.

Considine, J. D. "Review of Javon Jackson, *The Gospel According to Nikki Giovanni*." *Downbeat*, March 2022. https://downbeat.com/reviews/detail/the-gospel-according-to-nikki-giovanni.

Corbin, Alain. *Village Bells: Sound and Meaning in the 19th-Century French Countryside*. New York: Columbia University Press, 1994.

Coscarelli, Joe. "Kendrick Lamar vs. Drake Beef Goes Nuclear. What to Know." *New York Times*, May 6, 2024. https://www.nytimes.com/2024/05/06/arts/music/kendrick-lamar-drake-explainer.html?smid=nytcore-android-share.

Cox, Robert S. *Body and Soul: A Sympathetic History of American Spiritualism*. Charlottesville: University of Virginia Press, 2003.

Craig, Todd. "Open Season 2015: Hip-Hop's Responsibility in Civil Rights Lost." *Modern Language Studies* 45, no. 1 (Summer 2015): 46–55.

Crawley, Ashon T. "Blackpentecostal Breath." In *Notes Towards Becoming a Spill*, by Shikeith, 54–61. New York: Aperture, 2022.

Davenport, Reuben Briggs. *The Death-Blow to Spiritualism, Being the True Story of the Fox Sisters, as Revealed by the Authority of Margaret Fox Cane and Catherine Fox Jencken*. New York: G. W. Dillingham, 1888. Project Gutenberg, 2010. http://www.gutenberg.org/files/33506/33506-h/33506-h.htm.

Deveney, John Patrick. *Paschal Beverly Randolph: A Nineteenth-Century Black*

American Spiritualist, Rosicrucian, and Sex Magician. Albany: State University of New York Press, 1997.

Deveney, John Patrick. "Paschal Beverly Randolph and Sexual Magic." In *Hidden Intercourse: Eros and Sexuality in the History of Western Esotericism*, edited by Wouter J. Hanegraaff and Jeffrey J. Kripal, 355–67. Leiden: Brill, 2008.

Douglass, Frederick. *My Bondage and My Freedom*. 1855. New York: Library of America, 1996.

Douglass, Frederick. *Narrative of the Life of Frederick Douglass, an American Slave, Written by Himself*. 1845. New York: Signet, 1968.

Drake, Kayla. "Missouri Loosens Laws Criminalizing HIV Transmission After 30 Years of 'Faulty Assumptions.'" *NPR* July 15, 2021. https://news.stlpublicradio.org/government-politics-issues/2021-07-15/missouri-updates-hiv-laws-criminalizing-transmission-for-the-first-time-in-over-30-years.

Driscoll, Christopher M., Anthony B. Pinn, and Monica R. Miller, eds. *Kendrick Lamar and the Making of Black Meaning*. London: Routledge, 2020.

Du Bois, W. E. B. *The Souls of Black Folk*. Chicago: A. C. McGlurg, 1903. Reprint, University of North Carolina, *Documenting the American South*. https://docsouth.unc.edu/church/duboissouls/dubois.html.

duCille, Ann. *The Coupling Convention: Sex, Text, and Tradition in Black Women's Fiction*. New York: Oxford University Press, 1993.

Dyson, Michael Eric. *Holler If You Hear Me: Searching for Tupac Shakur*. New York: Basic Civitas Books, 2001.

Edwards, Brent Hayes. "Other Afterlives." *PMLA* 138, no. 2 (2023): 233–40.

Edwards, Erica. "The Formidable Work of the Present, A Powerhouse of a Book." *Los Angeles Review of Books*, June 13, 2011.

Eisenberg, Andrew J. "Space." In *Keywords in Sound*, edited by David Novak and Matt Sakakeeny, 193–207. Durham, NC: Duke University Press, 2015.

Elkins, Amy E. *Crafting Feminism: From Literary Modernism to the Multimedia Present*. New York: Oxford University Press, 2022.

Ellis, R. J., and Henry Louis Gates Jr. "'Grievances at the Treatment She Received': Harriet E. Wilson's Spiritualist Career in Boston, 1868–1900." *American Literary History* 24, no. 2 (2012): 234–64.

English, Daylanne K. *Each Hour Redeem: Time and Justice in African American Literature*. Minneapolis: University of Minnesota Press, 2012.

English, Daylanne K. "Race, Writing, and Time." In *Literature and Time*, edited by Thomas M. Allen, 225–41. Cambridge: Cambridge University Press, 2018.

English, Daylanne K. "Review of *Woody Guthrie's Modern World Blues*, by Will Kaufman; *Beyond the Crossroads: The Devil and the Blues Tradition*, by Adam Gussow; *Conjuring Freedom: Music and Masculinity in the Civil War's "Gospel Army*," by Johari Jabir; and *The Great Woman Singer: Gender and Voice in Puerto Rican Music*, by Licia Fiol-Matta." *American Literature* 93, no. 4 (2021): 718–22.

English, Daylanne K. *Unnatural Selections: Eugenics in American Modernism and the Harlem Renaissance*. Chapel Hill: University of North Carolina Press, 2003.

English, Daylanne K., and Alvin [now Ava] Kim. "Now We Want Our Funk Cut: Janelle Monáe's Neo-Afrofuturism." *American Studies* 52, no. 4 (2013): 17–30.

Eshun, Kodwo. "Further Considerations of Afrofuturism." *CR: The New Centennial Review* 3. no. 2 (2003): 287–302.

Eshun, Kodwo. *More Brilliant Than the Sun: Adventures in Sonic Fiction*. London: Quartet Books, 1998.

Evans, Rebecca. "Geomemory and Genre Friction: Infrastructural Violence and Plantation Afterlives in Contemporary African American Novels." *American Literature* 93, no. 3 (2021): 455–72.

Fabian, Johannes. *Time and the Other: How Anthropology Makes Its Object*. 1983. Reprint, New York: Columbia University Press, 2002.

Faust, Drew Gilpin. "'The Dread Void of Uncertainty': Naming the Dead in the American Civil War." *Southern Cultures* 11, no. 2 (2005): 7–32.

Faust, Drew Gilpin. *The Republic of Suffering*. New York: Alfred A. Knopf, 2008.

Felix, Mabel, Laurie Sobel, and Alina Salganicoff. "The Comstock Act: Implications Nationwide." KFF Website, April 15, 2024. https://www.kff.org/womens-health-policy/issue-brief/the-comstock-act-implications-for-abortion-care-nationwide/.

Felski, Rita. *The Limits of Critique*. Chicago: University of Chicago Press, 2015.

Ferguson, Christine. *Determined Spirits: Eugenics, Heredity and Racial Regeneration in Anglo-American Spiritualist Writing, 1848–1930*. Edinburgh: Edinburgh University Press, 2012.

Ferguson, Christine. "Eugenics and the Afterlife: Lombroso, Doyle, and the Spiritualist Purification of the Race." *Journal of Victorian Culture* 12, no. 1 (2007): 64–85.

Fielding, Bernard. "The Occult Lore of Bells." *Occult Review* (December 1918): 317–23.

Finley, Lana. "Paschal Beverly Randolph in the African American Community." In *Esotericism in African American Religious Experience*, edited by Stephen C. Finley, Margarita Simon Guillory, and Hugh R. Page Jr., 37–51. Leiden: Brill, 2014.

Fisher-Wirth, Ann. "The Allocations of Desire: 'This Is Just to Say' and Flossie Williams's 'Reply.'" *William Carlos Williams Review* 22, no. 2 (1996): 47–56.

Floyd-Thomas, Juan M. "The Good, the m.A.A.d, and the Holy: Kendrick Lamar's Meditations on Sin and Moral Agency in the Post-Gangsta Era." In *Kendrick Lamar and the Making of Black Meaning*, edited by Christopher M. Driscoll, Anthony B. Pinn, and Monica R. Miller, 69–98. London: Routledge, 2020.

Foley, Barbara. "Georgia on His Mind: Part 1 of Cane." In *Jean Toomer: Race, Repression, and Revolution*, 188–220. Urbana: University of Illinois Press, 2014.

Foley, Barbara. "'In the Land of Cotton': Economics and Violence in Jean Toomer's *Cane*." *African American Review* 32, no. 2 (1998): 181–98.

Foreman, Gabrielle P. "The 'Christian Recorder,' Broken Families, and Educated Nations in Julia C. Collins's Civil War Novel *The Curse of Caste*." *African American Review* 40, no. 4 (2006): 705–16.

Foreman, Gabrielle P., et al. "Colored Conventions National Convention of Colored Men Held in the City of Syracuse, New York in 1864, October 4, 5, 6, and 7, 1864." *Colored Conventions Project.* https://coloredconventions.org//.

Foreman, Gabrielle P., and Reginald H. Pitts. Introduction to *Our Nig; or, Sketches from the Life of a Free Black by Harriet Wilson* (1859), xxiii–l. New York: Penguin, 2005.

Frank, J., A. R. King, and D. J. Raine. *Accretion Power in Astrophysics.* 3rd ed. Cambridge: Cambridge University Press, 2002.

Freeman, Elizabeth. *Time Binds: Queer Temporalities, Queer Histories.* Durham, NC: Duke University Press, 2010.

Gates, Henry Louis, Jr. "Introduction: Writing 'Race' and the Difference It Makes." In *Race, Writing, and Difference,* edited by Henry Louis Gates Jr., 1–20. Chicago: University of Chicago Press, 1986.

Gates, Henry Louis, Jr. *The Signifying Monkey: A Theory of African-American Literary Criticism.* New York: Oxford University Press, 1988.

Gay, Ross. *Be Holding: A Poem.* Pittsburgh, PA: University of Pittsburgh Press, 2020.

Gay, Ross. "Beholding Black Life: A Conversation with Ross Gay, Frank Guridy, and Deborah Paredez. *Public Books,* June 1, 2022. https://www.publicbooks.org/beholding-black-life-a-conversation-with-ross-gay-frank-guridy-deborah-paredez/?utm_source=PUBLIC+BOOKS+Newsletter&utm_campaign=e5389b38c7-EMAIL_CAMPAIGN_2022_6_6&utm_medium=email&utm_term=0_d048c39403-e5389b38c7-47239089&mc_cid=e5389b38c7&mc_eid=78d37ce77a.

Gay, Ross. *The Book of Delights.* Chapel Hill, NC: Algonquin Books of Chapel Hill, 2019.

Gay, Ross. *Bringing the Shovel Down.* Pittsburgh, PA: University of Pittsburgh Press, 2011.

Gay, Ross. *Catalog of Unabashed Gratitude.* Pittsburgh, PA: University of Pittsburgh Press, 2015.

Gay, Ross, and Aimee Nezhukumatathil. *Lace & Pyrite: Letters from Two Gardeners.* Union, NJ: Get Fresh Publishing, 2014.

Gilroy, Paul. *The Black Atlantic: Modernity and Double Consciousness.* Cambridge, MA: Harvard University Press, 1993.

Gilroy, Paul. "'Lost in Music': Wild Notes and Organized Sound." In *Sound and Literature,* edited by Anna Snaith, 170–89. Cambridge, UK: Cambridge University Press, 2020.

Giovanni, Nikki. "All Eyez on U." In *Love Poems,* 62–64. New York: William Morrow, 1997.

Giovanni, Nikki. "A Very Simple Wish." In *The Collected Poetry of Nikki Giovanni: 1968–1998.* New York: Harper Perennial, 2003.

Goldsby, Jacqueline. "'I Disguised My Hand': Writing Versions of the Truth in Harriet Jacobs's *Incidents in the Life of a Slave Girl* and John Jacobs's 'A True Tale of Slavery.'" In *Harriet Jacobs and Incidents in the Life of a Slave Girl:*

New Critical Essays, edited by Deborah M. Garfield and Rafia Zafar, 11–43. Cambridge: Cambridge University Press, 1996.

Gregerson, Linda. "The Poem That Changed My Life: Ross Gay's 'Bringing the Shovel Down.'" Poets.org, November 30, 2016. https://poets.org/text/poem-changed-my-life-ross-gays-bringing-shovel-down.

Guillory, Margarita Simon. "Can I Be Both? Blackness and the Negotiation of Binary Categories in Kendrick Lamar's *Section.80*." In *Kendrick Lamar and the Making of Black Meaning*, edited by Christopher M. Driscoll, Anthony B. Pinn, and Monica R. Miller, 25–36. London: Routledge, 2020.

Gutierrez, Cathy. *Plato's Ghost: Spiritualism in the American Renaissance*. Oxford: Oxford University Press, 2009.

Hacker, David J. "A Census-Based Count of the Civil War Dead." *Civil War History* 57, no. 4 (2011): 306–47.

Hartman, Saidiya V. *Lose Your Mother: A Journey Along the Atlantic Slave Route*. New York: Farrar, Straus and Giroux, 2016.

Hartman, Saidiya V. *Scenes of Subjection: Terror, Slavery, and Self-Making in Nineteenth-Century America*. New York: Oxford University Press, 1997.

Hartman, Saidiya V. "The Time of Slavery." *South Atlantic Quarterly* 101, no. 4 (2002): 757–77.

Hayes, Terrance. Foreword to *The Golden Shovel Anthology: New Poems Honoring Gwendolyn Brooks*, edited by Peter Kahn, Ravi Shankar, and Patricia Smith, xxvii–xxix. Fayetteville: University of Arkansas Press, 2019.

Hayes, Terrance. "The Golden Shovel." In *Lighthead*, 6–8. New York: Penguin Books, 2010.

Hayes, Terrance. "Our Sermon Today Concerns the Dialectic." In *American Sonnets for My Past and Future Assassins*, 27. New York: Penguin, 2018.

Heffernan, James A. W. *Museum of Words: The Poetics of Ekphrasis from Homer to Ashbery*. Chicago: University of Chicago Press, 1993.

Hegel, Georg Wilhelm Friedrich. *The Philosophy of History*. Translated by John Sibree. New York: Cosimo, 2007.

Henriques, Julian. "Sonic Dominance and the Reggae Sound System Session." In *The Auditory Culture Reader*, edited by Michael Bull and Les Back, 451–80. Oxford: Berg, 2003.

Hiatt, Brian. "Kendrick Lamar: The Rolling Stone Interview." *Rolling Stone*, August 9, 2017. https://www.rollingstone.com/music/music-features/kendrick-lamar-the-rolling-stone-interview-199817/.

Hirschkind, Charles. "Religion." In *Keywords in Sound*, edited by David Novak and Matt Sakakeeny, 165–74. Durham, NC: Duke University Press, 2015.

Holloway, Karla F. C. "The Death of Culture." *Massachusetts Review* 40, no. 1 (Spring 1999): 31–43.

Holmes, Barbara A. Author Website. https://www.drbarbaraholmes.com/. Accessed July 27, 2022. Page no longer available.

Holmes, Barbara A. *Crisis Contemplation: Healing the Wounded Village*. Albuquerque, NM: CAC Publishing, 2021.

Holmes, Barbara A. "'We'll Make Us a World': A Post-Obama Politics of Embodied Creativity." In *Ain't I a Womanist, Too? Third Wave Womanist Religious Thought*, edited by Monica A. Coleman and Layli Maparyan, 184–200. Minneapolis: Augsburg Fortress, 2013.

Insko, Jeffrey, Michael Stancliff, Jeannine Marie DeLombard, Joy James, Brigitte Fielder, Jennifer C. James, and Teresa A. Goddu. "Abolition's Afterlives." *American Literary History* 5, no. 4 (Winter 2021): 1759–1824.

Iton, Richard. *In Search of the Black Fantastic: Politics and Popular Culture in the Post–Civil Rights Era*. New York: Oxford University Press, 2008.

Jackson, John L. "On Ethnographic Sincerity." *Current Anthropology* 51, no. S2 (2010): S279–87.

Jacobs, Harriet. *Incidents in the Life of a Slave Girl, Written by Herself*. 1861. University of North Carolina, *Documenting the American South*. https://docsouth.unc.edu/fpn/jacobs/jacobs.html.

Jameson, Fredric. "The End of Temporality." *Critical Inquiry* 29, no. 4 (2003): 695–718.

Jameson, Fredric. "Progress versus Utopia; or, Can We Imagine the Future?" *Science Fiction Studies* 9, no. 2, Special Issue, *Utopia and Anti-Utopia* (July 1982): 147–58.

JanMohamed, Abdul R. *The Death-Bound-Subject: Richard Wright's Archaeology of Death*. Durham, NC: Duke University Press, 2005.

Jarrett, Gene Andrew. *Deans and Truants: Race and Realism in American Literature*. Philadelphia: University of Pennsylvania Press, 2007.

Joseph, Chanté. "What Black Joy Means—And Why It's More Important Than Ever." *British Vogue*, July 29, 2020. https://www.vogue.co.uk/arts-and-lifestyle/article/what-is-black-joy.

Kachun, Mitch. "Slave Narratives and Historical Memory." In *The Oxford Handbook of the African American Slave Narrative*, edited by John Ernest, 22–35. New York: Oxford University Press, 2014.

Kafer, Alison. *Feminist, Queer, Crip*. Bloomington: Indiana University Press, 2013.

Kanno-Youngs, Zolan. "US Watched George Floyd Protests in 15 Cities Using Aerial Surveillance." *New York Times*, June 19, 2020. https://www.nytimes.com/2020/06/19/us/politics/george-floyd-protests-surveillance.html.

Keeling, Kara. *Queer Times, Black Futures*. New York: New York University Press, 2019.

Kestenbaum, Sam. " "I'm an Israelite": Kendrick Lamar's Spiritual Search, Hebrew Israelite Religion, and the Politics of a Celebrity Encounter." In *Kendrick Lamar and the Making of Black Meaning*, edited by Christopher M. Driscoll, Anthony B. Pinn, and Monica R. Miller, 274–99. London: Routledge, 2020.

Key, André E. "Damnation, Identity, and Truth: Vocabularies of Suffering in Kendrick Lamar's *DAMN*." In *Kendrick Lamar and the Making of Black*

Meaning, edited by Christopher M. Driscoll, Anthony B. Pinn, and Monica R. Miller, 300–320. London: Routledge, 2020.

King, Martin Luther, Jr. *Where Do We Go from Here: Chaos or Community?* Boston: Beacon Press, 1967.

Kornbluh, Anna. *The Order of Forms: Realism, Formalism, and Social Space*. Chicago: University of Chicago Press, 2019.

Kornbluh, Anna. "We Have Never Been Critical: Toward the Novel as Critique." *Novel: A Forum on Fiction* 50, no. 3 (2017): 397–408.

Krysl, Marilyn. Introduction to *Obsession: Sestinas in the Twenty-First Century*, edited by Carolyn Beard Whitlow and Marilyn Krysl, xiii–xvi. Dartmouth, NH: Dartmouth College Press, 2014.

Kucich, John J. *Ghostly Communion: Cross-Cultural Spiritualism in Nineteenth-Century American Literature*. Hanover, NH: Dartmouth College Press, 2004.

Laski, Gregory. *Untimely Democracy: The Politics of Progress After Slavery*. New York: Oxford University Press, 2018.

LaValle, Victor. "Recognition." *New York Times Magazine*, "The Decameron Project," July 7, 2020: 1–15. https://www.nytimes.com/interactive/2020/07/07/magazine/victor-lavalle-short-story.html.

Legaspi, Althea. "Kodak Black Pleads Guilty to First-Degree Assault and Battery in Sexual Misconduct Case." *Rolling Stone*, April 28, 2021. https://www.rollingstone.com/music/music-news/kodak-black-pleads-guilty-to-first-degree-assault-and-battery-in-sexual-misconduct-case-1162747/.

Levine, Caroline. *Forms: Whole, Rhythm, Hierarchy, Network*. Princeton, NJ: Princeton University Press, 2015.

Lloyd, Vincent W. *Religion of the Field Negro: On Black Secularism and Black Theology*. New York: Fordham University Press, 2017.

Luciano, Dana. "Forum: Afterlives of 19th-Century American Racism." *J19* 6, no. 1 (2018): 167–74.

Maddala, Vivek. "A Composer Breaks Down the Music Theory Behind Kendrick Lamar's 'United in Grief.'" *Stereogum*, June 6, 2022. https://www.stereogum.com/2188951/a-composer-breaks-down-the-music-theory-behind-kendrick-lamars-united-in-grief/columns/in-theory/.

Marez, Curtis. *Farm Worker Futurism: Speculative Technologies of Resistance*. Minneapolis: University of Minnesota Press, 2016.

Mark, Julian. "AI Can Bring the Notorious B.I.G.'s Voice Back to Life. Should It?" *Washington Post*, May 10, 2023. https://www.washingtonpost.com/technology/2023/05/10/ai-voices-biggie.

Marsh, Steve. "Kendrick Lamar: Rapper of the Year." *GQ*, November 12, 2013. https://www.gq.com/story/kendrick-lamar-men-of-the-year-rapper.

Marshall, Nicholas. "The Great Exaggeration: Death and the Civil War." *Journal of the Civil War Era* 4, no. 1 (2014): 3–27.

Martin, Theodore. "Temporality and Literary Theory." *Oxford Research*

Encyclopedia of Literature. December 22, 2016. https://doi.org/10.1093/acrefore/9780190201098.013.122.
Mayfield, T. J. "Mississippi View of COVID-19 and Kidney Failure." *Clinical Journal of the American Society of Nephrology* 18, no. 5 (May 2023): 549–50.
McDowell, Deborah E. "Tending the Tradition: Gayl Jones and the Beacon Black Women Writers Series." *Palimpsest: A Journal on Women, Gender, and the Black International* 13, no. 2 (2024): 17–36.
McGarry, Molly. *Ghosts of Futures Past: Spiritualism and the Cultural Politics of Nineteenth-Century America*. Berkeley: University of California Press, 2008.
McKittrick, Katherine. *Demonic Grounds*. Minneapolis: University of Minnesota Press, 2006.
Mead, Margaret, and James Baldwin. *A Rap on Race*. Philadelphia: Lippincott, 1971.
Meckel, Richard A. *Save the Babies: American Public Health Reform and the Prevention of Infant Mortality, 1850–1929*. 2nd ed. Rochester, NY: University of Rochester Press, 2015.
Miller, Monica R. "Can Dead Homies Speak? The Spirit and Flesh of Black Meaning." In *Kendrick Lamar and the Making of Black Meaning*, edited by Christopher M. Driscoll, Anthony B. Pinn, and Monica R. Miller, 159–74. London: Routledge, 2020.
Mitchell, W. J. T. *Picture Theory*. Chicago: University of Chicago Press, 1994.
Morrison, Toni. "No Place for Self-Pity, No Room for Fear." *The Nation*, March 23, 2015. https://www.thenation.com/article/archive/no-place-self-pity-no-room-fear/.
Moten, Fred. *Black and Blur*. Durham, NC: Duke University Press, 2017.
Moten, Fred. "The Case of Blackness." *Criticism* 50, no. 2 (2008): 177–218.
Muñoz, José Esteban. *Cruising Utopia: The Then and There of Queer Futurity*. New York: New York University Press, 2009.
Napolin, Julie Beth. "b.O.s. 13.4 / *Numbers Station [Red Record]*." *ASAP Journal*, August 13, 2020. https://asapjournal.com/node/13-4-numbers-station-red-record-julie-beth-napolin/.
Napolin, Julie Beth. "Scenes of Subjection: Women's Voices Narrating Black Death." *Sounding Out!* (blog), December 9, 2016. https://soundstudiesblog.com/2016/12/19/scenes-of-subjection-womens-voices-narrating-black-death/.
Nartonis, David K. "The Rise of 19th-Century American Spiritualism, 1854–1873." *Journal for the Scientific Study of Religion* 49, no. 2 (2010): 361–73.
Nava, Alejandro. *In Search of Soul: Hip Hop, Literature and Religion*. Oakland: University of California Press, 2017.
Nersessian, Anahid. *The Calamity Form: On Poetry and Social Life*. Chicago: University of Chicago Press, 2020.
Nunley, Vorris L. *Keepin' It Hushed*. Detroit, MI: Wayne State University Press, 2011.
Ogbunu, Brandon C. "How Afrofuturism Can Help the World Mend." *Wired*, July 15, 2020. https://www.wired.com/story/how-afrofuturism-can-help-the-world-mend/#:~:text=A%20century%20later%2C%20as%20a,consider%20universes%20of%20better%20alternatives.

O'Leary, Chris. *Ashes to Ashes; The Songs of David Bowie, 1976–2016*. London: Repeater Books, 2018.

O'Leary, Chris. "Pushing Ahead of the Dame: David Bowie, Song by Song: 'Bleed Like a Craze, Dad.'" December 17, 2012. https://bowiesongs.wordpress.com/2012/12/17/bleed-like-a-craze-dad/.

"Our Present Needs." *Savannah Tribune*, August 6, 1898, 2. *African American Newspapers 1827–1998*. Database. Accessed September 27, 2025.

Oxford English Dictionary. "apocalypse (n.)." https://doi.org/10.1093/OED/4668314849. Accessed July 22, 2024.

Pegg, Nicholas. *The Complete David Bowie*. 2016. London: Titan Books, 2000.

Pelly, Jenn. "Janelle Monáe's 'Electric Lady' Video Features T.I., Estelle, Esperanza Spalding, T-Boz, Her Mom." *Pitchfork*, July 30, 2014. https://pitchfork.com/news/56092-janelle-monaes-electric-lady-video-features-ti-estelle-esperanza-spalding-t-boz-her-mom/.

Perry, Imani. *Prophets of the Hood: Politics and Poetics in Hip Hop*. Durham, NC: Duke University Press, 2004.

Peterson, Carla L. "Mapping Taste: Urban Modernities from the *Tatler* and *Spectator* to *Frederick Douglass's Paper*." *American Literary History* 32, no. 4 (2020): 691–722.

Peterson, Marina. *Atmospheric Noise: The Indefinite Urbanism of Los Angeles*. Durham, NC: Duke University Press, 2021.

Pickens, Therí Alyce. *Black Madness :: Mad Blackness*. Durham, NC: Duke University Press, 2019.

Pickens, Therí Alyce, ed. "Blackness and Disability." Special Issue. *African American Review* 50, no. 2 (2017).

Pinn, Anthony B. *Deathlife: Hip Hop and Thanatological Narrations of Blackness*. Durham, NC: Duke University Press, 2024.

Pinn, Anthony B. "Introduction: Making a World with a Beat: Musical Expression's Relationship to Religious Identity and Experience." In *Noise and Spirit: The Religious and Spiritual Sensibilities of Rap Music*, edited by Anthony B. Pinn, 1–26. New York: New York University Press, 2003.

Quashie, Kevin. *Black Aliveness; or, A Poetics of Being*. Durham, NC: Duke University Press, 2021.

Ramazani, Jahan. Introduction to *Yeats and the Poetry of Death: Elegy, Self-Elegy, and the Sublime*, 1–13. New Haven, CT: Yale University Press, 1990.

Ramírez, Catherine S. "Afrofuturism/Chicanafuturism." *Aztlán* 33, no. 1 (2008): 185–94.

Randolph, Paschal Beverly. *After Death; or, Disembodied Man*. Boston: printed by the author, 1868, Reprint, London: Forgotten Books, 2012.

Randolph, Paschal Beverly. *Dealings with the Dead: The Human Soul, Its Migrations and Its Transmigrations, By the Rosicrucian*. Boston: printed by the author, 1861–62. Reprint, London: Forgotten Books, 2012.

Randolph, Paschal Beverly. *Eulis! The History of Love: Its Wondrous Magic,*

Chemistry, Rules, Laws, Modes, Moods, and Rationale. Toledo: printed by author, 1874. Reprint, Toledo, OH: Randolph Publishing Company, 1906.

Randolph, Paschal Beverly. *The "Learned Pundit" and "Man with Two Souls": His Curious Life, Works, and Career. The Great Free-Love Trial. Randolph's Grand Defence. His Address to the Jury, and Mankind. The Verdict*. Boston: Randolph Publishing House, 1872.

Randolph, Paschal Beverly. Letter to the Editor. *New Orleans Tribune*, December 8, 1864.

Randolph, Paschal Beverly. *Love and Its Hidden History: Also, The Master Passion; or, The Curtain Raised on Woman, Love, and Marriage, Female Beauty; Its Attainment, Culture, and Retention, with Hints for the Increase of Woman's Power. A Book for Woman, Man, Wives, Husbands, and Lovers, Loving the Unloved, and the Yearning Ones of the World*. Boston, MA: Randolph and Company, 1870.

Randolph, Paschal Beverly. *Seership! The Magnetic Mirror. A Practical Guide to Those Who Aspire to Clairvoyance-Absolute. Original and Selected, from Various European and Asiatic Adepts*. Toledo, OH: printed by author, 1870. Reprint, Toledo, OH: K. C. Randolph, 1896. Internet Archive, https://archive.org/details/SeershipTheMagneticMirror.

Randolph, Paschal Beverly. *Tom Clark and His Wife, Their Double Dreams and the Curious Things That Befell Them Therein; or, The Rosicrucian's Story*. New York: Sinclair Tousey, 1863. Project Gutenberg, 2011. https://www.gutenberg.org/cache/epub/35366/pg35366-images.html.

Rankine, Claudia. "The Condition of Black Life Is One of Mourning." *New York Times Magazine*, June 22, 2015. https://www.nytimes.com/2015/06/22/magazine/the-condition-of-black-life-is-one-of-mourning.html.

Rath, Richard Cullen. *How Early America Sounded*. Ithaca, NY: Cornell University Press, 2003.

Reed, Anthony. *Freedom Time: The Poetics and Politics of Black Experimental Writing*. Baltimore: Johns Hopkins University Press, 2014.

Reed, Anthony. *Soundworks: Race, Sound, and Poetry in Production*. Durham, NC: Duke University Press, 2021.

Rice, William H. "Two Work Songs in Cane." *Black American Literature Forum* 23, no. 3 (1989): 593–99.

Rich, Adrienne. "Terza Rima." In *Fox: Poems, 1998–2001*, 41–53. New York: W. W. Norton, 2001.

Robinson, Kristin. "How AI Brought Biggie Back from the Dead." *Billboard*, May 11, 2023. https://www.billboard.com/pro/notorious-big-timbaland-ai-collab-raises-questions/.

Rose, Tricia. *Black Noise: Rap Music and Black Culture in Contemporary America*. Middletown, CT: Wesleyan University Press, 1994.

Rosenberg, Charles E. *The Cholera Years: The United States in 1832, 1849, and 1866*. 2nd ed. Chicago: University of Chicago Press, 1987.

Ross, Marlon B. "Kenneth W. Warren's *What Was African American Literature?* A Review Essay." *Callaloo* 35, no. 3 (2012): 604–12.

Rothman, Sheila. *Living in the Shadow of Death: Tuberculosis and the Social Experience of Illness in American History*. New York: Basic, HarperCollins, 1994.
Rueb, Emily S. "He Emerged from Prison a Potent Symbol of HIV Criminalization." *New York Times*, July 14, 2019. https://www.nytimes.com/2019/07/14/us/michael-johnson-hiv-prison.html.
Rutter, Emily. Introduction to *Revisiting the Elegy in the Black Lives Matter Era*, edited by Tiffany Austin, Sequoia Maner, Emily Rugh Rutter, and Darlene Anita Scott, 9–26. New York: Routledge, 2020.
Sanchez, Sonia. *Does Your House Have Lions?* Boston: Beacon Press, 1997.
Sanchez, Sonia. "For Tupac Amaru Shakur." In *Like the Singing Coming Off the Drums*, 118–23. Boston: Beacon Press, 1998.
Santamarina, Xiomara. "Fugitive Slave, Fugitive Novelist: *The Narrative of James Williams* (1838)." *American Literary History* 31, no. 1 (2019): 24–46.
Scarborough, Joe. Interview. "Gov. Walz: 'People like JD Vance Know Nothing about Small Town America.'" *MSNBC News*, July 23, 2024. YouTube Video. https://youtu.be/tviViJqpgpY?si=4RXzVeIo7jK64oEA.
Schafer, R. Murray. "The Soundscape." In *The Sound Studies Reader*, edited by Jonathan Sterne, 95–103. London: Routledge, 2012.
Schafer, R. Murray. *The Soundscape: Our Sonic Environment and the Tuning of the World*. 1977. Reprint, Rochester, VT: Destiny Books, 1994.
Schafer, R. Murray. *The Tuning of the World: Toward a Theory of Soundscape Design*. Philadelphia: University of Pennsylvania Press, 1980.
Schalk, Sami. *Bodyminds Reimagined: (Dis)ability, Race, and Gender in Black Women's Speculative Fiction*. Durham, NC: Duke University Press, 2018.
Schmidt, Leigh Eric. *Hearing Things: Religion, Illusion, and the American Enlightenment*. Cambridge, MA: Harvard University Press, 2000.
Sedgwick, Eve Kosofsky. "Paranoid Reading and Reparative Reading; or, You're So Paranoid, You Probably Think This Essay Is About You." In *Touching Feeling*, 124–51. Durham, NC: Duke University Press 2002.
Selisker, Scott. "Review." *African American Review* 44, no.4 (2011): 717–19.
Share, Don. "Introduction: The Golden Shovel." *Poetry Magazine*, February 1, 2017. https://www.poetryfoundation.org/poetrymagazine/articles/92023/introduction-586e948ad9af8. Accessed August 22, 2022.
Sharpe, Christina. *In the Wake: On Blackness and Being*. Durham, NC: Duke University Press, 2016.
Shikeith. "Bio." Artist's Website. https://shikeith.com/bio. Accessed August 5, 2024.
Shikeith. "The Moment You Doubt Whether You Can Fly, You Cease Forever to Be Able to Do It." Art Installation, 2014. https://shikeith.com/the-moment-you-doubt-whether-you-can-fly. Accessed August 5, 2024. Page no longer available.
Shikeith. *Notes Towards Becoming a Spill*. New York: Aperture, 2022.
Shulman, Michael. "Janelle Monáe Peels the Onion." *New Yorker*, January 8, 2023. https://www.newyorker.com/culture/the-new-yorker-interview/janelle-monae-peels-the-onion.
Smith, Danez. *Don't Call Us Dead*. Minneapolis: Graywolf Press, 2017.

Smith, Danez. *Homie: Poems.* Minneapolis: Graywolf Press, 2020.

Smith, Dinitia. "A Slave Story Is Rediscovered, and a Dispute Begins." *New York Times*, October 28, 2006. https://www.nytimes.com/2006/10/28/books/a-slave-story-is-rediscovered-and-a-dispute-begins.html.

Smith, Mark M. *Listening to Nineteenth-Century America.* Chapel Hill: University of North Carolina Press, 2001.

Smith, Suzanne E. *To Serve the Living: Funeral Directors and the African American Way of Death.* Cambridge, MA: Harvard University Press, 2010.

Smith, Tracy K. *The Body's Question.* Minneapolis: Graywolf Press, 2003.

Smith, Tracy K. *Life on Mars: Poems.* Minneapolis: Graywolf Press, 2012.

Smith, Tracy K. *Ordinary Light: A Memoir.* New York: Vintage Books, 2015.

Smith, Tracy K. "Realm of Shades." In *Bearden's Odyssey: Poets Respond to the Art of Romare Bearden*, edited by Kwame Dawes and Matthew Shenoda, 90. Evanston, IL: TriQuarterly Books/Northwestern University Press, 2017.

Smith, Tracy K. "Realm of Shades." In *Wade in the Water: Poems*, 13. Minneapolis: Graywolf Press, 2018.

Smith, Tracy K. *Wade in the Water: Poems.* Minneapolis: Graywolf Press, 2018.

Spillers, Hortense. "Mama's Baby, Papa's Maybe: An American Grammar Book." 1987. In *Black, White, and in Color: Essays on American Literature and Culture*, 203–29. Chicago: University of Chicago Press, 2003.

Spillers, Hortense. "Moving on Down the Line: Variations on the African-American Sermon." 1988. In *Black, White, and in Color: Essays on American Literature and Culture*, 251–76. Chicago: University of Chicago Press, 2003.

Spires, Derrick R. "Genealogies of Black Modernities." *American Literary History* 32, no. 4 (2020): 611–22.

Sterne, Jonathan. "Hearing." In *Keywords in Sound*, edited by David Novak and Matt Sakakeeny, 65–77. Durham, NC: Duke University Press, 2015.

Stevens, Wallace. "Anecdote of the Jar." *Poetry* 1 (October 1919): 8.

Stockman, Farah. "This Is the Music America Needs." *New York Times*, August 5, 2023. https://www.nytimes.com/2023/08/05/opinion/gangstagrass-music-america.html.

Stoever, Jennifer Lynn. *The Sonic Color Line: Race and the Cultural Politics of Listening.* New York: New York University Press, 2016.

Strauss, Matthew. "2Pac's Estate Threatens Drake with Legal Action over 'Taylor Made Freestyle.'" *Pitchfork*, April 24, 2024. https://pitchfork.com/news/2pacs-estate-threatens-drake-with-legal-action-over-taylor-made-freestyle/.

Tal, Kalil. "That Just Kills Me: Black Militant Near-Future Fiction." *Social Text* 71, no. 2 (2002): 65–91.

Tate, Greg. "Come Join the Zombie Parade: Deborah Grant." In *Flyboy 2: The Greg Tate Reader*, 219–23. Durham, NC: Duke University Press, 2016.

Tate, Greg. "Review of Kendrick Lamar, *To Pimp a Butterfly*." *Rolling Stone*, March 19, 2015. https://www.rollingstone.com/music/music-album-reviews/to-pimp-a-butterfly-119818/.

Tobin, Jaqueline L., and Raymond G. Dobard, PhD. *Hidden in Plain View: A Secret Story of Quilts and the Underground Railroad.* New York: Doubleday, 2010.

Toikkanen, Jarkko. "Intermedial Experience and Ekphrasis in Wordsworth's 'Slumber.'" *Partial Answers: Journal of Literature and the History of Ideas* 17, no. 1 (2019): 107–24.

Toomer, Jean. "Autobiographical Selection." In *Cane* (1923), edited by Darwin T. Turner, 140–45. New York: W. W. Norton, 1988.

Toomer, Jean. "Cotton Song." In *Cane* (1923), edited by Darwin T. Turner, 11. New York: W. W. Norton, 1988.

Toomer, Jean. "Georgia Dusk." In *Cane* (1923), edited by Darwin T. Turner, 15. New York: W. W. Norton, 1988.

Tranen, Joshua. "Dreaming About Balloons: An Interview with Shikeith Cathey." *Yale Daily News*, April 7, 2017. https://yaledailynews.com/blog/2017/04/07/dreaming-about-balloons-an-interview-with-shikeith-cathey/.

Treves, A., L. Maraschi, and M. Abramowicz. "Basic Elements of the Theory of Accretion." *Publications of the Astronomical Society of the Pacific* 100, no. 626 (April 1988): 427–51.

Urban, Hugh B. "The Beast with Two Backs: Aleister Crowley, Sex Magic and the Exhaustion of Modernity." *Nova Religio: The Journal of Alternative and Emergent Religions* 7, no. 3 (2004): 7–25.

Urban, Hugh B. "'Magia Sexualis': Sex, Secrecy, and Liberation in Modern Western Esotericism." *Journal of the American Academy of Religion* 72, no. 3 (2004): 695–731.

Waldman, Katy. "What Covid Did to Fiction." *New Yorker*, June 10, 2024. https://www.newyorker.com/magazine/2024/06/17/what-covid-did-to-fiction.

Walker, Alice. *In Search of Our Mother's Gardens.* 1967. New York: Houghton Mifflin, 1983.

Walker, David. *Appeal to the Coloured Citizens of the World.* 1829. Reprint, New York: Hill and Wang, 1995.

Walker, David. "The Humbug in American Religion Ritual Theories of Nineteenth-Century Spiritualism." *Religion and American Culture: A Journal of Interpretation* 23, no. 1 (2013): 30–74.

Warren, Calvin L. *Ontological Terror: Blackness, Nihilism, and Emancipation.* Durham, NC: Duke University Press, 2018.

Warren, Kenneth W. *What Was African American Literature? The W. E. B. Du Bois Lectures.* Cambridge, MA: Harvard University Press, 2011.

Watkins, Ralph C. "Rap, Religion, and New Realities: The Emergence of a Religious Discourse in Rap Music." In *Noise and Spirit: The Religious and Spiritual Sensibilities of Rap Music*, edited by Anthony B. Pinn, 184–93. New York: New York University Press, 2003.

Weheliye, Alexander G. *Habeas Viscus: Racializing Assemblages, Biopolitics, and Black Feminist Theories of the Human.* Durham, NC: Duke University Press, 2014.

Weheliye, Alexander G. *Phonographies: Grooves in Sonic Afro-Modernity*. Durham, NC: Duke University Press, 2005.

Wells-Barnett, Ida B. *The Red Record: Tabulated Statistics and Alleged Causes of Lynching in the United States*. 1895. Project Gutenberg, 2005. https://www.gutenberg.org/files/14977/14977-h/14977-h.htm.

White, Edward. "In the Joints of Their Toes." *Paris Review* (blog), November 4, 2016. https://www.theparisreview.org/blog/2016/11/04/in-the-joints-of-their-toes/.

Wilderson, Frank B., III. *Afropessimism*. New York: Liveright, 2020.

Wilderson, Frank B., III. "An Afropessimist on the Year Since George Floyd Was Murdered: Notes of a (Minneapolis) Native Son. *The Nation*, June 14/21, 2021. https://www.thenation.com/article/society/george-floyd-afropessimism/.

Wilderson, Frank B., III. "Color Theory." *Harper's Magazine*, April 9, 2020. https://harpers.org/archive/2020/04/color-theory/.

Wilford, John Noble. "How Epidemics Shaped the Modern Metropolis." *New York Times*, April 15, 2008. http://www.nytimes.com/2008/04/15/science/15chol.html.

Wilson, Harriet. *Our Nig; or, Sketches from the Life of a Free Black by Harriet Wilson*. 1859. New York: Penguin, 2005.

Wilson, Harriet. Preface to *Our Nig; or, Sketches from the Life of a Free Black, in a Two-Story White House, North*. 1859. Project Gutenberg, 2011. https://www.gutenberg.org/ebooks/584.

Winters, Joseph R. "Beyond Flight and Containment: Kendrick Lamar, Black Study, and an Ethics of the Wound." In *Kendrick Lamar and the Making of Black Meaning*, edited by Christopher M. Driscoll, Anthony B. Pinn, and Monica R. Miller, 212–27. London: Routledge, 2020.

Winters, Joseph R. "Contemporary Sorrow Songs: Traces of Mourning, Lament, and Vulnerability in Hip Hop." *African American Review* 46, no. 1 (Spring 2013): 9–20.

Winters, Joseph R. *The Disturbing Profane: Hip Hop, Blackness, and the Sacred*. Durham, NC: Duke University Press, 2025.

Womack, Ytasha. *Afrofuturism: The World of Black Sci-fi and Fantasy Culture*. Chicago: University of Chicago Press, 2013.

Wright, Michelle M. *The Physics of Blackness: Beyond the Middle Passage Epistemology*. Minneapolis: University of Minnesota Press, 2015.

Yang, Angela, and Saba Hamedy. "Drake Pulls 'Taylor Made Freestyle' after Tupac Estate Threatens Action for Apparent Use of AI Voice." NBC News, April 26, 2024. https://www.nbcnews.com/pop-culture/pop-culture-news/drake-pulls-taylor-made-freestyle-tupac-estate-threatens-action-appare-rcna149592.

Young, Kevin. *The Grey Album: On the Blackness of Blackness*. Minneapolis: Graywolf Press, 2012.

Yusoff, Kathryn. *A Billion Black Anthropocenes or None*. Minneapolis: University of Minnesota Press, 2018.

Zafar, Rafia. "Of Print and Primogeniture; or, The Curse of Firsts." *African American Review* 40, no. 4 (2006): 619–21.

Index

NOTE: Page numbers in *italics* denote illustrations. Nineteenth-century Spiritualist and author Paschal Beverly Randolph is abbreviated as "Randolph" in this index.

Daylanne K. English is Professor of English at Macalester College in St. Paul, MN. She is the author of *Unnatural Selections: Eugenics in American Modernism and the Harlem Renaissance* and *Each Hour Redeem: Time and Justice in African American Literature.*

Printed and bound by CPI Group (UK) Ltd, Croydon, CR0 4YY

15/10/2026

14983212-0001